CONTENTS

◀ LEARNING ABOUT THE JOB

Marines and sailors on board a transport bound for Tarawa begin to familiarize themselves with the island of Betio, mid-November 1943. (Naval History and Heritage Command)

ON THE COVER

2d Division Marines training for Tarawa. (Hatch Collection, National Museum of the Pacific War)

Library of Congress Cataloging-in-Publication Data

Names: Rogers, Daniel E., 1962- author.
Title: The Battle of Tarawa / Daniel E. Rogers.
Other titles: Naval history 1042-1920
Description: Annapolis, MD : Naval Institute, [2022] | Series: Naval history special edition | Title from cover.
Identifiers: LCCN 2021052644 | ISBN 9781591147039
Subjects: LCSH: Tarawa, Battle of, Kiribati, 1943. | Tarawa Atoll (Kiribati)—History, Military.
Classification: LCC D767.917 R64 2022 | DDC 940.54/26681--dc23/eng/20211103
LC record available at https://lccn.loc.gov/2021052644

BACKGROUND AND PREPARATION

The origins of U.S. involvement in the western Pacific. The U.S. fleet at the Battle of Manila Bay, May 1898. (Naval History and Heritage Command)

INTRODUCTION: THE EBB AND FLOW OF THE PACIFIC WAR, 1941–1943

In the late autumn of 1943, as the second anniversary of the Japanese attack on Pearl Harbor approached, World War II in the Pacific was about to enter a third phase.

In the first period, from December 1941 to May 1942, the Japanese army and navy had expanded with few checks other than those imposed by geography. In the second phase, from May 1942 through November 1943, the United States and its allies had begun to stymie the Japanese on land in New Guinea and the Solomon Islands, and at sea in the Coral Sea, at Midway, and elsewhere. A third phase would commence in November 1943 with nearly simultaneous major U.S. offensives in the Solomon and Gilbert Islands. The assault on the Gilberts was the opening move in a U.S. effort to drive toward Japan through the Central Pacific. Over the next year and a half, this drive would lead to the Marshall and Mariana Islands, Peleliu, Iwo Jima, and Okinawa.

The American strike on the Gilberts was codenamed Operation Galvanic. Many tens of thousands of Marines, soldiers, sailors, and airmen from the United States were brought into combat against Japanese ground, naval, and air forces. At stake was control of three equatorial coral atolls, along with the seas around and the skies above them. In just one week of November 1943, close to 5,000 Japanese died in battle, alongside more than 1,700 Americans. Many thousands more on the U.S. side were casualties. In terms of lives lost daily for each contested square mile, for the United States this was the deadliest combat of the war up to that point.

The most immediately famous and historically significant combat during these bloody days involved the U.S. 2d Marine Division attacking Betio Island

in the Tarawa Atoll. Known instantly as the Battle of Tarawa, this was the costliest brief engagement that the Marine Corps had yet known. The lethality and close quarters of the fighting there were conveyed in still images and motion pictures that were quickly sent home, bringing to the American public its first real visual appreciation of the Pacific war's brutality.

Tarawa was a battle of other firsts. It was the first Pacific landing that the Japanese heavily contested on the beach. It was the first attack on a defended coral atoll. It marked the first use of amphibious landing craft for assault troops, allowing them to ride over a fringing coral reef directly onto the beach—or beyond. It was the first time the U.S. Navy and U.S. Army Air Forces attempted to reduce all defenders of a targeted island to helplessness just prior to the arrival of assault troops. And there would be more firsts, each allowing U.S. commanders to learn from mistakes as the war moved to islands ever closer to Japan.

If the war in the Pacific had an "end of the beginning" (to echo Winston Churchill), it came at Tarawa.

THE CENTRAL PACIFIC IN U.S. NAVY STRATEGY

Since their acquisition by the United States after the Spanish-American War in 1898, the Philippine Islands had been left in an unavoidably vulnerable position with respect to Japan. There was no continuous line of communication from the mainland United States to the Philippines, nor bases across the Pacific for refueling and repairing the U.S. Navy ships needed to supply and, if necessary, defend or liberate the islands. The closest major U.S. possessions were Guam and Oahu (1,600 miles and 5,300 miles away, respectively).

Planning for this dilemma began even before World War I, but accelerated and intensified after Japan received a League of Nations mandate over Germany's former possessions in the Marshall, Mariana, and Caroline Islands. Japan was now a world power whose possessions lay astride the U.S. path to the Philippines. The Navy's Plan Orange for a potential war against Japan, in its 1924 formulation, envisaged the seizure of bases in the Central Pacific on the way to rescuing the Philippines and winning a decisive naval encounter with Japan. By the late 1930s, however, this plan was no longer feasible, since it had relied upon Japan's being the only U.S. enemy. Therefore, the Rainbow 5 plan, devised on the eve of World War II, put the United States on a defensive stance in the Pacific while Germany was being defeated first. Nevertheless, the mindset had been established that a Central Pacific drive and the seizure of bases would be the preferred Navy strategy in the next war.

THE U.S. MARINE CORPS AS AMPHIBIOUS ASSAULT FORCE

There would be no seizure of bases, in the Central Pacific or elsewhere, without troops. The United States Marine Corps had been positioning itself to be the source of those troops for most of the decade before World War II. This new role would mark a profound transition for the Corps. For much of their history, the Marines' primary function had been to serve as defenders of Navy ships, ship boarding parties, naval base guards, and expeditionary troops in small wars such as those in the Caribbean and Latin America. In World War I, the Corps had joined frontline action already long in progress, rather than fighting its way in from the coast. But in 1933, the Secretary of the Navy accepted a Marine Corps proposal to create the Fleet Marine Force, a permanent large element that would serve with the fleet and train to seize bases or to land while being opposed.

To carry out this new role, the Marine Corps had to design a method, virtually from scratch, for the conduct of amphibious warfare. The most recent major example of landing troops on a hostile shore, the British–Australian–New Zealand–French effort known as the Gallipoli Campaign (1915), had proven a disastrous lesson in how lack of planning is reflected in poor battlefield performance. In 1933, in order to ensure future operations would be well organized, the Marine Corps schools at Quantico turned their officers into inventors of doctrine, and by 1934 they had produced a *Tentative Manual for Landing Operations*, later also to be adopted mostly intact by the Navy and Army. When World War II came, therefore, the Marines had studied and trained in such matters as naval gunfire support of landing troops; aerial support; moving Marines from ships to shore; establishing a beachhead; and loading, unloading, and delivering supplies to combat forces ashore.

JAPAN IN THE GILBERTS: BACKGROUND

World War II had begun for Japan not in 1941, but in 1937, when it attacked south from Manchuria in an

attempt to subdue China. The war against China had gone neither quickly nor especially well, since China had nearly limitless reserves of manpower and land to counter its disadvantages in military preparedness and technology.

In an ongoing attempt to starve the Chinese forces of outside support, by 1941 Japan had seized much of the coast of China and taken over Indochina from Vichy France. These Japanese moves led to a U.S. oil embargo against Japan, as well as to the Japanese leadership's stark realization that its effort to create a Greater East Asia Co-Prosperity Sphere dominated by itself might well soon be halted for lack of fuel. Other than acquiescing in the U.S. demand that China be freed, Japanese policy makers came to see their only option as seizing oil and other raw materials in what came to be known as the Southern Resources Area dominated by the Dutch East Indies (today's Indonesia) and in British possessions on the Malay Peninsula.

The 7 December 1941 attack on Pearl Harbor that brought the United States so resolutely into war against Japan had been designed to neutralize any U.S. Navy threat to the acquisition of the Southern Resources Area or to the erection of a buffer of island bases to protect both that area and the Japanese homeland. By 1943, Japan's defensive outer barrier included: (1) the long line of islands acquired under a League of Nations mandate when Germany was defeated in World War I (the Carolines, Marshalls, and Marianas); (2) Wake Island, a U.S. atoll base, captured in December 1941; (3) Guam, also captured in December 1941; (4) portions of New Guinea, the Solomon Islands, and the Bismarck Islands, captured in 1942; (5) two Aleutian Islands, Attu and Kiska, taken in 1942; and (6) the Gilbert Islands, seized in 1941.

The Japanese navy occupied Makin in the Gilberts on 10 December 1941. Tarawa was reconnoitered on 24 December 1941. These islands would help protect the Marshalls from U.S. interference based in Samoa or the Ellice Islands, more than 1,000 miles to the southeast. The Japanese 4th Fleet needed few men to take the Gilberts from their nominal British rulers, who had not defended the islands, nor did the Japanese station many troops on them. There was no significant strengthening by the Japanese until after a U.S. Marine raid under Lieutenant Colonel Evans Carlson on 17 August 1942. That raid was designed to distract the Japanese from the Guadalcanal operation in the Solomons, then only ten days old. Carlson's raid may have been counterproductive, however, for not only did it cost the lives of 30 Marines, it also alerted the Japanese to U.S. interest and capabilities in the area. The Japanese navy began an immediate construction and reinforcement program in the Gilberts.

The island of Betio at the southwest corner of Tarawa Atoll was selected as the main Japanese base. Airfield construction started in October 1942, and it was completed by March 1943. At the same time, albeit at a slower pace, fortifying Betio as a true citadel began. Reinforced positions that would permit attackers to be defeated before or shortly after landing were designed and constructed. Large caliber naval weapons, and many varieties of smaller guns, were installed all over the island.

The guns were manned by soldiers the Japanese called *rikusentai*. Often inaccurately compared to U.S. Marines, the rikusentai were nonetheless part of the Japanese navy who, like the Marines, carried out assignments on land that were similar to some traditionally fulfilled by the Marines. Their branch of the navy was known as the Special Naval Landing Forces (SNLF), which deployed two major components to Tarawa in 1943: the 7th Sasebo SNLF, with nearly 1,600 officers and men; and the 3rd Special Base Force. The 7th Sasebo was organized into rifle companies, a weapons battery, an antiaircraft battery, and a tank and flamethrower unit. The 3rd Special Base Force included a

Main Japanese Weapons

- 8-INCH VICKERS NAVAL GUNS
- 140-MM GUNS
- 127-MM TWIN MOUNT GUNS
- 80-MM ANTI-BOAT GUNS
- 75-MM DUAL PURPOSE (ANTIAIRCRAFT/ANTI-BOAT)
- 75-MM MOUNTAIN GUNS
- 70-MM HOWITZERS
- 37-MM ANTI-TANK GUNS
- 13-MM MACHINE GUNS (TWIN AND SINGLE MOUNT)
- 7.7-MM MACHINE GUNS
- LIGHT TANKS WITH 37 MM GUNS
- .25-CALIBER RIFLES
- 50-MM GRENADE THROWERS ("KNEE MORTARS")
- ANTI-BOAT MINES
- BAYONETS
- SWORDS (OFFICERS)

Japanese Fortifications

At Tarawa on an unprecedented and massive scale, and to a far lesser extent at Makin and Abemama, the Japanese garrisons erected sophisticated, robust, and mutually supporting fortifications in the water and on land. The carnage of the three days at Tarawa stemmed from the inability of the U.S. Navy and Army Air Forces to neutralize these positions before the battle, and from the Marines' struggles to overcome them during the battle.

The Japanese pinned all their hopes on these positions. If they held, the Japanese navy and air force might have the time to get to the Gilberts and damage and chase away the U.S. fleet. But they were static positions, except for a few light tanks that might be placed in semi-sheltered locations. That meant the initiative on Betio was in the hands of the U.S. Marines. It also meant that if Japanese communications were severed, which in fact they almost immediately were, these positions would become islands of increasingly desperate and lonely resistance, leading any survivors to commit suicide after they depleted their ammunition and began to fear the shame of capture.

The Japanese fortifications at Tarawa started in the water around all sides of Betio. Anti-boat mines littered the southern and western oceanside approaches. Later in the battle, when these shorelines had been cleared of Japanese soldiers and it was deemed safer for U.S. boats and amtracs to operate there, some vessels still struck these mines and lost their crews. The lagoon side had not been mined yet. Although there were indications such mining was next on base commander Rear Admiral Kieji Shibazaki's agenda, the U.S. decision to strike in November 1943 rather than wait for a more propitious moment, in December or January 1944, resulted in a much less dangerous experience for LVTs, LCVPs, and LCMs "(see page 13). Off all coasts there were also barbed wire fences capable of snagging small craft and men wading in; LVTs could usually push through them, but not always. The southern and western coasts also had concrete tetrahedrons that would force approaching craft into small openings into which Japanese artillery pieces and machine guns were aimed and ready to fire. In a less organized and more spur-of-the-moment sense, the hulk of the *Saidu Maru* and the 800-yard-long pier also served as Japanese fortified positions, from which enfilading fire could be directed at passing boats and wading Marines.

On land, Japanese sheltered firing positions included pillboxes made of coconut logs covered with coral sand, steel pillboxes, reinforced concrete blockhouses, rifle pits, foxholes, and gun positions for the larger artillery. In many cases, these positions were connected by trenches allowing for reinforcement, repositioning, and resupply.

Most of the island coast was ringed by a seawall constructed of coconut logs that were linked together with steel rods. Sometimes firing positions were included within sections of this seawall. The wall's position relative to the edge of the lagoon varied with the tide. At high tide, the lagoon waters often lapped up against the wall or were very close to it. At lower tides, such as the morning of D-Day, the wall could be 20 or more yards inland. Its height therefore varied from a foot to more than five feet. It offered limited dry cover to landing Marines, but proved to be an impassable barrier for LVTs and tanks, which required either demolition of the wall or luck in finding a break in it in order to advance to the heart of the island.

U.S. casualties were so severe because for much of the battle, these fortifications allowed sufficient numbers of Japanese soldiers to survive preliminary bombardments and then direct accurate, incapacitating fire on boats and individuals. These emplacements could often be vanquished only with flamethrowers, explosive charges, hand grenades, or 75-mm fire from howitzers, medium tanks, or self-propelled mounts. Since the use of grenades required an exposed close approach, as did employing explosive charges carried by engineers, many Marines would die trying to get the explosives through the firing slits. Meanwhile, the large reinforced concrete positions were impermeable to all U.S. fire except for explosive charges tossed into firing slits or ventilation shafts.

construction battalion and labor units to which forcibly conscripted Korean laborers were attached. In all, nearly 5,000 men at Tarawa awaited the U.S. initiative in the Central Pacific.

Betio would be a prime example of how the Japanese Z Plan was to work on the outer fringes of its empire. According to the Z Plan, garrisons such as the one at Tarawa would be expected to hold out until the surface fleet, submarine fleet, and air forces could converge to engage and wipe out the attacking U.S. naval forces. Meanwhile, Makin would be less heavily fortified as a seaplane base. Abemama (spelled "Apamama" in many contemporary U.S. documents) would only be lightly garrisoned, with no air base. Together they formed the front door to the Japanese Empire that U.S. forces would have to kick down in November 1943.

THE SCENE OF BATTLE: THE GEOGRAPHY OF THE GILBERT ISLANDS

The Gilbert Islands lie a little north and west of the intersection of the equator with the International Date Line. They are approximately halfway between Hawaii and the east coast of Australia. The closest island chain to the Gilberts is the Marshall Islands, held by the Japanese since 1914, the nearest of which (Mili Atoll) lies about 200 miles to the north-northwest of Makin Atoll.

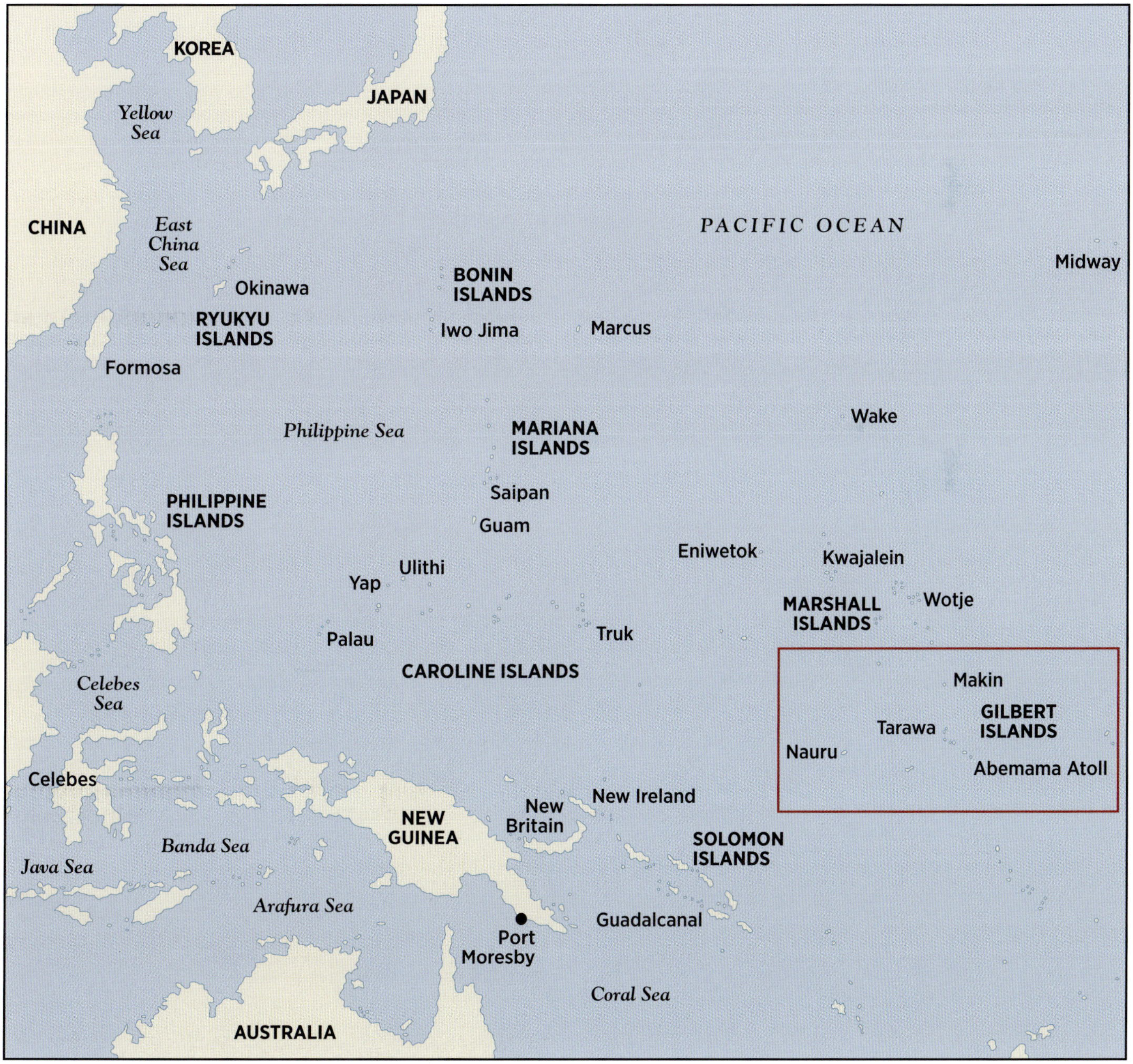

Tarawa Atoll

The major objective of the U.S. assault on the Gilberts, Tarawa Atoll was nearly 3,000 miles due north of the base of the 2d Marine Division in Wellington, New Zealand. Shaped like a triangle, Tarawa has a 20-mile-long western side that is a reef below sea level forming an obstacle to navigation except for a less-than-one-mile-wide opening into the lagoon about three-and-one-half miles north of Betio. The southern edge of the atoll is 18 miles long and contains 5 islands; the eastern edge of the atoll is 24 miles long and contains approximately 40 islands.

For Operation Galvanic, Betio Island at Tarawa was codenamed Helen, and the atoll itself was Longsuit. Betio, located at the southwestern corner of the atoll, provided an ideal location for an airstrip due to its length and orientation with respect to the prevailing winds. At its western edge, Betio is about 800 yards wide, but tapers to only 20 yards wide on its southeastern tip. On maps with north at the top, Betio suggests the appearance of a bird lying on its back, with the island's 800-yard-long central pier serving as its legs, the northwest point its beak, and the southeastern tip its tail. No point on Betio is more than 10 feet above sea level.

Fresh water was available mostly by storing rain water. The island was covered with coconut palm trees, except for the airfield and areas near the beaches. The

U.S. Navy model used to prepare for bombardment of Betio from the due west. (Naval History and Heritage Command)

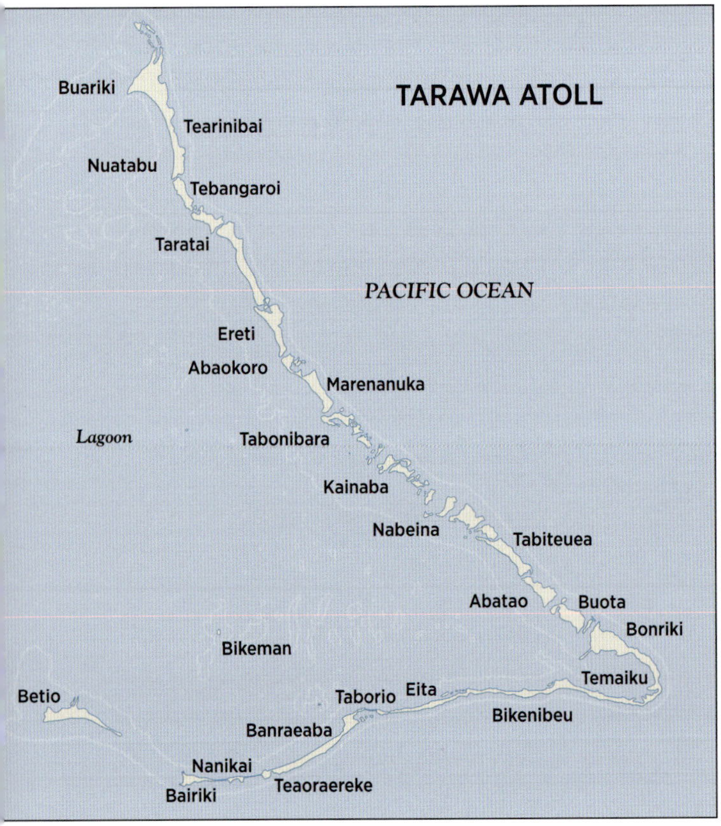

September 1943 reconnaissance photo as Betio is being bombed. (Naval History and Heritage Command)

Low-level, oblique angle reconnaissance photo of the sort very useful for determining position and types of Japanese crew-serviced weapons and fortified positions. From September 1943. (Naval History and Heritage Command)

beaches were 30 to 50 yards wide at low tide, while at high tide they vanished completely. The entire island was surrounded by a coral reef that ran from 500 to 1,200 yards off shore. The island next to Betio was Bairiki, which could be reached on foot at low tide.

Makin and Abemama Atolls

Codenamed Kourbash during Operation Galvanic, Makin Atoll lies about 100 miles north of Tarawa. Like Tarawa it is a triangle, but Makin Atoll does not contain as many islands. Moreover, only the islands on the southern edge of the triangle (Butaritari and Kuma) were large enough for military bases, with an elevation similar to that on Betio. The vegetation was far more lush, providing countless naturally occurring concealed firing positions. Butaritari, shaped like a claw hammer with the hammer's head on the west, made for a very long beach exposed to landings from the sea. There were several short piers or wharfs in the center of the island on the lagoon side, where the small Japanese contingent had its base.

Abemama Atoll had the codename Boxcloth. The islands targeted by the Marines here lie about 100 miles southeast of Betio. The topography and elevations are similar to those of Tarawa and Makin. There were no piers, and the extremely small Japanese garrison confined itself to the southeastern portion of the atoll.

THE GILBERTS IN THE CROSSHAIRS, 1943

Of all the specks of land dotting the Pacific Ocean—thousands of islands, inhabited or not—how did the U.S. political and military establishment come to focus on Tarawa and the other Gilbert Islands in late 1943?

The driving force behind this decision was Admiral Ernest Joseph King, Chief of Naval Operations and Commander-in-Chief, U.S. Fleet. By early 1943, the Allies had made progress in the Solomon Islands with the conquest of Guadalcanal, and while there was still a long way to go there, the steady buildup in ships, supplies, and manpower in the Pacific meant that other possibilities would be opening.

Specifically, King realized that the route across the Central Pacific, from Hawaii through the Marshalls and Carolines, as first proposed by Plan Orange, was now more feasible. At the Casablanca Conference of January 1943, attended by President Franklin Roosevelt, Prime Minister Winston Churchill, and their senior military and naval staffs, King argued that the Allies would be ill-advised after Guadalcanal to allow Japan to regain

the initiative or strengthen its defenses. An Allied offensive was in order.

The British representatives recoiled at this proposal. They wished to remain tightly focused on defeating Germany first. But their own insistence at Casablanca that a cross-channel invasion of France must wait until Italy had been invaded and driven from the war worked against them. This kind of peripheral assault on Hitler would mean substantial naval forces, including landing craft for amphibious assaults, would be lying idle and could therefore be used in the Pacific. After the U.S. Army chief of staff, General George C. Marshall, supported King, the British ultimately acquiesced. Provided that no additional resources were diverted to the Pacific, they agreed that an offensive posture would be acceptable there for 1943.

U.S. planning then got under way. At first, King believed the goal of the United States in the Pacific should be reaching China by driving through the Marshall and Caroline Islands. Only later would he and others decide that the Carolines could be bypassed, and the offensive steered to the northwest to the Marianas, and then close to Japan itself at Iwo Jima and Okinawa. Regardless of his target, however, King faced a formidable American foe to this thinking in General Douglas MacArthur, who wished to make the main—indeed the only—thrust to Japan from his own theater in the Southwest Pacific.

MacArthur was perhaps too ambitious for his own good at this stage. When he proposed a plan (Elkton) in February 1943 for seizing the Japanese base at Rabaul in New Britain that would require more divisions of troops than could be conceivably devoted to it, the Joint Chiefs of Staff (JCS) could not approve. With MacArthur denied a major engagement on New Britain, substantial U.S. Navy resources would be freed in 1943 that could be dedicated to the start of a Central Pacific drive beginning in the Marshalls.

As early as February 1943, King began consulting with Admiral Chester W. Nimitz, Commander-in-Chief, Pacific Fleet and Commander-in-Chief, Pacific Ocean Areas. Any drive beginning in the Marshalls would be Nimitz's to conduct. As the JCS began planning for the Central Pacific push, two things became obvious: (1) attacking the Marshalls, held by Japan since the end of World War I, would be a dangerous leap into the dark if the United States did not obtain good intelligence on if or how the Japanese had fortified the islands; and (2) an attack on the Marshalls under such circumstances would require more resources and manpower than the United States would have available.

It was then that the Gilberts came into focus as the best initial target for the Central Pacific offensive. The JCS planners realized that effective aerial photoreconnaissance of the Marshalls required

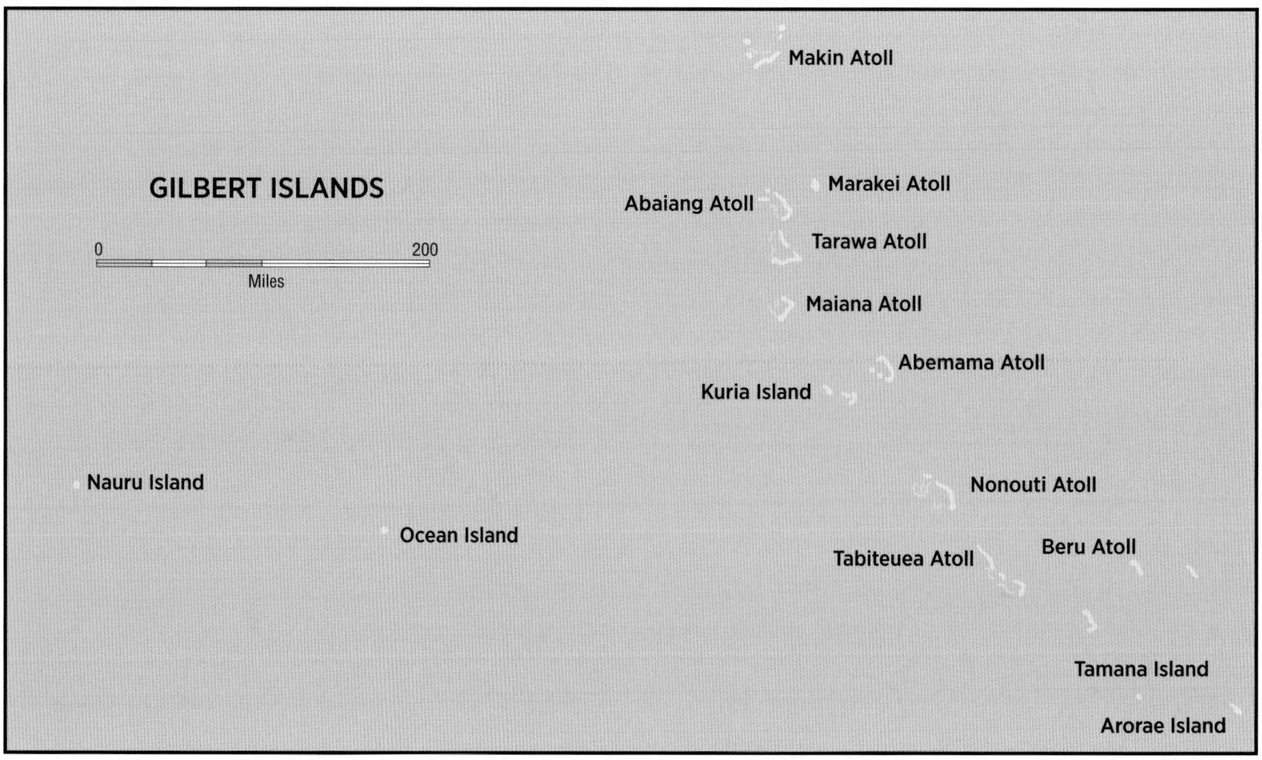

repeated overflights, that land-based aircraft alone could visit the Marshalls with sufficient frequency, and that the Gilberts were the only suitable islands close enough to serve as air bases. The JCS staff further understood that Japanese control of the Gilberts represented a continuing threat to U.S. bases in the Ellice and Samoan Islands, and that shipping to Australia and New Zealand would be less complicated if the Japanese were pushed back from the Gilberts to the Marshalls.

The originator of the Gilberts campaign, Chief of Naval Operations Adm. Ernest J. King. (Naval History and Heritage Command)

On 20 July 1943, the Joint Chiefs themselves, having considered these points, directed Nimitz to begin preparing attacks on Tarawa and Abemama in the Gilberts and nearby Nauru Island on 15 November 1943. Subsequent planning put the entire Pacific Fleet at Nimitz's disposal for the operations, along with the 2d Marine Division and the 27th Infantry Division of the U.S. Army. Nauru, to be assigned to the 27th, was located 440 miles south-southwest of Tarawa and had been added to the operation in order to deny the Japanese an air base from which to attack the Gilberts so readily.

Nimitz chose Vice Admiral Raymond Spruance, then his chief of staff, to lead the newly designated Central Pacific Force. Under Spruance, a new V Amphibious Force (VAF), led by Rear Admiral Richmond Kelly Turner, would be in overall command of the ships and landings, while a new V Amphibious Corps (VAC) under Marine Major General Holland M. Smith would train the landing troops. Spruance, Turner, and Smith, along with the staffs of the divisions or regiments spearheading the assaults, all participated in planning, training, and execution of what was now called Operation Galvanic.

One of their first conclusions was that Nauru was too far away, and too difficult topographically, to risk invading at the same time as Tarawa and Abemama. They pressed Nimitz and then King to substitute Makin, a lightly defended atoll about 100 miles north of Tarawa being used as a seaplane base. King was easy to convince, especially as Makin was much closer to the next objective (the Marshalls) than Nauru, Tarawa, or Abemama. Since Makin was so much more weakly defended, only a reinforced regiment of the 27th Division would be required for its assault, rather than the entire division. As planning and training proceeded, D-Day was moved back five days, to 20 November 1943. This date was as far as the attack could be delayed while still leaving sufficient time for the Marshalls to be hit by late January or early February. And 20 November provided for a rising tide after sunrise, believed to be key to successful landings.

NAVY, MARINE CORPS, AND ARMY PLANNING FOR GALVANIC

V Amphibious Force commander Rear Admiral Turner divided the attacking elements of Galvanic into Northern and Southern Attack Forces. He would command the northern one himself (Task Force 52), destined for Makin, as it was the closest to potential Japanese fleet counterattacks from the Carolines or Marshalls. Rear Admiral Harry Hill commanded the Southern Attack Force (Task Force 53) destined for Tarawa. Spruance, in overall command of Galvanic, elected not to exercise any tactical control, but came along as an observer and chose to witness the Tarawa landings from his flagship, the cruiser USS *Indianapolis* (CA-35), which was also to participate in the bombardment of Tarawa. Turner wanted Major General Holland Smith of V Amphibious Corps at his side at Makin, even though most of the Marines for whom Holland Smith was theoretically responsible would be 100 miles away at Tarawa.

The U.S. fleet expansion begun before the Pearl Harbor attack had led to a massive influx of new sailors

and reserve officers requiring realistic training. The Central Pacific Force consequently spent the summer of 1943 in fleet maneuvers, and its faster elements—the new carriers and fast battleships—conducted raids on far-flung Japanese-held islands (such as Marcus, Wake, Tarawa, and Makin). Meanwhile, aerial photoreconnaissance, both carrier-based and land-based, was providing extraordinarily accurate intelligence about the numbers of Japanese troops at Tarawa and Makin, their dispositions, their fortifications, and their weapons. In one particularly innovative move, counting the Japanese latrines constructed over the water at Tarawa led to a highly precise count of the total number of defenders present (nearly 5,000). The submarine USS *Nautilus* (SS-168) took sea level photos and measured tides and currents. Several British Commonwealth citizens who had formerly lived in the Gilberts were identified and flown to Hawaii to consult on one particularly important and vexing issue: determining the likely level of the high tide at Tarawa on the day chosen for the assault, 20 November.

That day was selected because it provided a rising tide in the early morning. This would allow for several hours of more accurate daylight naval and aerial bombardment before the arrival at high tide of the assault waves in landing craft. Australians and New Zealanders with maritime experience at Tarawa were not united in their views about the likely depth of the water over Tarawa's fringing reef in the lagoon at high tide on 20 November. Most believed it would be about 5 feet. One, Frank Holland, argued that it would likely be 3 feet, which would be insufficient for the main American landing craft—LCVPs (landing craft, vehicle, personnel) and LCMs (landing craft, mechanized)—to get close to the beach, since their draft when loaded was approximately 4 feet. No one could know for sure, and the margin for error was going to be slender no matter what.

As it turned out, 20 November fell during a period of apogean neap tides, when the positions of the moon and sun relative to the Earth were likely to cause the water to hover very close to its average daily level, with neither a high nor low tide that would be pronounced. While Turner could not have known this, he was aware that the tide might be so low as to prevent landing craft such as had been used in the Solomons and New Guinea from getting close to the beach on D-Day. Men might have to wade, and supplies might have to be manhandled or sent in on rubber boats from the reef's edge, between 500 and 800 yards from the beaches.

The planning staff of Major General Julian Smith's 2d Marine Division also knew of these problems. The division D-3 officer (responsible for operations and training), Lieutenant Colonel David M. Shoup, therefore proposed using amphibious tractors (LVTs: landing vehicles, tracked) to lead the attack. Shoup's suggestion was embraced by both Julian and Holland Smith, the latter of whom pressed so forcefully for the use of the vehicles that Turner relented on his initial

A Short History of the 2d Marine Division

In February 1941, the rapid expansion of the U.S. Marine Corps led to the activation of the 2d Marine Division for the first time. Two already existing infantry regiments, the 6th and the 8th Marines, supplied cadres for forming a new infantry regiment, the 2d Marines. These three were joined by an artillery regiment, the 10th Marines, and an engineer regiment, the 18th Marines. In rapid succession, the 2d, 8th, and 6th Marines all served on Guadalcanal, albeit often while attached to the 1st Marine Division. After Guadalcanal was deemed secure in February 1943, the entire 2d Marine Division was relocated to the Wellington, New Zealand, area for rest, recuperation, and training. The cool climate was especially important to aid in the treatment of thousands of malaria cases.

Major General Julian C. Smith replaced Major General John Marston as commanding general of the division in May 1943. Smith saw to its rebuilding and the integration of replacement Marines over the coming months, as the Marines forged strong relationships with the local population who saw them as their defenders against possible Japanese attack. (Most of the New Zealand army was away fighting with British Commonwealth forces in the Mediterranean and elsewhere.) In early August 1943, Vice Admiral Spruance arrived in Wellington to inform Julian Smith and his top staff that the 2d Marine Division was to assault Tarawa the following November.

opposition to the LVTs; he had believed them to be unreliable. But there were not enough LVT-1s in the South Pacific to train with; and the newer models, LVT-2s, being shipped from San Diego, would barely make it to Tarawa by 20 November.

The 2d Marine Division planners looked at Betio in terms of its geography, topography, and hydrology; considered the Japanese posture; and recommended attacking the northwestern portion of the island, through the narrow entrance into the atoll's lagoon. Here the Japanese had been slowest to place mines and other obstacles off shore. Moreover, the lagoon waters would be calmer, without heavy surf or troublesome currents. The disadvantage of this approach was that it required the landing craft to travel more than ten miles once they had been loaded with their Marines or equipment in the designated transport staging area.

To reduce the substantial threat to U.S. troop transports from Japanese ships, submarines, and aircraft in the Marshalls and Carolines, Nimitz pressed for the entirety of Galvanic to be concluded and the troop transports on their way back out within only a few days. His rush would frustrate the 2d Marine Division's staff. They had asked for artillery to be landed on Bairiki island (next to Betio) a day or more before the main landings, and for lengthy preliminary aerial and naval bombardments, as well as a decoy landing intended to keep the defenders away from the actual points of attack. But all these were rejected by Spruance and Nimitz for reasons of time and resources.

The denials made some sense. The Bairiki artillery plan would alert the Japanese to the imminent attack, giving them extra time to sortie their fleet while the vulnerable troop transports lay off shore as fat targets for dive bombers, torpedo bombers, and submarines. For the same reason, U.S. Navy attack forces arriving in the Gilberts for days of massive preliminary bombardments might attract a Japanese response that would arrive before Galvanic was completed. And a decoy landing would require more ships, especially submarine-hunting destroyers, than could be rounded up.

If all these limitations were not enough to stun the leadership of the 2d Marine Division, there would be

One of the Japanese latrines over the water, whose placement in the open allowed for an accurate estimate of the numbers of defenders on the island by photoanalysts. (Hatch Collection, National Museum of the Pacific War)

another one they would have to accept. One of the three reinforced infantry regiments from the 2d Marine Division, the 6th Marines, would be held back for Turner's use as a corps reserve, to be deployed at either Tarawa or Makin as needed, and only if needed, and only on Turner's command.

Julian Smith was shaken by these orders and asked for instructions in writing, so as to be absolved from any blame for attacking too directly and with too few Marines. Holland Smith obliged him with orders on paper. Then Julian Smith and his staff finalized their plans under these less than optimal conditions. Rather than landing two regiments abreast (the 2d and 8th Marines) and having the 6th Marines under his control as a division reserve, Julian Smith had to initially move just a single reinforced regiment toward Betio. This was to consist of the three battalions of the 2d Marines (with one of the three, the 1st Battalion, 2d Marines [1/2], held in reserve by the 2d Marines' commanding officer). They were augmented by the 2d Battalion of

Main Landing Craft

Landing vehicle, tracked (LVT)

This amphibious vehicle was the brainchild of a civilian, Donald Roebling, who originally designed it to navigate the Florida Everglades. The LVT was propelled, both at sea and on land, by tracks, and thus was often known as an amphtrac or amtrac. It moved considerably faster on land (12 mph) than on the water (6 mph). The vehicle came to the attention of the Marine Corps, who wished to consider it for a supply vehicle in amphibious landings. The original variant, the LVT-1 (Alligator), was unarmored and could carry a payload of 4,500 pounds, or 18 men. It often carried two .30-caliber machine guns. The newer LVT-2 (Buffalo) was faster (20 mph land, 7.5 mph water) and carried four machine guns (three .30-caliber, one .50-caliber). Neither of these first two variants had a ramp for cargo or personnel; everyone and everything had to come and go over the sides. The LVTs were not heavily armored, meaning relatively small caliber weapons could penetrate the fronts and sides, and artillery could obliterate them if a shell hit directly.

These vehicles carried the initial assault waves at Tarawa and Makin.

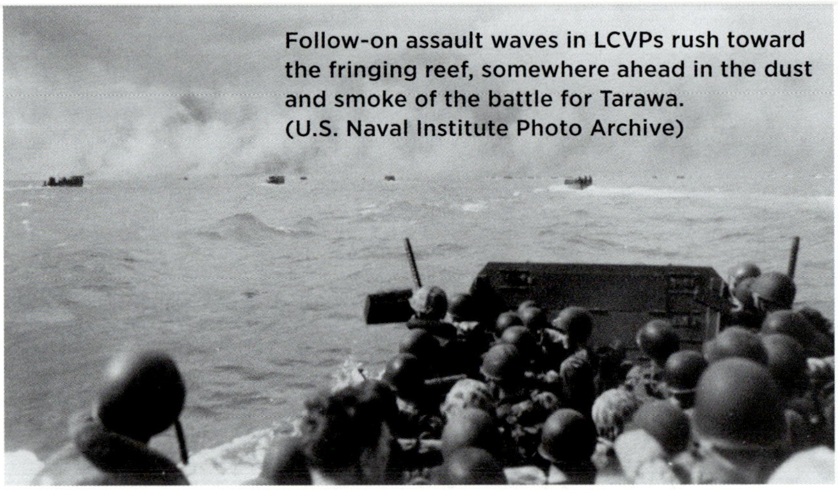

Follow-on assault waves in LCVPs rush toward the fringing reef, somewhere ahead in the dust and smoke of the battle for Tarawa. (U.S. Naval Institute Photo Archive)

Those that survived the first run shuttled in Marines and soldiers from succeeding waves, transported injured back to medical care on board ships, and ferried in the most vital supplies.

Landing craft, vehicle, personnel (LCVP)

These carried more men and equipment to invasion beaches around the world than any other. They were also known as Higgins Boats after their inventor, Andrew Jackson Higgins. They could carry 36 men, a 6,000-pound vehicle, or 8,100 pounds of cargo at a speed of 9 knots. They were shallow draft (slightly more than 3 feet) and were armed with two .30-caliber machine guns. A front ramp could be lowered once the craft's crew had deliberately beached the LCVP, and the assault troops could quickly disembark without the risk of submerging themselves or their gear in water or suffering injury from falling.

These craft carried the bulk of the Marines who landed at Tarawa, as well as many of the supplies brought to its pier. For most of the battle, the LCVPs were incapable of getting any closer than 500 yards of the beach, due to the lower than normal range of tides that left too little water to float the Higgins boats.

Landing craft, mechanized (LCM)

The largest of the craft, these were used to transport men and equipment to the beaches in the Gilberts. Several variants were in use. All could carry a single tank or other motor vehicle, or up to 60 men. With twin propellers, they could move as fast as 12 knots, and drew about the same amount (3 to 4 feet) as a Higgins boat.

the 8th Marines (2/8), with all four battalions known collectively as Combat Team 2 (CT 2). Smith would keep the remaining two battalions of the 8th Marines (1/8 and 3/8) as his division reserve. Whereas Julian Smith and others had learned in school at Quantico that an amphibious assault required a three-to-one manpower advantage in order to succeed, his initial advantage would be more in the range of five-to-three.

According to their plan, CT 2 would land in LVTs (at H-Hour, 0830 on D-Day) along the northwest shore of Betio. The 3d Battalion, 2d Marines (3/2) would hit on the westernmost beach, designated Red 1. The 2d Battalion, 8th Marines, would land on the easternmost, Red 3. And in the middle, the 2d Battalion, 2d Marines would hit Red 2. The entire western shore of Betio was designated Green Beach, and the western portion of the southern shore as Black Beaches 1 and 2, although neither figured into the first plans for the attack.

If all worked perfectly, the preliminary bombardments would allow the assault waves to establish a deep enough beachhead to enable the succeeding waves arriving in LCVPs and LCMs to land intact, even if the Marines they carried had to wade across the reef or be shuttled in by the first waves' now empty LVTs. Together, several thousand Marines would then push quickly across the western, widest portion of Betio. They would pivot to the east, their left, and squeeze the Japanese into the pinpoint eastern tip of Betio, annihilating them. If the plan succeeded, it might require a single day. Garrison troops and airplanes could be landed, and the assault regiments could re-embark for Hawaii before Japanese naval elements could arrive.

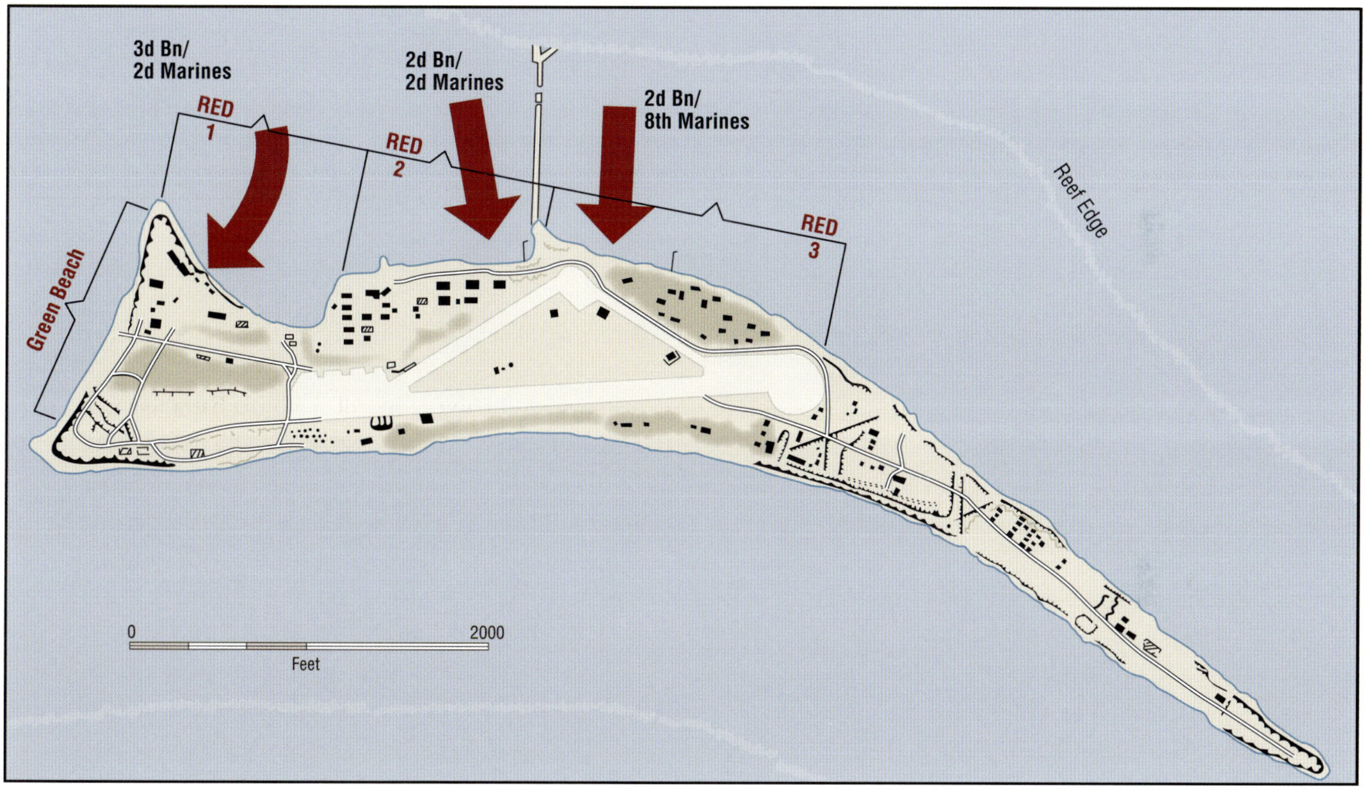

Meanwhile, in devising their attack on Makin, the planners of U.S. Army Major General Ralph Smith's 27th Infantry Division had less time, since only in late September was their target shifted away from more daunting Nauru and their troop requirement lessened. Still, like the 2d Marine Division, the 27th would use LVTs for the initial waves. Their assault would be focused on the largest island of the Makin Atoll, Butaritari. It was longer than Betio—16 miles—and had a wider western beach facing the sea, nearly three miles. Yet most of Butaritari was narrow, and much of the western portion was swampy with lush vegetation, which created substantial impediments to rapid movement.

The 165th Regimental Combat Team of the 27th Infantry Division would put two battalions ashore on the western side of Butaritari Island, and a couple of hours

later a third battalion would proceed through the lagoon onto the central portion of the island. The hope was to draw the Japanese to the west in order to weaken the defenses of the more vital central portion of the island, which the U.S. forces had dubbed the Citadel. Artillery landed on the western beaches could, meanwhile, shell the Citadel. Although he had reservations about Ralph Smith's complex plan, Holland Smith approved it. Like the plan for Tarawa, the one for Makin seemed to call for a day's battle under ideal circumstances. Makin's attackers would have the added advantage of slightly heavier fire support because of the presence of more battleships guarding against the approach of a Japanese fleet from the Marshalls or Carolines.

Chaplains

Prior to departure from New Zealand, the 2d Marine Division's chaplains served to bolster morale among the Marines and to aid in maintaining good relations with the religiously and civically minded among the local populace. On board the transports for Efate and finally Tarawa, more Marines started paying close attention to what the Navy chaplains had to offer. Protestant chaplain Lieutenant Wyeth Willard recorded 22 services on the 19 days on board the USS *Sheridan* (APA-51), with more than 5,000 Marines and sailors in attendance. He interviewed all the Marines of his landing team (1/8) individually to ensure that he had accurate information about next of kin and religious affiliation. Willard conducted baptisms in one of the transport's rear observation turrets.

The Roman Catholic chaplain of the 2d Marines, Lieutenant Francis Kelly, found himself summoned by the new regimental commander, Colonel Shoup, on 19 November, on board the transport USS *Zeilin*. "Padre, I want you to pray for me," Shoup, nominally a Protestant, stated. Kelly was not sure what kind of prayer Shoup was requesting. When he asked for clarification, Shoup made known his greatest concerns at that hour: "I want you to pray that I don't make any mistakes out on that beach; no wrong decisions that will cost any of those boys an arm or a leg or a hand, much less a life. I want you to pray for that, Padre."

In the U.S. operation in Guadalcanal, chaplains had remained in reserve until a firm presence ashore had been established by the assault waves. Ordinarily, their duty was to help with casualties. Willard, however, requested permission to land with the Marines from his battalion (1/8). He was convinced that Marines would receive his spiritual message far more willingly if he were seen to be taking the same risks as they were. At first this request was denied, but after trying repeatedly with the battalion and regimental leadership, he was ultimately allowed to board the landing craft with 1/8, spend the night of D-Day with them, then wade ashore as they faced withering Japanese fire at sunrise on D+1. As it turned out, Willard's and the other chaplains' primary duty ashore was locating and burying the many hundreds of dead rather than assisting with the care of the wounded.

NAVY CHAPLAINS AT TARAWA ASSIGNED TO THE 2D MARINE DIVISION

Division Chaplain

- Lt. William Lumpkin (Protestant/Episcopalian)

2d Marines

- Lt. Norman Darling (Protestant/Methodist)
- Lt. Francis Kelly (Roman Catholic)

6th Marines

- Lt. William O'Neill (Roman Catholic)
- Lt. Gordon Tollefson (Protestant/Lutheran)

8th Marines

- Lt. John Loughlin (Roman Catholic)
- Lt. Douglas Vernon (Protestant/Presbyterian)
- Lt. W. Wyeth Willard (Protestant/Baptist)

10th Marines

- Lt. Harry Boer (Protestant/Reformed)
- Lt. (j.g.) Charles Riedel (Roman Catholic)

18th Marines

- Lt. Arthur Chatten (Protestant/Lutheran)
- Lt. (j.g.) Malcolm MacQueen (Protestant/Baptist)
- Lt. (j.g.) Joseph Wieber (Roman Catholic)

Biographies of Commanders

Admiral Chester William Nimitz Sr. (1885–1966), at Pearl Harbor as Commander-in-Chief, Pacific Ocean Areas

Nimitz, a native of Fredericksburg, Texas, graduated from the U.S. Naval Academy in 1905, after having failed to gain entrance to the U.S. Military Academy. In one of his earliest assignments, he was in command of the destroyer USS *Decatur* (DD-5) when it ran aground in the Philippines, leading to his court-martial and lifelong willingness to extend second chances to fellow officers. He was assigned to the submarine force before and during World War I, and he held various surface and submarine commands between the wars. When the United States entered World War II, Nimitz was chief of the Navy's Bureau of Navigation, responsible for personnel. President Roosevelt selected him to command the Pacific Fleet after the attack on Pearl Harbor, and

After the U.S. Marines had taken Betio Island, Tarawa Atoll, Adm. Chester Nimitz, CINCPAC, inspected the island. L-R: Cdr. Lamar (not shown), Rear Adm. John H. Hoover, Rear Adm. F. P. Sherman, Nimitz, Brig. Gen. Price, and Maj. Gen. J. C. Smith, 27 Nov. 1943. (Naval History and Heritage Command)

later he became Commander-in-Chief, Pacific Ocean Areas, with command over all Allied naval, land, and air forces in the theater.

After successfully overseeing the Central Pacific offensive that captured the Gilberts, Marshalls, Marianas, Peleliu, Iwo Jima, and Okinawa, Nimitz represented the United States at the surrender of Japan in Tokyo Bay on 2 September 1945. He served as Chief of Naval Operations at the rank of fleet admiral from 1945 to 1947, after which he retired from active duty.

Vice Admiral Raymond Ames Spruance (1886–1969), at Tarawa as Commander, Central Pacific Force

Born in Baltimore, Spruance grew up there and in Indianapolis. He graduated from the Naval Academy in 1907, and for the first part of his career specialized in engineering. After various assignments and ship commands, he was serving as a rear admiral and cruiser division commander under Vice Admiral William Halsey as the United States entered World War II. When Halsey was hospitalized in May 1942, he recommended Spruance to replace him to lead the USS *Enterprise* and USS *Hornet* (CV-8) into the Battle of Midway in June. After success in that engagement, Spruance served as chief of staff to Admiral Nimitz and commander of the Central Pacific Force, later to become the U.S. Fifth Fleet. He planned the Gilberts operation and was on the USS *Indianapolis* at Tarawa, where he was content to observe and not issue tactical instructions. Spruance then led U.S. efforts in the Marshalls and Marianas, and at Iwo Jima and Okinawa. For the latter operations, he was awarded the Navy Cross. He retired at the rank of admiral in 1948.

Major General Holland McTyeire Smith (1882–1967), at Makin as Commander of the V Amphibious Corps

Born in Hatchechubbee, Alabama, Smith graduated from Alabama Polytechnic Institute (later Auburn University). He then attended law school at the University of Alabama. At first a member of the Alabama National Guard, in 1905 Smith left his unsatisfying legal career upon receiving a commission as a second lieutenant in the Marine Corps. His first assignment after training was in the Philippines. It was there he earned the nickname "Howlin' Mad" from his men. He was on the front lines in France in World War I. Between the wars he became a proponent of using the Marine Corps as amphibious shock troops, and as the United States entered World War II, he was the acknowledged master of the subject and was ordered to train Army and Marine Corps units. Admiral Nimitz named Smith the commanding general of the V Amphibious Corps (VAC) in September 1943. His first command in a combat setting in World War II would come almost immediately, in the Gilbert Islands. Thereafter he commanded VAC at Saipan and Task Force 56 at Iwo Jima. Smith retired from active duty at the rank of general in 1946.

Rear Admiral Richmond Kelly Turner (1885–1961), at Makin as Commander, V Amphibious Force and Northern Attack Force

Tactical commander of the amphibious assault on the Gilberts, Rear Adm. Richmond Kelly Turner. (Naval History and Heritage Command)

Turner was born in Portland, Oregon, and attended the U.S. Naval Academy, graduating in 1908. He served on destroyers and battleships before taking flight training in 1927. On the eve of World War II, Turner was Director of War Plans in Washington, D.C. He bore some of the responsibility for the failures of communication between intelligence officials, the naval and political leadership, and base commanders in Hawaii that allowed the Japanese to achieve surprise in their attack on Pearl Harbor in December 1941. Turner held tactical command of the first U.S. amphibious operation of the Pacific war, at Guadalcanal in August 1942, and many major ones thereafter, including those at the Russell Islands, New Georgia, the Gilbert Islands, the Marshall Islands, the Mariana Islands, Iwo Jima, and Okinawa. He was promoted to the rank of admiral in 1945 and retired from active duty in 1947.

Major General Julian Constable Smith (1885–1975), at Tarawa as Commanding General of the 2d Marine Division

Smith was a native of Elkton, Maryland, and a graduate of the University of Delaware. He was commissioned a second lieutenant in the Marine Corps in 1909, and saw service at sea, in Mexico, and in Nicaragua, where, as a major, he won the Navy Cross in 1933. As World War II erupted in Europe, Smith was a naval observer at the U.S. Embassy in London. As a major general, in 1942 he took command of Fleet Marine Force Training in New River, North Carolina, and was given command of the 2d Marine Division in New Zealand in May 1943, just before its assignment to assault Tarawa. Smith returned with the 2d Marine Division to its new base on the island of Hawaii, but in April 1944 was moved from division leadership to serve as commanding general of the administrative command of Fleet Marine Forces in the Pacific. Prior to his retirement from active duty in 1946, Smith also served as commanding general of the Department of the Pacific and commander of the Marine Corps Recruit Depot at Parris Island, South Carolina.

The commanding general of the 2d Marine Division at Tarawa, Maj. Gen. Julian C. Smith, wearing glasses on left, with Rear Admiral Harry Hill (two stars on helmet, to the right). (U.S. Naval Institute Photo Archive)

General Ralph Corbett Smith (1893–1998), at Makin as Commander of the 27th Infantry Division's elements

Born in South Omaha, Nebraska, Smith attended Colorado State College. He served in the Colorado National Guard before receiving a commission in the U.S. Army as a second lieutenant in 1916. He was part of the U.S. expedition against Pancho Villa and served on the front lines in France in World War I, where he was wounded during the Meuse-Argonne Offensive. In November 1942, he was named commander of the 27th Infantry Division, which had been an element of the New York National Guard prior to being federalized in 1940. Smith continued as division commander through the Makin (1943) and Saipan (1944) operations. He was relieved of command of the division at Saipan by Marine Lieutenant General Holland Smith due to the perceived slow movement of his soldiers when compared with nearby Marine divisions. He was subsequently named commander of the 98th Infantry Division in Hawaii, and military attaché to France. Ralph Corbett Smith retired from the Army in 1946.

Maj. Gen. Ralph C. Smith (U.S. Army)

THE BATTLE OF TARAWA

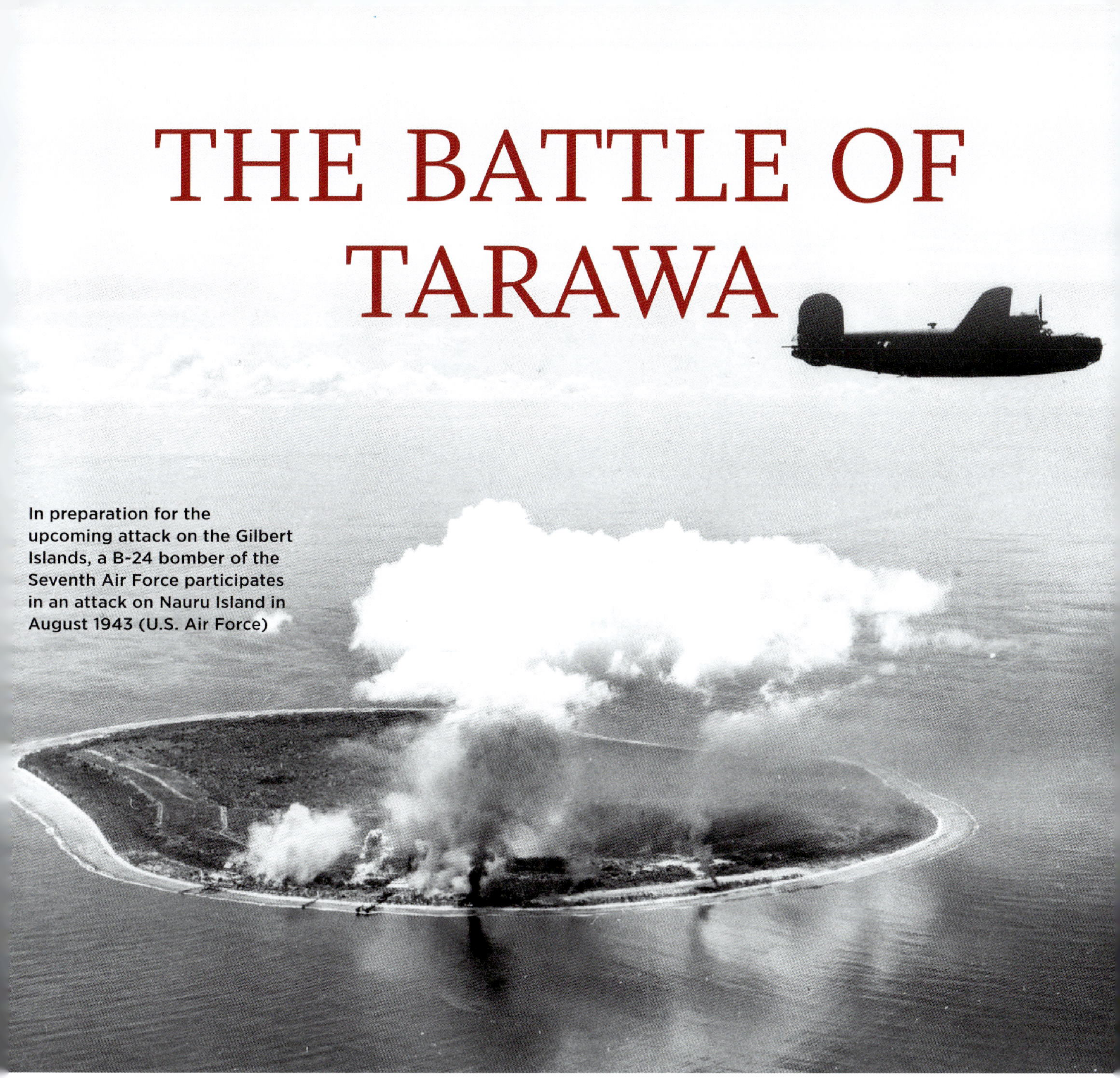

In preparation for the upcoming attack on the Gilbert Islands, a B-24 bomber of the Seventh Air Force participates in an attack on Nauru Island in August 1943 (U.S. Air Force)

PRELIMINARY AERIAL RECONNAISSANCE AND BOMBARDMENT

Until October 1942, the Gilbert Islands were not accessible to U.S. air power except by naval aviation, which had concentrated its dwindling number of carriers in operations and combat around the Solomon Islands. During that same autumn of 1942, the U.S. Army Air Forces first set up a base for operations at Funafuti, in the Ellice Islands (today's Tuvalu), 800 miles southeast of Tarawa. From Funafuti, the 7th Air Force (7 AF) could now operate its B-24 Liberators over the Gilberts, although the bombers were not permanently based at Funafuti until 1943.

The 7 AF first conducted small-scale reconnaissance flights over the Gilberts in January and February 1943, but there was not a major air raid until April 1943. Both Tarawa and Nauru were struck then, as a result of which the Japanese in the Gilberts first learned of the Liberator staging area at Funafuti and retaliated against it, destroying several U.S. bombers. The B-24s were quickly withdrawn to Hawaii, and it would not be until September 1943 that another full-scale mission to Tarawa was scheduled.

This operation, from 17 to 19 September, was the most valuable of all U.S. air missions to Tarawa. The 7 AF component was conducted as a coordinated assault and reconnaissance mission with a Navy carrier task force under Rear Admiral Charles A. Pownall, consisting of the carriers *Lexington* (CV-16), *Princeton* (CVL-23), and *Belleau Wood* (CVL-24). By this time, Funafuti had been augmented by four other new bases in the region from which bombers could reach Tarawa: Canton, Nanumea, Baker, and Nukufetau. The 2d Marine Division staff would be able to draft highly detailed and accurate maps marking the locations and types of Japanese crew-serviced weapons and fortified buildings on Betio due to these September missions. The B-24s also dropped 30 tons of general purpose bombs during the September 1943 operation. While the damage to Japanese installations from the raid would do little to ease the Marines' task when they landed in November, the Japanese were convinced by the attack that basing planes on Betio was a bad idea. They withdrew their medium bombers and never again used Betio as an active air base.

The final phase of preliminary aerial assaults on the Gilberts occurred during the week before the U.S. landings. On D minus 7 (13 November 1943), B-24s dropped 126 20-pound fragmentation cluster bombs on Betio from an altitude of 8,500 feet, as well as 55 500-pound general purpose bombs from 15,000 feet. The Liberators returned on D minus 6, D minus 3, and D minus 1; on the last occasion they were again joined by carrier aircraft in their attacks. Moreover, the B-24s took care to bomb Japanese airfields in the Marshall Islands from which the Japanese might counterattack Tarawa and Makin during the U.S. landings.

The overall effect of these attacks was to acquire first-rate intelligence, but the inaccuracy of the higher-level bombing did little to damage the defenders' fortified positions. Perhaps the greatest effect, and one impossible to calculate precisely, was the Japanese expenditure of their irreplaceable ammunition on antiaircraft fire. For instance, the troops on Betio may have used as much as 70 percent of their existing 13-mm machine gun ammunition against attacking U.S. aircraft during preliminary raids, saving the Marines from facing these rounds later.

STEAMING FOR TARAWA AND D-DAY ON BETIO, 0000–0600

Admiral Harry Hill's Task Force 53 (Southern Attack Force) reached Tarawa after midnight on D-Day, 20 November. It had taken a roundabout path: Leaving New Zealand on 1 November, it had steamed to the northwest and reached Efate in the New Hebrides by 5 November in order to conduct final rehearsals. It left Efate on 13 November and reached its D-Day position, 10 miles west of Betio, just past midnight on 20 November. As it left Efate bound for Tarawa, Task Force 53 first steamed northeast, passing south of the Ellice Islands, then due north, and finally northwest, in the process linking up for nearly two days with Turner's Task Force 52 (Northern Attack Force), which was bound for Makin. With this combined approach from

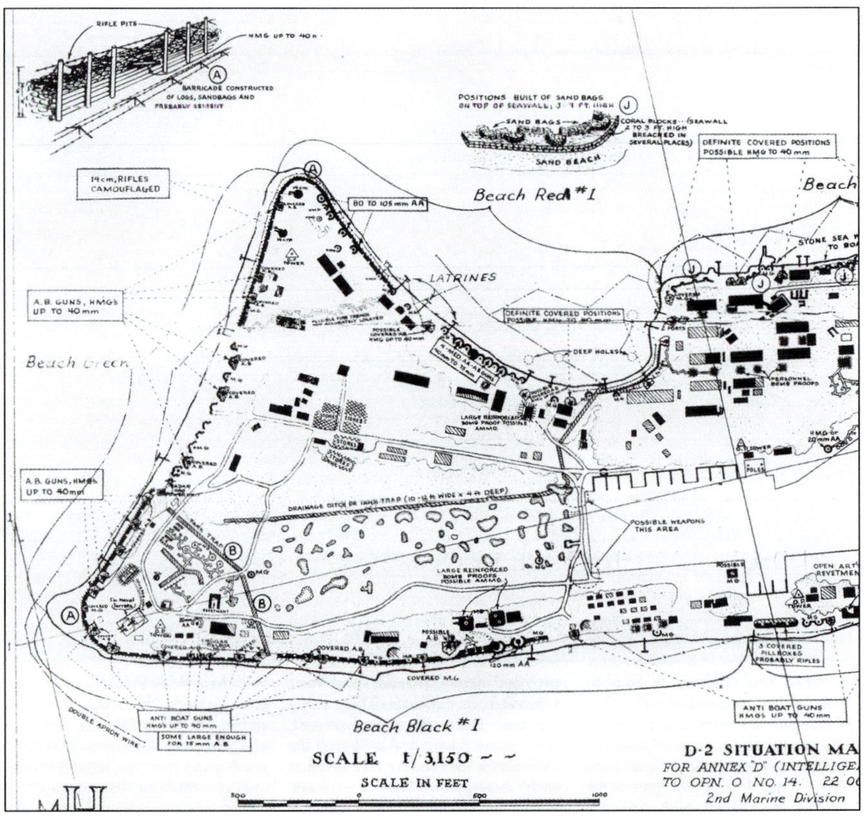

2d Marine Division intelligence map of Betio prepared in October 1943. (U.S. Marine Corps)

the southeast, the chances of discovery by Japanese air or naval forces were greatly reduced.

Task Forces' Approach to Gilberts

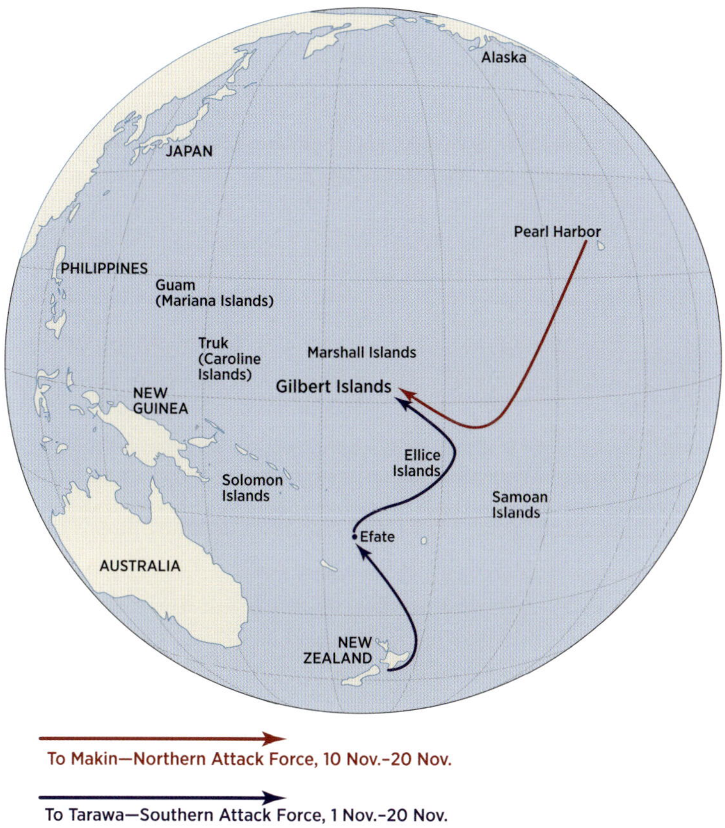

The arrival of all the ships called for by the Galvanic plan required an intricate choreography. The main task forces, consisting mostly of transports, cargo vessels, destroyers, cruisers, and battleships, departed separately from the LSTs (landing ships, tank), which were much slower and therefore needed a head start. Moreover, the LSTs carrying the newer LVT-2s arrived only at the very last minute. Still, the schedule worked flawlessly. Although a Japanese reconnaissance plane was spotted and shot down, the convoys were not discovered by the Japanese in such a way as to lead to any counterattacks prior to D-Day.

One of the most important final tasks was performed by the submarine USS *Nautilus*. She left Pearl Harbor on 8 November and arrived at Tarawa on 18 November. Her job was to perform last-minute reconnaissance at Tarawa and then transport a Marine unit to Abemama. But confusion about her presence near Tarawa and the appropriate signaling protocol led to a near-disaster when she was spotted at night on radar by the approaching Task Force 53 and subjected to naval shelling by the destroyer USS *Ringgold* (DD-500). The *Nautilus* was hit in her conning tower by a dud 5-inch shell before diving, and only heroic efforts at damage control kept the submarine from sinking with all hands before she could surface again safely, effect repairs, and continue to her mission at Abemama.

Few on the 16 troop transports headed for Tarawa slept well that last night. Some Marines were served their "breakfast" of steak and eggs well before midnight. Final religious services were held. Many Marines alternated between hope that they would easily triumph in battle and fear that the Japanese might have already denied them such a victory by having stealthily withdrawn, as they had done at Kiska in the Aleutian Islands before the U.S. assault there the previous August. If so, the Marines might stay relatively safe, but they would not get the chance to fight for which they had joined up.

Sun and Moon Data for One Day

U.S. Naval Observatory Astronomical Applications Department

Betio (Longitude E 172° 56', Latitude N 1° 21')

Saturday, 20 November 1943	**Universal Time + 12h**
Sun	
Begin civil twilight	**05:50**
Sunrise	**06:12**
Sun transit	**12:14**
Sunset	**18:15**
End civil twilight	**18:37**
Moon	
Moonrise	**00:14**
Moon transit	**06:26**
Moonset	**12:38**

Phase of the moon on 20 November 1943: last quarter at 10:43

Any who were not already up and eating were awakened by reveille sounded at 0045 on 20 November. For 961 Marines and sailors involved in the attack on Betio during the next three days, it would be the final morning summons to duty.

Sailors on the command bridge of the USS *Maryland* (BB-46), Hill's flagship, spotted Betio visually at 0250 beneath a third-quarter moon that had been rising in the east since just after midnight. At 0355, the transport group commander, Captain Herbert B. Knowles, reported that the transports were in position to begin disembarking Marines. LCVPs were being lowered into the water from all the transports, into which the first assault waves quickly began to descend via rope ladders for their ride to nearby staging areas. There, they would "crossdeck"—move directly from one boat to the next, over the gunwales—into the LVTs that had arrived separately on board LSTs. By 0430 the Marines of the LVT waves were mostly off the transports. H-Hour, the time set for their arrival on the beaches, was four hours away.

As the transports responded to an order from Hill to shift position in order not to mask the fire from his battleships toward Betio, the LVTs and LCVPs had to follow in the dark as best they could. At 0441, a Japanese gun fired a red star cluster over the south shore of Betio, signaling the defenders to be ready to fight. The Japanese knew the Americans were there and did not mind letting them know. At 0505, the destroyer USS *Meade* (DD-602) began to lay a smoke screen in front of the battleship *Colorado* (BB-45) just as morning twilight was commencing, in order to hide the sparks from the catapult about to launch the *Colorado*'s observation plane. Apparently the smoke was not sufficient, for the Japanese opened fire on the *Colorado* at 0507 with one of the 8-inch naval guns of the shore battery. The Battle of Tarawa had begun.

The preliminary naval bombardment was not set to start for an hour yet, but silencing the Japanese guns with counterbattery fire was paramount. The *Colorado* and the *Maryland* began firing back with their main batteries of 16-inch guns. On board the transport USS *Zeilin* (APA-3), *Time-Life* war correspondent Robert Sherrod saw the flames as the guns fired, then heard their roar as the sound reached him seconds later. Before long, he and everyone else beheld a massive fireball erupting from Betio, indicating that one of the magazines of the largest guns had been hit by the battleship salvos. The U.S. counterbattery fire continued until 0542, when Hill ordered it to stop in order to clear the way for the first carrier-based aerial attack of the morning to begin as scheduled, in the final half hour of twilight before sunrise at 0612.

Rear Admiral Keiji Shibazaki (1894–1943), at Tarawa as commander of the Japanese garrison forces

Shibazaki was born in Kasai, on the largest Japanese island of Honshu. He attended the Imperial Japanese Naval Academy, graduating in 1915. He then held assignments on various types of ships. In the 1930s, he also served as the aide to a member of the Japanese Imperial family and as a field commander of the Special Naval Landing Forces (rikusentai) for 19 months in China. Shibazaki arrived at Tarawa on 20 July 1943 to assume command, having recently been promoted to rear admiral. He devoted the four months at his disposal to improving fortifications, gunnery, and morale. Shibazaki would perish during the battle's first day, 20 November, not long after having allegedly attempted to stiffen the morale of his men by proclaiming that "one million Americans could not take Tarawa in one hundred years."

Yet no planes arrived, either on time or in the minutes that followed. The Navy held its fire while the Japanese continued theirs. Hill's efforts to contact the aircraft were frustrated by the failure of his radios, which the blast effect from the *Maryland*'s main battery had temporarily disabled. While he waited for the planes to appear, shells from the shore batteries began striking close to the troop transports. In some cases, the transports reported shrapnel strikes against their hulls or shells ricocheting off the water and flying over. They immediately steamed ahead to the north to get out of range of the shore fire, complicating operations but not affecting the initial assault waves that were already long gone and into their LVTs, circling just outside the atoll waiting for clearance to enter the lagoon.

At 0559, the Japanese commander, Rear Admiral Keiji Shibazaki, radioed to his headquarters that Betio was under attack and the Americans had launched landing craft. This was precisely the scenario foreseen

The Replacement of Colonel William M. Marshall as Commander of Combat Team 2

Until ten days before Combat Team 2 was to initiate the assault on Tarawa, the 2d Marines' regimental commander, Colonel William McNary Marshall (1893–1960), was set to lead the Marines who landed in the initial waves. Marshall had been a Marine officer since 1917, but the closest he had come to combat experience was in the Marines' Caribbean expeditions between the wars.

In early 1942, Marshall was a colonel and the commanding officer of the 6th Marines, who were stationed with the 1st Provisional Marine Brigade in Iceland. In 1943, he was named regimental commander of the 2d Marines in New Zealand. When the 2d Marines were named as the main regiment for the initial Tarawa assault, that meant much would depend on Marshall's temperament, judgment, and leadership.

Col. William McNary Marshall, March 1942. (Courtesy of family)

His health interfered dramatically. Earlier in his career, Marshall had nearly been retired due to persistent hypertension. He spent at least the last two weeks of July 1943 in the base hospital in Wellington. The precise problem remains a mystery. At the Efate rehearsals in early November, on the way from New Zealand to Tarawa, Marshall showed outward signs of not being up to the task. He appeared to fall asleep at meetings and became forgetful. Some Marines believed he was having what they called a nervous breakdown. Many historical accounts called it a heart attack. Julian Smith wrote to his wife while on board the USS *Maryland* bound for Tarawa that he had replaced Marshall with David Shoup because Marshall "could not physically or nervously stand the strain." Thus it was that Lieutenant Colonel Shoup, previously the 2d Marine Division's operations and training officer, was promoted to colonel and given his first combat command just ten days before D-Day.

Marshall was left behind at Efate as the 2d Division steamed for Tarawa, and was then sent back to the United States. He spent extended portions of 1944 at St. Elizabeths, a federal psychiatric hospital in Washington, D.C. While in private Smith alluded to a psychological basis for Marshall's relief, in later published accounts he vaguely cited an illness and stated that Marshall's retirement was for physical disability. Marshall wrote to Smith in January 1944 to thank him for giving him a "break" on his last fitness report, and to state, "the only cure for what I have is to figure out how to make a 100 percent comeback, either as an 'average' Colonel or in some other line of war work."

Marshall retired from active duty in October 1944 and died, of a heart attack, at the age of 66 in his native Colorado.

by the Japanese in their counterattack plan. They began moving submarines and land-based airplanes toward the Gilberts, yet no significant surface units could approach due to the recent depletion of Japanese naval aviation in action around Rabaul. Shibazaki and his nearly 5,000 men would have no hope of rescue.

INTO THE LAGOON AND TO THE BEACH: D-DAY, 0600–0930

Hill waited until 0605 before giving up on the arrival of the planes from the carriers and ordering the naval bombardment to resume. In the 23 minutes since he had stopped the counterbattery bombardment, the Japanese had been free to target U.S. ships without a response, and to move their men around without danger. The naval bombardment had only just begun again when the planes finally turned up. Some sort of miscommunication had occurred during the final planning at the end of October in Hawaii, resulting in the carriers' thinking that their planes were to be expected at sunrise (which they calculated as 0611). But Hill, who had already left for Efate, was never informed. Now in the first light of D-Day, he again ordered ship-based fire to cease, while the planes bombed and strafed for about ten minutes before retiring. At 0620, Hill was free to begin the originally scheduled naval bombardment at "William Hour" (W-Hour).

The Southern Attack Force's plan for Tarawa foresaw 75 minutes of naval fire to commence upon the conclusion of the initial air strike. The goals were to engage in counterbattery fire to knock out any Japanese heavy guns still firing at the Navy, and to have fire support ships close drastically on the island, some as near as 2,000 yards, in order to destroy all previously identified coastal

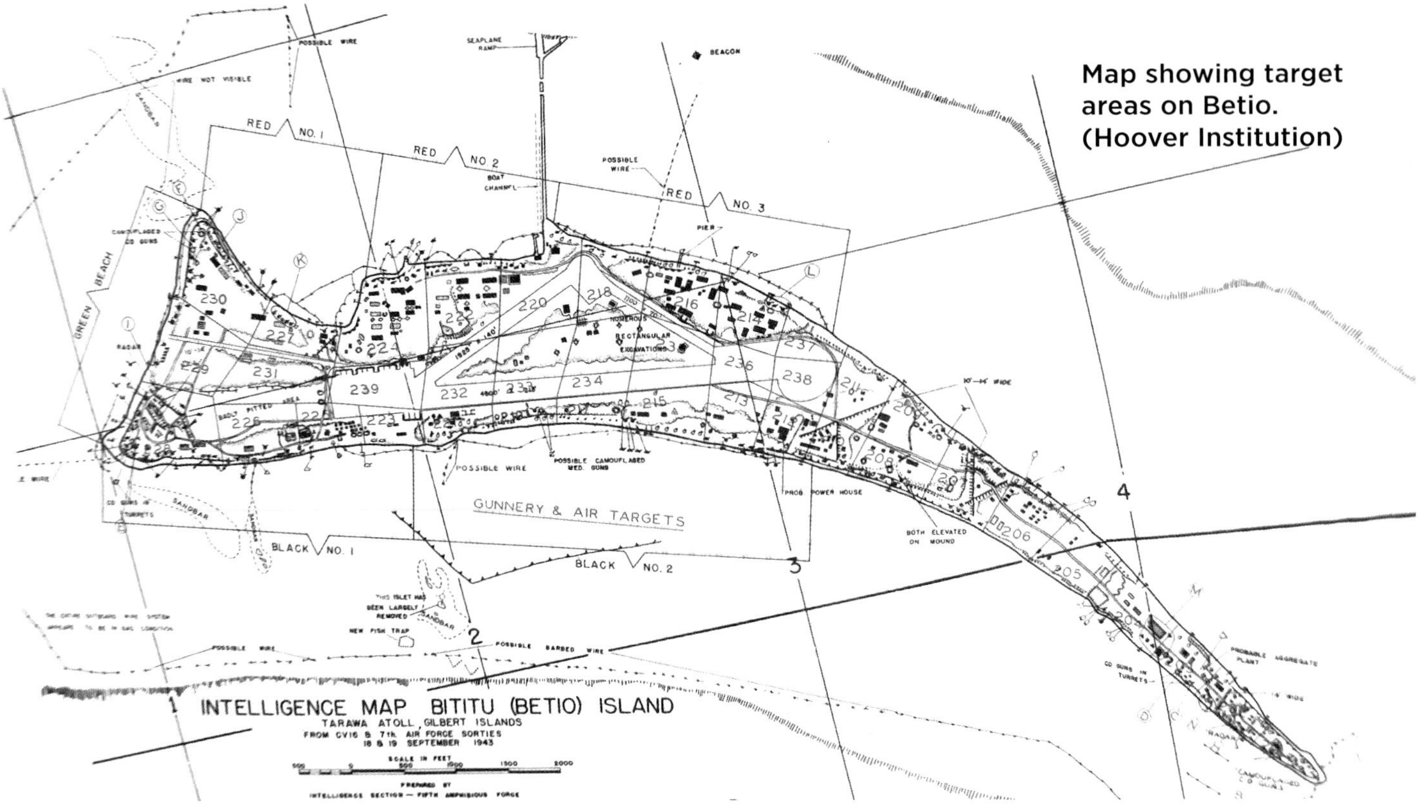

Map showing target areas on Betio. (Hoover Institution)

guns. After a ten-minute built-in pause, a second phase, to last 45 minutes, was more directly targeted at the invasion beaches and their fortified emplacements, although other areas would also be blanketed by fire designed to neutralize Japanese positions. During this second phase, the fire support ships would shift from south of Betio Island to its west. This position was necessary so that any ricochets—which were likely due to the extremely flat trajectory of shells fired from close range with the standard quantity of propellant used in naval surface warfare—would not hit the gathering landing forces and their support ships in the lagoon to Betio's north.

A second aerial assault on the beaches would take place immediately prior to the landings at H-Hour (originally 0830). After H-Hour, naval fire support would occur as called for by the Marine units and their attached Navy spotters. All of Betio was divided into areas assigned a three-digit designation beginning with the numeral 2. For instance, the area just south of the base of the long pier was area 220; the northwest tip (the Bird's Beak) was 230; and the stubby Burns Philp wharf off Red Beach 3 lay in 216. Preliminary naval fire was mostly directed at entire areas rather than at specific structures within them. The areas, at their largest, measured about 700 feet by 800 feet; at the smallest (area 201, at the extreme southeastern tip of Betio), 700 feet by 300 feet.

Three thousand tons of shells would be fired over two and a half hours. The preliminary naval and aerial bombardment on D-Day was not without positive effects for the U.S. forces, although it vastly underperformed hopes and expectations:

- Most critically, Japanese wired communication was obliterated, and since the Japanese did not appear ready to make use of runners and written messages, they had no centralized control of all their forces at any time during the battle.
- An unknown number of Japanese were killed or rendered ineffective by the bombardment—but, again, not anywhere near the number hoped.
- Some of the larger naval guns that might have even more seriously disrupted the landings were knocked out, along with some of the smaller, but still potent, dual-purpose antiaircraft guns.
- Camouflage, in the form of screens, netting, or sand poured on top of emplacements, was loosened, shifted, or destroyed. This degradation of the camouflage was not only useful but essential to rapid Marine victory on Betio.
- However, almost all reinforced positions along the beaches and inland were intact: firing emplacements for rifles and machine guns shielded by walls of coconut-tree logs, conical steel pillboxes, and steel-reinforced concrete shelters protected

most of the firing positions that would waylay the Marines coming ashore and on the island for the next four days.

Outside the lagoon, the bombardment appeared impressive to the Navy as well as to Marines on LVTs. Rear Admiral Howard F. Kingman, commander of the fire support group who had earlier boasted that his naval fire would "obliterate" Tarawa, believed "it was almost impossible for any human being to be alive on Betio." Correspondent Sherrod, however, who had initially shared Kingman's awe at the apparent power of the bombardment, soon noted that Japanese shells began landing near the transports, one a mere 50 yards from the *Zeilin*, on board which he was watching.

The first American ship to enter the Tarawa lagoon was the minesweeper USS *Pursuit* (AM-108). She approached the entrance to the lagoon from the northwest just before sunrise, accompanied by a second minesweeper, the USS *Requisite* (AM-109), and two destroyers, the USS *Dashiell* (DD-659) and USS *Ringgold*. The *Pursuit* lowered gear to search for acoustic and magnetic mines and began clearing a safe path for the rest of her small convoy and all the LVTs, LCVPs, and other ships and boats subsequently to enter the lagoon. She immediately came under Japanese fire from shore, which she answered with her own 3-inch gun. The two destroyers came to the *Pursuit*'s assistance and began a full day of fire support with their 5-inch guns.

Having taken on as a pilot a New Zealand reserve naval officer familiar with Tarawa, and accompanied by two LCVPs to lay a smokescreen, the *Pursuit* first approached the lagoon entrance at 0620. She found no mines there or inside the lagoon, confirming in just a few minutes the wisdom of the northern approach plan of Julian Smith, division chief of staff Merritt A. Edson, and Shoup. Whatever trials awaited the Marines and Navy in the north side's lagoon, the mines and obstacles on the south and west beaches would have been costlier. When she was finished looking for mines, the *Pursuit* put out marker buoys to indicate the line of departure (LOD). Each assault wave bound for the three beaches would start there simultaneously, and the ensuing wave would follow several minutes later.

Meanwhile the *Ringgold*, firing and being fired upon by shore batteries, was hit twice, each time by a dud. Although damaged, she was able to continue throughout the battle, providing fire support from the lagoon, recovering wounded, and providing initial care to them before transferring them out to the transports. At 0715, the *Pursuit* assumed a position to mark the LOD and turned on her searchlight, so that the approaching LVTs could see her through the smoke generated to shield her from the shore batteries.

The *Pursuit* quickly noticed a problem with the LVTs of the initial assault waves: they were late. Her radar allowed her to calculate, and report to Hill, that the LVTs were 24 minutes behind schedule. At 0803, Hill reacted by delaying H-Hour by 15 of those 24 minutes. Not only could the LVTs not make up any of the 9 minutes Hill had already been unwilling to concede to them; they fell even farther behind. By the time the first wave crossed the line of departure at 0825, the LVTs were a full 39 minutes behind. At 0823, Hill partially bowed to the inevitable once again, just as the first wave was reaching the LOD, by postponing H-Hour to 0900, 30 minutes later than originally scheduled.

The delay stemmed from several factors. Starting with the first predawn shifting of the transport area, the LVTs had never been able to catch up again. The LVT-2s coming directly from Samoa had never trained with the LVT-1s or the LCVPs that were delivering the Marines for their crossdeck transfers. In the dark and twilight, they had required more time than expected. The older LVT-1s in the first waves were in generally subpar mechanical condition and were slower by design than the LVT-2s in the second wave. But the superior speed and condition of the LVT-2s did no good, since they were stuck several minutes behind the LVT-1s of the first wave.

Once again, the Navy's airplanes were not kept fully informed of the changes, and they appeared on time by their own schedule, at 0825, for a five-minute bombardment near the landing beaches immediately prior to the originally scheduled H-Hour. This attack was successfully called off and rescheduled for 0855, five minutes ahead of the new, final H-Hour. When the planes re-arrived at 0855 and executed their final pre-landing attacks, naval fire was suspended on Hill's order, to avoid danger to or interference with the planes, and then to prevent any chance of placing rounds among the landing craft. Although Julian Smith and Edson argued that the Marines needed the continuing naval fire to hinder last-minute Japanese preparations, Hill would not budge. From 0900 until the first waves began arriving at their beaches between

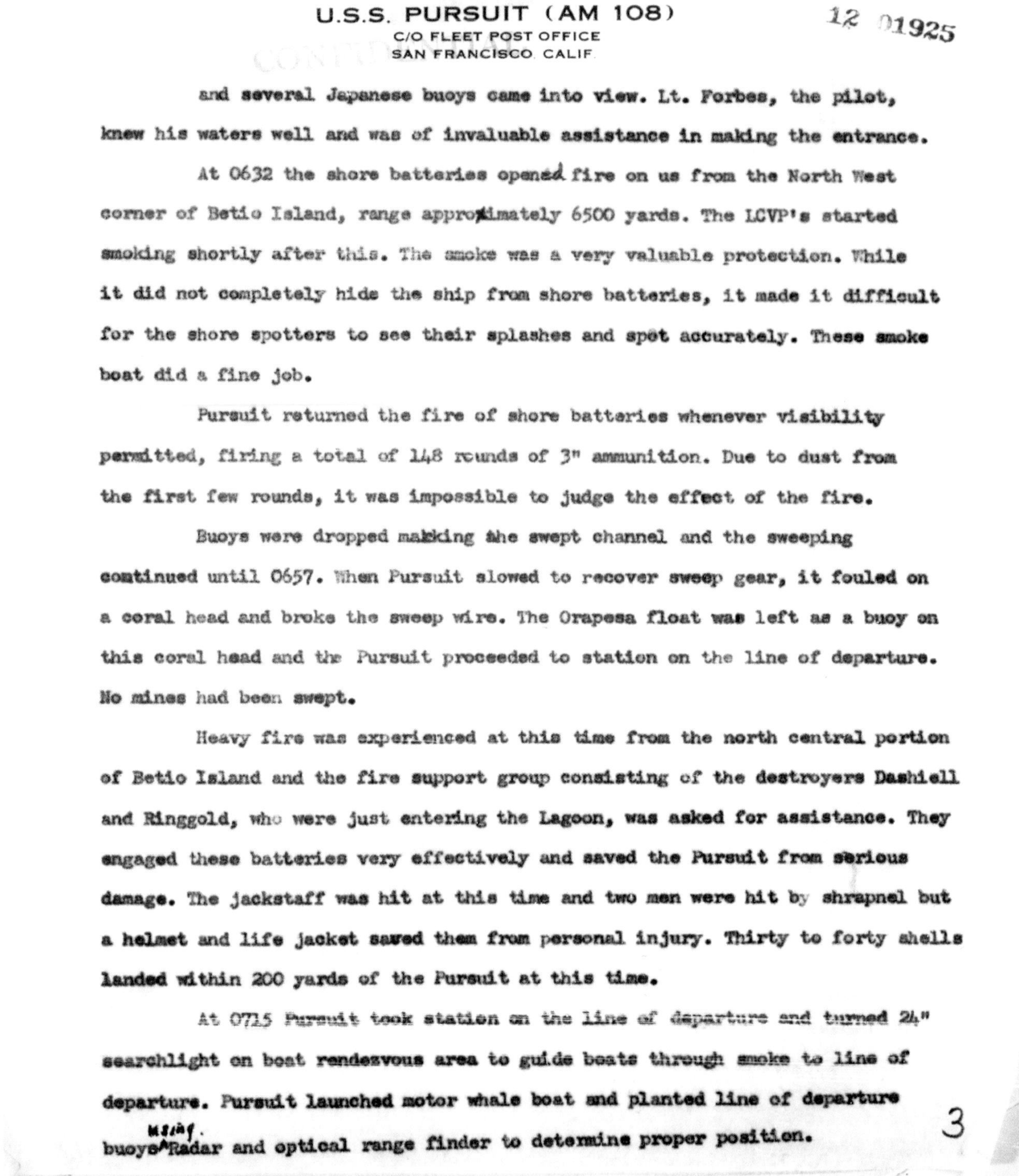
U.S.S. PURSUIT (AM 108)
C/O FLEET POST OFFICE
SAN FRANCISCO, CALIF.

12 01925

and several Japanese buoys came into view. Lt. Forbes, the pilot, knew his waters well and was of invaluable assistance in making the entrance.

At 0632 the shore batteries opened fire on us from the North West corner of Betio Island, range approximately 6500 yards. The LCVP's started smoking shortly after this. The smoke was a very valuable protection. While it did not completely hide the ship from shore batteries, it made it difficult for the shore spotters to see their splashes and spot accurately. These smoke boat did a fine job.

Pursuit returned the fire of shore batteries whenever visibility permitted, firing a total of 148 rounds of 3" ammunition. Due to dust from the first few rounds, it was impossible to judge the effect of the fire.

Buoys were dropped makking the swept channel and the sweeping continued until 0657. When Pursuit slowed to recover sweep gear, it fouled on a coral head and broke the sweep wire. The Orapesa float was left as a buoy on this coral head and the Pursuit proceeded to station on the line of departure. No mines had been swept.

Heavy fire was experienced at this time from the north central portion of Betio Island and the fire support group consisting of the destroyers Dashiell and Ringgold, who were just entering the Lagoon, was asked for assistance. They engaged these batteries very effectively and saved the Pursuit from serious damage. The jackstaff was hit at this time and two men were hit by shrapnel but a helmet and life jacket saved them from personal injury. Thirty to forty shells landed within 200 yards of the Pursuit at this time.

At 0715 Pursuit took station on the line of departure and turned 24" searchlight on boat rendezvous area to guide boats through smoke to line of departure. Pursuit launched motor whale boat and planted line of departure buoys using Radar and optical range finder to determine proper position.

3

USS *Pursuit* after action report. (National Archives)

0910 and 0922, the Japanese were free to regain their composure, observe the lagoon, and move troops from the south coast to the north to meet the initial waves of Marines.

Also at 0855, the first Marines to directly engage the Japanese at Tarawa began their assault. Combat Team 2's scout and sniper platoon, assisted by combat engineers, landed at the pierhead from LCVPs with the mission of eliminating any Japanese positions that could pour enfilading fire from the 700-yard-long structure onto the LVTs approaching Betio on either side. This unit, led by Lieutenant William Deane Hawkins, consisted of three sections, one of which was a combat engineer unit led by Lieutenant Alan Leslie.

Hawkins' Marines first secured the seaplane ramp that descended at the end of the pier over the edge of the reef. Gasoline had been stored in barrels there, and Japanese small arms fire began striking all around

Aerial view of ships formation during battle operation of Tarawa. Landing craft, looking like waterbugs, make for the beach. (U.S. Naval Institute Photo Archive)

Marine-laden landing craft form the first wave and head for the beach at Tarawa. (U.S. Naval Institute Photo Archive)

Marines arriving on a secure beach later in the battle wade ashore through the surf. Landing boats and barges brought them to within 500-800 yards of the beach but the coral bottom prevented the boats from coming any closer to the shore. (U.S. Naval Institute Photo Archive)

them. Hawkins, four of his men, and Leslie with his flamethrower moved down the pier toward the beach, seeking to kill or eliminate any threats. Leslie set some shacks ablaze that he believed to be housing snipers, and the conflagration spread to the pier, creating a gap that would hamper later American efforts to use the pier for resupply.

Satisfied to the best of their knowledge that the top of the pier had been cleared, and that Marines in the LVTs would be spared fire from their flank, Hawkins and the others returned to their LCVPs and struggled, like all in LCVPs that day, to get ashore. They could not know that many more Japanese lurked under the pier or would make their way down there. They had done their best to eliminate a serious immediate threat to the first waves, killed the first Japanese to face the Marines on Betio, and lost no men in the process.

LVTs of the first waves move ashore. (Hatch Collection, National Museum of the Pacific War)

LVT Experiences in the Initial Waves

LVTs provided a way for Marines to arrive on shore in great numbers, more or less simultaneously, with quite limited protection from opposing fire. Their rapid movement once in contact with the reef or on land, and some thin armor retrofitted to the vehicles, offered but scant protection from opposing fire. Major Henry C. Drewes, commander of the 2d Amphibian Tractor Battalion, supervised the installation of machine guns on the previously unarmed LVT-1 supply vehicles. Two forward facing .50-caliber guns were placed on each vehicle, and many had at least one .30-caliber gun mounted in the rear. Thus, the LVTs provided the only targeted suppression of Japanese machine gun nests and rifle pits in the beach area as the first waves drew closer.

The LVT gunners and drivers were highly vulnerable, however. The thin armor could not stop the Japanese 13-mm machine gun rounds, and the Marine gunners had to be at least partially exposed in order to aim. The 2d Amphibian Tractor Battalion would suffer the highest casualty rate of any unit in the battle. Drewes himself was killed in action in the lagoon during the initial landings.

The 15–20 Marines who could be crowded into what had originally been designed as cargo space were vulnerable to rounds piercing the sides and front of the LVTs. They were also subject to repeated Japanese attempts to hit them with shells designed to burst in the air above them and rain down shrapnel.

The *Saidu Maru*, a sunken trawler, used as a concealed firing position by Japanese defenders who waded out to it. (Hatch Collection, National Museum of the Pacific War)

This method failed, though, because the Japanese had constructed the shells poorly; upon exploding, they virtually disintegrated rather than breaking apart into lethal metal shards. Once the Marines arrived and sought to disembark, they had to clamber up and over the sides, exposing themselves to enemy fire and dropping many feet to the ground.

The LVTs took fire from all manner of other weapons in the lagoon: a few remaining anti-boat guns; dual-purpose antiaircraft guns now leveled at the water; machine guns; grenade launchers; and small arms. The machine gun and rifle fire came not only from emplacements around the water's edge, but also from under the pier and the hulk of the trawler *Saidu Maru*, in the lagoon at the reef's edge near the boundary of beaches Red 1 and 2.

Donald Tyson, "All Might Not Go As Expected,"

***PROCEEDINGS*, NOVEMBER 1999, PP. 54–55**

At a predetermined point offshore, everyone was ordered to get down in the tractor and prepare for the final run to the beach. As we neared the island, our machine guns opened fire, and the blasts from our two .50-calibers were ear-splitting. Any thought that no one had survived our naval onslaught was dispelled quickly, as the Japanese unleashed an intensive barrage. The Browning Automatic Rifle (BAR) man firing our port .50-caliber gun died instantly, as the first rounds of enemy rifle and machine gun fire raked our Amtrac. Simultaneously, a steady stream of bullets began coming in one side of the tractor and going out the other with a pinging sound—except when someone's body got in the way. Our starboard-side .50-caliber gunner was killed, and a replacement for the port-side gun jumped up, grabbed the cocking handle and pulled it back, but he was killed before firing a shot. Our gunner on the .30-caliber machine gun had been hit, too. At about this time, an antiboat gun shell tore into our starboard track, causing the tractor to make a half right-turn stop. The port side then dropped into a small shell hole, exposing part of the inside to the beach.

We had been on board our Amtrac for almost five hours, and during that period, equipment was scattered everywhere about the interior. As our occupants began to debark, I started trying to round up my gear, which included a five-gallon can of diesel oil for the flamethrower, a pack loaded with blocks of TNT, and my rifle. By this time, everyone had gone over the side, except Corporal Mohacsi and myself. Boot camp had taught us always to pick up an automatic weapon when available; therefore, I left my rifle in favor of the BAR lying in the bottom of the tractor. Quickly, I began removing the BAR magazines from the shoulder harness of our first casualty and putting them inside my dungaree jacket. One of the wounded men—because he was in tremendous pain—begged me to drag a dead man off his legs. I made him as comfortable as possible and then decided to take stock of my own situation before jumping into the water.

3d Battalion, 2d Marines (3/2) (component of Combat Team 2)

CO: Major John Fred Schoettel

Time of Arrival: 0910

Target/Goal: Large guns at northwest tip of Betio, inland on western portion of island.

RED BEACH 1 IN THE INITIAL ASSAULT

The honor of arriving on shore first at Betio fell to the 3d Battalion, 2d Marines (3/2) on Beach Red 1. The plan was for two of its companies to arrive in LVTs and proceed inland past the beach before disembarking over the sides of the LVTs, which would return to the reef's edge to ferry in subsequent waves from the LCVPs that might be stranded there by the low water.

I Company of 3/2 would land on the right (to the west) and seize the northwest tip of Betio (the Bird's Beak), including whatever remained of its largest

naval guns. K Company of 3/2 had what appeared to be the most dangerous line of attack of any that morning: into the heart of a cove, or "re-entrant," the only concave section of the entire assault area, which potentially would expose K Company's Marines to fire from ahead and each side. Such fire did in fact occur, accompanied by machine gun fire from the *Saidu Maru*, meaning K Company was being hit from *four* sides. Not surprisingly, it suffered severe casualties in the water and once ashore. According to the plan, I and K Companies were to link with each other, while K Company was to establish contact with Marines from 2/2 to the east on Red 2. L Company of 3/2 was to arrive in the first waves of LCVPs immediately following I and K.

Nothing worked according to plan or anything close to it, and this approach to Betio proved so dangerous that it would not be used thereafter in the battle for any reinforcements or supplies. I Company landed more securely than K, but was pinned down behind an exceptionally high portion of the seawall, 5 feet tall in places, that often made it fatal for Marines trying to climb over with rifles or other weapons. LVTs could surmount the seawall neither here nor at lower points.

K Company's Marines on the left were either pinned on the beach or became casualties, except for the few who managed to penetrate inland on their own initiative. They had little central direction, because 17 of the battalion's 37 officers became casualties on D-Day. All of the assault engineers from the 18th Marines who had been detached to 3/2 became casualties in the water or else on the beach, thus making it impossible for Marines wishing to advance to surmount the pillboxes or other positions that required explosives or flamethrowers to overcome. All in all, the assault companies of 3/2 lost half their men, either killed or wounded, within the first two hours. Only when the succeeding waves of L Company began to wade ashore on the extreme right and attack on Green Beach would anything resembling progress begin.

The battalion commander, Major John Schoettel, at the reef's edge in an LCVP and unable to judge events ashore accurately, believed his battalion had been essentially wiped out while landing or wading in. The fierce Japanese resistance led him to stay in his boat in the lagoon for many hours.

Red Beach 1 Status at 1000: Marines pinned on beach in center of cove and at northwest tip. Scattered remnants find way to push as far as 50 yards inland before encountering emplacements thwarting any further advance.

RED 3 INITIAL ASSAULT WAVES

2d Battalion, 8th Marines (2/8) (component of Combat Team 2)

CO: Major Henry Pierson Crowe

Time of Arrival: 0917

Target/Goal: Left (east) flank of U.S. positions, Burns Philp wharf, northeastern taxiway, junction of taxiways at top of airfield.

Of all the initial assault battalions, 2/8 arrived with the fewest casualties and the most cohesion. In part this was due to the suppressive naval gunfire of the preliminary bombardment, in part due to luck, and in part due to the crowding of the entire battalion into a far narrower portion of their assigned beach, Red 3, than had been planned.

Heavy fire from the eastern tip of Betio and from the area of the Burns Philp wharf drove units from 2/8 designated for the extreme left flank of the U.S. positions significantly to their right (west). Some of the most poignant early photographs taken during the battle show the intense crowding here at the seawall. Yet 2/8 suffered the fewest casualties of the three initial assault battalions: no more than 25 of 552 in the first three waves.

The plan called for Company F of 2/8 to be on the left and drive south and east upon landing. Company E was to move due south onto the airfield's northeastern taxiway and the junction of that taxiway with the northwestern one. G Company, arriving next via LCVPs, was to come into the center and help exploit the earliest gains.

Here as elsewhere, the seawall prevented the advance of LVTs. Only a few found a gap, most significantly the one carrying Lieutenant Aubrey Edmonds, E Company's executive officer. He drove through this gap and onto the airfield before ordering everyone out. Naturally assuming other Marines would be nearby, they instead were shocked to discover they were alone and vulnerable. They held their position for hours, but ultimately had to withdraw back to their battalion behind the seawall on Red 3. Edmonds was seriously wounded as he followed his men back. Sergeant Melvin McBride, taking charge

of what was left of his platoon after both its leader and platoon sergeant fell, also led men over the wall early to stake out an isolated position, before they too were forced to withdraw some while later.

The battalion commander of 2/8, Major Henry P. Crowe, jumped into the water with his headquarters unit from their LCVP, carrying a shotgun and moving fast not only to avoid the Japanese fire but also to establish personal command. Crowe reached Red 3 only four minutes after his battalion's final LVTs. His battalion's radios were the only ones to arrive fully functional, and he would be a key link between all landed troops and the ships off Betio during the early portion of the battle. Crowe attempted to motivate his battalion to move over the wall and inland as planned, but while his Marines complied, many became casualties as they faced the most daunting emplacements on all of Betio—concrete reinforced "bombproofs"—and would find their progress hindered by them throughout the battle.

Status at 1000: Two significant, but totally isolated advances onto the airfield. Heavy fire from east pins most of 2/8 into a narrow segment of Red 3 behind the seawall. Fortified positions prevent any major advances over the seawall. Crowe in full command with radio communications.

RED BEACH 2 INITIAL ASSAULT WAVES

2d Battalion, 2d Marines (2/2) (component of Combat Team 2)

CO: Lieutenant Colonel Herbert Raudenbusch Amey Jr. (KIA)

Time of Arrival: 0922

Target/Goal: Center of U.S. lines, northwest taxiway, site of CT 2 command post.

The most devastated of the three initial landing battalions was 2/2. In addition to Japanese fire, 2/2 faced barbed wire that slowed its LVTs and in some cases stopped them, despite training tests showing the LVTs could drive right through.

E Company of 2/2 was to land on the right (west) and establish contact with K Company of 3/2 on Red 1, while F Company was to land on the left (east) closest

Marines from 2/8 near their battalion commander's initial command post on Red 3, between the seawall and the lagoon. (Naval History and Heritage Command)

to the pier. The battalion commander, Lieutenant Colonel Herbert Amey, chose to put more of his rifle units in LVTs as opposed to heavy weapons units as the other battalion commanders had done, meaning his G Company, a rifle company, would land in LVTs to assist and exploit gains by E and F Companies more quickly.

The heaviest and deadliest Japanese fire of the battle came from an area the Marines called the Pocket, at the boundary between Red 1 and Red 2. This fire played havoc with 2/2's arrival. E Company was practically destroyed; five of its six officers were killed on or in the water, or on the beach. One of its platoons, like others to follow, was driven to the right by the fire from the Pocket and ended up on Red 1, cut off from the rest of the battalion. One platoon of G Company landed all the way at the Bird's Beak. Those who made it ashore on Red 2 had to seek cover from murderous fire behind the seawall or in shell holes. Almost all the combat engineers had been

Tanks in Action

The Marines employed two types of tanks in their assault on Tarawa: the diesel-engine variant of the Sherman medium tank (M4A2) with a 75-mm main gun; and the light Stuart (M3A1) with a 37-mm main gun.

Given the immense contribution made by the only two medium tanks that survived for the entire three-day battle, it is clear that if more had been able to make it ashore and had been integrated effectively with infantry units, the battle could have been won more quickly and with far fewer U.S. casualties. But getting the tanks ashore, whether medium or light, proved to be the most difficult task of all.

Fourteen M4A2s of C Company of the I Marine Amphibious Corps (IMAC) tank battalion were assigned to the 2d Marine Division for the assault on Tarawa. C Company consisted of three platoons of four tanks each, plus two headquarters tanks. The company commander was First Lieutenant Edward Bale, who commanded the tank *Cecilia* (the crews gave all the tanks names that began with their company designator, the letter C). Their medium Sherman tanks were brought to Tarawa on board the USS *Ashland*, a dock landing ship, which could launch mechanized landing craft by flooding her well deck, lowering her stern gate, and disgorging them. Each LCM carried one tank. The light tanks, by contrast, were deep down in the cargo holds of the transports assigned to the battalions they were supposed to support. It proved impossible to extricate and hoist them onto LCMs swiftly enough to employ them early in the battle.

On D-Day at Tarawa, the LCMs carrying the medium tanks faced the same problem as every other boat, except rubber ones: they would have to stop 500–800 yards from the beach and launch their tanks at the reef's edge. The medium tank company had been prepared for this and was counting on the courage of Marines willing to walk in front of the tanks to guide them around depressions or shell holes that might flood out their electrical systems and strand them in the lagoon. Many Marines died walking slowly and directly ahead of the tanks, but most of the tanks made it ashore. Several did stall in deep water and had to be abandoned, but none of the crew members drowned.

Two platoons of the medium tanks came ashore on Red 3, and one on Red 1. Those on Red 3 were directed inland quickly by the 2/8 battalion commander, Major Crowe, who needed the tanks to suppress and eliminate the fire from Japanese fortified positions. Yet this was exactly how *not* to best employ the tanks, because without infantry close by to support them, they were blind to some dangers and vulnerable to others (swarming Japanese soldiers on foot with explosives, for example).

By D+1, only two medium tanks were left operable: one with Major Michael Ryan's men on Green Beach (*China Gal*, taken over by company commander Bale after his *Cecilia* was disabled) and *Colorado* on Red 3, east of the main pier. Both would pour essential 75-mm fire into Japanese emplacements impervious to any smaller rounds that did not, by extraordinary shooting, go straight through the emplacements' slender firing slits. The light tanks with 37-mm main guns played a vital support role in the drive of 1/6 across the southern part of the island on D+2, when they helped cover the advance of *China Gal*, whose mobile 75-mm gun was irreplaceable.

Water, poor radio communication with infantry, and the seawalls that prevented the tanks from going inland at points of their choosing proved to be the most serious obstacles to effective use of tanks at Tarawa. As with every facet of the operation, the missed opportunities, mistakes, and shortcomings would be addressed and remedied in order to enable a far more potent use of tanks in upcoming amphibious assaults.

killed. This meant any advances that small numbers of Marines might make inland could not be exploited past fortified emplacements that would have been silenced by explosives or flamethrowers. Only a few Marines made it as far as 50 yards inland in spots, but there was no coordinated advance along the whole beach.

The most grievous blow to 2/2 came as Amey approached Red 2. He transferred his headquarters unit from an LCM to a returning LVT. When the LVT became fouled on barbed wire, rather than wait for it to extract itself and find a better way to shore, Amey ordered everyone into the water for a short wade to the beach. Walking in beside Associated Press war correspondent William Hipple, Amey was struck by machine gun fire 50 yards from shore and killed instantly. His executive officer, Major Howard Rice, in a separate boat for just such a contingency, could not land and ultimately only came ashore much later, well over to the west on Red 1. The senior officer present on Red 2 was Lieutenant Colonel Walter I. Jordan, an observer from the 4th Marine Division gaining experience for its upcoming first deployment. Jordan assumed command, as best he could, of men who did not know him and were so depleted as to be nonfunctional for the time being. In just the act of coming ashore, 2/2 had suffered 30 percent casualties.

The only bright spot for 2/2 and the entire 2d Division was the discovery that the pier offered some limited protection to Marines wading in. Red 2 would thus be an arrival point for men and supplies throughout the remainder of the battle.

Status at 1000: Scattered elements as far as 50 yards inland. Most confined to seawall or shell holes. Command of battalion badly disrupted; CO dead. No contiguous line along the beach or inland, heavy opposition to any advance from the Pocket on the right.

HOLDING ON AND LANDING THE FIRST REINFORCEMENTS: D-DAY 0930–1200

1st Battalion, 2d Marines (1/2) (Combat Team 2 reserve)

CO: Major Wood Barbee Kyle

Time of Commitment: 1100

Target/Goal: Help establish beachhead on Red 2 by reinforcing badly depleted and disorganized remnants of 2/2.

3d Battalion, 8th Marines (3/8) (component of 2d Marine Division reserve)

CO: Major Robert Henry Ruud

Time of Commitment: 1103

Target/Goal: Reinforce 2/8 on Red 3; establish contact with Marines on and behind the left edge of Red 2; help establish momentum toward east and south on the Marines' extreme left flank at the eastern edge of Red 3.

Waves four through six of the initial assault, carrying battalion command groups, medium tanks (M4A2, Sherman) on LCMs, follow-on rifle companies, and heavy weapons companies, were all boated in landing craft that could not clear the reef. There was no reliable, steady, consistent shuttle of returning LVTs from the first three waves to bring Marines in the later waves to the beach. Some did in fact make the transfer (such as Lieutenant Colonel Herbert Amey of 2/2, and, as recounted shortly, Colonel David Shoup).

If other Marines of these subsequent waves wished to join the first waves ashore, they had no choice but to wade in water 3 to 6 feet deep, and then steadily shallower as the reef sloped up to the beach. Here and there, potholes created by shell craters or natural formations could drop Marines in over their heads—dangerous or fatal if they were carrying so much equipment that they sank to the bottom. Due to the preliminary bombardment and movement of the LVTs on tracks, the lagoon waters over the reef had been churned a chalky white, often rendering the bottom invisible to the Marines. In many spots, barbed wire presented still another challenge.

Vastly more dangerous than the holes was the Japanese fire directed at the Marines. Every minute that had passed between the cessation of the preliminary bombardment at 0900 and the arrival of Marines was another minute the Japanese could gather themselves, remember their training and mission, and direct accurate fire on boats and Marines in the water. These follow-on waves from LCVPs and LCMs suffered high casualties and loss of cohesion. Flying above in a scout plane catapulted off the USS *Maryland*, Navy pilot Lieutenant Commander Robert A. MacPherson recorded in his log: "The water seemed never clear of tiny men, their rifles held over their heads, slowly wading beachward. I wanted to cry."

Machine guns, rifles, and plunging fire from grenades picked many off in the water, where they fell below the surface, their wounds turning the milky waters pink. The larger Japanese guns, such as the 120-mm anti-boat guns on the eastern tip and 75-mm dual-purpose antiaircraft guns throughout the island, began to find the range of LCVPs and LCMs on the reef's edge, sometimes scoring direct hits that obliterated the boats and many of the men in them.

One such vehicle, an LVT, was carrying an engineering unit to Red 2 to support the efforts of 2/2 against fortified positions. The unit included Staff Sergeant William J. Bordelon. When the LVT was destroyed by Japanese fire, he was one of the few survivors. Bordelon led the others to the temporary shelter of the seawall and began to plan his efforts to silence the fire from pits and pillboxes so that those following could make it to the beach.

Bordelon and another Marine from his unit quickly gathered their dynamite and fashioned four explosive charges. Bordelon exposed himself to Japanese fire as he threw the first of these charges into the nearest machine gun positions. He was successful in eliminating them, but was wounded by Japanese fire and shrapnel. He then crawled inland to an enclosed position that had been especially effective against arriving Marines. Bordelon pushed explosives through the firing slits and was shot in the arm again. His final explosive charge blew up as he was throwing it, wounding him further. He refused all treatment.

Before he could return to his demolition work, Bordelon noticed a wounded Marine in the water struggling to get to shore. He ran out to help, pulling the man to safety. As he and Sergeant Elden Beers went to work on yet another position, Beers was struck

CT 2's Commander Comes Ashore

"COMBAT LEADERSHIP AMID CHAOS," *NAVAL HISTORY*, DECEMBER 2018

Colonel David Shoup had been the commander of the 2d Marines for a mere ten days. His movement from the transport USS *Zeilin* to the predetermined location for his command post on Red 2, a mere 15 yards from the water's edge in the center of expected Marine positions, turned into an odyssey. His first, albeit minor, wounds were inflicted when Japanese shells, overpacked with explosives and evidencing what Shoup called "poor metallurgy," took small chunks out of his nose and wrists as they impacted like supersonic grains of sand rather than as large chunks of metal. In its lack of precision, the Navy's preliminary bombardment had left many Japanese positions fully operational. LVTs, LCVPs, and Marines in the water were facing heavy fire from many directions and a variety of weapons. Shoup's planning was beginning to unravel.

Like all of the LCVPs, the one carrying Shoup grounded where the water over the reef was only 4 feet deep—hundreds of yards offshore. Shoup ordered a returning LVT to take his team from the Higgins boat to shore. Betio's long, wide northern pier offered the only limited protection from Japanese fire. Shoup's LVT first went down the eastern side of the pier, until it ran into such heavy fire that it had to return to the end of the pier and travel down the western side. The vehicle was disabled some 400 yards out, and at about 1030, Shoup ordered his men into the water next to the pier.

Then and there the legend of Shoup was born. He halted several leaderless and weaponless Marines who were heading back into the lagoon, ordering them to turn around and take weapons off the dead. In so doing, he gave the men a purpose and a leader, both of which he believed to be keys in surmounting the fear of combat. The retreating Marines complied.

Shortly thereafter, on the verge of drawing his sidearm to brandish at a group of stopped Marines, Shoup barked: "Are there any of you cowardly sons of bitches got the guts to follow a Colonel of the Marines?" These men, too, came along behind him. Later during the battle, perhaps reflecting on this powerful experience, Shoup would advise officers who were bemoaning the lack of courageous Marines: "You've got to say, 'Who'll follow me?' And if only ten follow you, that's the best you can do, but it's better than nothing."

As he approached Red 2, a mortar shell exploded near Shoup. He was knocked down in the water, his knee nearly dislocated. His dungarees were shredded and covered in blood (a gaping wound, caused either by shell fragments, coral shards, or both, would become infected over the coming days). Still under fire, he emerged from the water and made his way to the predesignated spot for CT 2's command post, against the lagoon-side wall of a Japanese bunker on Red 2 that held active enemy troops. Shoup reached the post at about noon with only four of the officers originally assigned to serve as CT 2's headquarters staff. In time, he would marvel: "to think that the show was run" with only his operations officer, the commander of an artillery battalion, the communications officer, the regimental surgeon, and whichever stray Marines Shoup commandeered for special missions.

down by a grenade blast. Bordelon pulled Beers to safety, before finding a grenade launcher with which to continue his attacks. He was wounded by small arms fire yet again, but pulled a Marine with him to cover before trying to press on. When he raised himself to fire the grenade, he was shot dead. For his bravery, Bordelon would be recognized with the Medal of Honor, the first one earned in the Battle of Tarawa.

Despite his struggles and the threat to his radios from the water, Shoup was able to establish radio contact with his battalion commanders while he was next to the pier. Schoettel reported what appeared to be the total destruction of his battalion (3/2) to Shoup. At 1015, Shoup ordered Schoettel to land on Red 2 due to the apparent inability to put any Marines ashore on Red 1. At 1018, Schoettel responded, "We have nothing left to land."

Shoup turned his attention elsewhere, as he had already decided to commit the reserve element under his direct control, 1st Battalion, 2d Marines (1/2). He ordered Major Wood Kyle's battalion to land on Red 2 to help establish momentum and rebuild cohesion among the Marines there. Kyle moved to the reef's edge, but found the low water blocking the way for his LCVPs. He began to round up returning LVTs—which took time, and there were not enough for his entire battalion. By 1100 he had enough for his A and B Companies, while C Company would remain in their LCVPs pending arrival of more LVTs, which did not materialize until after 1300.

As they moved toward Red 2, A and B Companies faced the full fury of Japanese fire from that beach and the Pocket. Three boats were hit by shell fire during the transfer of men from LCVPs to LVTs. Many other LVTs were hit and disabled by shell fire and machine gun fire on the way in. Those LVTs to the right, most exposed of all to heavy fire, started drifting even farther rightward toward Red 1 as they avoided the most concentrated fire. Four officers and 110 men from 1/2 landed on Red 1, to be absorbed into the units from 2/2 and 3/2 that had already landed there, intentionally or not, and were now under the command of Major Michael Ryan of 3/2 (more on whom follows).

On Red 2 (the intended destination of 1/2's Marines), no more than 400 men arrived fit to continue the assault. They had been picked off in the water and subjected to the same intense opposition on the beach as the initial assault waves. They were bunched up

Colonel David Monroe Shoup (1904–1983), at Tarawa as Commanding Officer of the 2d Marines

A native of Battle Ground, Indiana, Shoup attended DePauw University, partly on an ROTC scholarship. He was commissioned an Army second lieutenant upon graduating in 1926. Shoup quickly resigned that commission in order to accept one in the Marine Corps. He served on board ships, in China, and stateside in various postings. In 1941, he traveled with the 6th Marines to Iceland and served there until 1942,

(Naval History and Heritage Command)

when he was assigned to the 2d Marine Division in the Pacific as its operations and training officer (D-3), at the rank of lieutenant colonel. He was wounded in combat while observing other units assault Rendova in the Solomon Islands in 1943. Just ten days before the assault on Tarawa, he was named to lead the 2d Marines. For his actions at Tarawa, he received the Medal of Honor and a gold star (subsequent award) for the Purple Heart received at Rendova. After the war, Shoup's assignments included commanding the 1st and 3d Marine Divisions. In 1959, President Eisenhower nominated Shoup to be Commandant of the Marine Corps, a position he held from 1960 until his retirement in 1963 from active duty.

The central pier choked with supplies during the battle. (Hatch Collection, National Museum of the Pacific War)

toward the left, or pier side, of Red 2, because they had discovered what Shoup and so many others had, that the pilings offered the only cover while wading ashore. While Kyle made it to Red 2 and a battalion on that beach now had a commander it knew, it was badly understrength and would not see all of its surviving units landed until the next day. For the moment, they could only hold on until Shoup gave them a mission.

Now it was time for Julian Smith to consider whether the division reserve units still under his direct control should be committed. They consisted largely of the two infantry battalions from the 8th Marines that had not been attached to CT 2, 1/8 and 3/8, along with these battalions' reinforcing units such as engineers and artillery. Smith chose to work through the headquarters of the 8th Marines and its commanding officer, Colonel Elmer E. Hall. The general directed Hall to send 3/8 to the line of departure and to place it under Shoup's control. Shoup received this charge at 1103 and immediately ordered 3/8 to land on Red 3, to aid 2/8 in its mission to hold the Marines' left flank and expand south and east.

Shoup, still in the water by the pier, observed the carnage during 3/8's landing. Using LVTs here was out of the question, as Kyle had commandeered all available ones and was using them on Red 2. So 3/8, under the command of Major Robert Ruud, waded in from the edge of the reef, facing the same kind of deadly fire as Marines to their west. Only 100 Marines, about 30 percent of those who attempted to land in Ruud's first wave, survived. Shoup tried, with limited success, to gesture to subsequent waves from 3/8 to wade in his direction, toward the meager protection offered by the pier.

By the time Ruud saw his fourth wave attempt to reach shore, it was obvious that his battalion had been so depleted by the casualties coming ashore that it would be able to offer little assistance to efforts to establish momentum on Red 3. Regimental commander Colonel Hall could see this as well, and he ordered Ruud to stop trying until further notice. Only at the end of the afternoon would the remaining elements from 3/8 gather at the head of the pier and reach Red 3 by 1730. Ruud's surviving Marines from K Company had already been integrated fully into Crowe's 2/8 battalion; Ruud, on Shoup's orders, sent Marines from other companies to the right to help establish contact between 2/8 and 1/2 inland from the base of the pier.

On the extreme western portion of the island, 3/2's L Company commander, Major Michael P. Ryan, was in an LCVP of the fourth wave. Mentally prepared for wading in by the knowledge that the water might be too low, Ryan and his men nonetheless had one of the longest wading experiences of the day, due to the length of the reef off Red 1: 700 yards. Ryan was originally designated to come ashore somewhere in the middle of Red 1, but as he saw the bloodbath developing ahead, he noticed off to his right a single Marine at the Bird's Beak climbing over the seawall. He decided it was a sign that coming ashore there might meet with less opposition and directed his men

far to the right. This would prove to be one of the single most important spontaneous decisions by a Marine during the entire battle.

Ryan's men landed not on the extreme right of Red 1; instead they proceeded past the northwest tip of the island altogether, and began to come ashore on the northern extremes of Green Beach, which had been named such but not designated for the initial assault. Ryan began reassembling whichever Marines were there into a more cohesive unit that could penetrate inland.

Soon he and the Marines with him would be joined by two medium tanks with 75-mm guns. These two tanks from C Company, I Marine Amphibious Corps, had proceeded from the dock landing ship USS *Ashland* (LSD-1) to the reef on LCMs. The tanks were deposited and guided in by Marines on foot to help them steer clear of holes that might drown out their vulnerable electrical systems. After landing, C Company Commander First Lieutenant Edward Bale had not been able to proceed directly ahead from the middle of Red 1 in his tank *Cecilia* due to the intact seawall there. Wounded and dead Marines littered the beach in both directions, so in order to avoid running over them, Bale led the tanks with him back into the water to head west to look for a gap. Now without their guides, several of the tanks fell into holes that disabled them. Only Bale's *Cecilia* and another tank named *China Gal* emerged from the water on the northern edge of Green Beach. These two tanks were now perfectly positioned to help Ryan move past fortified positions and expand the area under his control all the way to the southern shore of Betio.

First Lieutenant Roy Elrod

"WE WERE GOING TO WIN, OR WE WERE GOING TO DIE THERE" BY FRED ALLISON, *NAVAL HISTORY*, OCTOBER 2016

The attitude of the Marines was that we were going to win. We never thought that we weren't winning; there were more Japanese bodies lying around than ours. . . . I have never talked to another Marine that was there that didn't feel the same way I did. Nobody had any intention of going back. We were there to stay; we were going to win, or we were going to die there. I wasn't about to walk back out through that surf with all the rounds that were coming there.

MAKING IT WORK: D-DAY 1200 TO D+1 0600

At about 1200, Colonel Shoup arrived at the spot previously designated for his command post in the center of Red 2 and 50 yards inland, in the middle of the Marines' expected initial positions. Lieutenant Colonel Evans Carlson, acting as an observer and accompanying Shoup from the *Zeilin*, helped Shoup ashore after he was wounded. Carlson then received Shoup's assignment to head back to the water in order to personally carry a message to Julian Smith: Carlson was to tell the division's commanding general that Shoup intended to hold on, which was an inspiring report on the one hand. But it also revealed what everyone knew: The efforts so far were lagging behind the best hopes placed in them, and no outcome, however negative, could yet be excluded. Shoup also asked Carlson to indicate that Red 2 near the pier should be used for reinforcements and supplies, which were needed badly already.

On board the *Maryland*, Julian Smith and Harry Hill were realizing that the options under their sole control had dwindled. Since 3/8's disastrous commitment after 1100, the only elements left to Smith's discretion were 1/8 and the division support group containing Marines such as military policemen, headquarters units, and very small service detachments. To free 1/8 for immediate deployment and still maintain a viable reserve, Smith needed the 6th Marines transferred to his control immediately. Hill agreed. Hill transmitted a request to Admiral Turner at Makin at 1331 reading: "CG 2d Marine Division [J. Smith] requests release of CT 6 to 2d Mar. Div. Issue in doubt. I concur." The ominous terse warning that "doubt" existed sufficed; the same words had famously been used by the commander of the Marine garrison on Wake

Island just before its capitulation to the Japanese in December 1941.

Shortly thereafter, and upon agreeing with Holland Smith that the 6th Marines would not be needed at Makin, Turner radioed his approval of the request. Julian Smith was now free to move 1/8 ashore wherever and whenever he felt it would most support existing positions or help create momentum for an advance. At 1343, guessing that the 6th Marines would come into to his control soon, he had ordered 1/8 into landing craft and moved to the line of departure.

Julian Smith had several options for using 1/8. He could once again endeavor to reinforce the weak center position on Red 2; he could try to bolster Red 3 on the left flank; or he could attempt something far more daring. He had sought to learn Shoup's preferences, but his radioed queries had not reached CT 2's command post. So on his own, Smith opted for the riskiest but potentially also most rewarding plan: landing 1/8 through the lagoon on the northeastern tip of Betio's "tail," well east of Red 3, and having it move west to establish contact with the positions held by 2/8 and 3/8, thus relieving pressure on them. At 1625, he sent word to the regimental commander, Colonel Hall, to land all remaining Marines of his regiment at 1745 on the newly designated, unnamed beach on the extreme east of Betio.

The communications breakdown that had been afflicting the entire operation interfered again: Smith assumed that Hall got the order to land, but Hall never did. Observation airplanes radioed a report of Marines moving ashore at Red 2, which Smith's division headquarters took to mean that Hall was moving his men ashore on the wrong beach. In fact, 1/8 was still in its LCVPs near the line of departure, waiting. There these Marines would stay, all night long, bereft of any supplies except what they had on their persons, being jostled about by the waves, crowded into boats designed only for the shortest of voyages.

While this confusion proceeded, Smith intervened in a battalion-level command matter within CT 2. When he became aware that Major John Schoettel of 3/2 was still afloat beyond the reef and out of contact with his landed Marines, Smith ordered, "Direct you land at

The Odyssey of Dutch Hermle

The assistant division commander of the 2d Marine Division was Brigadier General Leo "Dutch" Hermle, who had earned a law degree before entering the Marines and had served in the U.S. garrison in Iceland with David Shoup, William Marshall, and others of the 2d Marine Division. The expected progression of control ashore was that Shoup would be in command of CT 2 for the first hours of the assault; then Hermle would take over if further 2d Division elements outside CT 2 began arriving, as they had when 3/8 and 1/8 were committed; and then at some point Julian Smith himself would come ashore when the advance of Marine positions created a more secure environment from which he could command on Betio's soil.

At 1343 on D-Day, Smith ordered Hermle to leave the transport *Monrovia* (APA-31) and make his way to the pierhead to survey the situation for himself and report back to Smith. He reached the designated spot by 1740, about half an hour before sunset, but could no longer establish direct radio contact with Smith. He was able only to communicate briefly and intermittently with Shoup and Crowe half a mile away, who again implored the division leadership for supplies. In what he thought was the absence of instructions to the contrary, Hermle chose to remain on the pier and organize the supply effort.

But at 1750, Smith had actually sent a message ordering Hermle to proceed ashore to Shoup's command post and assume leadership of all landed Marines. Hermle did not receive the order. He stayed on the pier and did good work moving men and supplies shoreward all night long. Hermle only returned to the water early the day following D-Day (D+1), carrying a message he had received from Shoup that he wanted 1/8 to land on Red 2 next to the pier. At 0513, Hermle finally got a message back to Smith from the *Ringgold* and learned that he had earlier been ordered to take command. Smith decided to leave Shoup in charge and directed Hermle to report to him on the *Maryland*.

D+1 would therefore be the day that Shoup, not Hermle, oversaw the turning of the battle decisively in the Marines' favor.

any cost, regain control of your battalion and continue the attack." Schoettel complied, but not where he or Smith thought he should be. He waded ashore on Red 2 in the middle of the afternoon and reported to Shoup in person. There would be no way for him to move to his battalion's landed Marines under Major Ryan's command across the Pocket on Green Beach. Schoettel and his party were temporarily given the responsibility of guarding Shoup's command post, which was located against one wall of a still-occupied Japanese structure.

In this same stretch of D-Day afternoon, one of the key events in the entire battle would occur. At about 1500, the Japanese base commander, Rear Admiral Shibazaki, was likely outside his bombproof command post near the eastern edge of Red 3 with his senior staff, about to move to the southern shore in order to allow his headquarters to be used for the care of wounded Japanese troops. The group was spotted in the open, and one of the destroyers in the lagoon, either the *Ringgold* or the *Dashiell*, fired 5-inch airbursting shells designed to rain down metal fragments.

The Japanese senior staff were all killed on the spot. Already isolated and stationary in their fortified positions, now the Japanese troops on much of the island would be leaderless as well. In Shibazaki's absence, at 1630 someone in the Japanese command sent out the last recorded message toward their Marshall Islands communications ship. It was a situation report that made no mention of Shibazaki and informed the distant Japanese naval leadership of the continuing arrival of Marines and supplies through the lagoon.

On and immediately inland from the three D-Day beaches, few advances were made in the afternoon. Any potential gains on Red 1 had been stymied by the seawall and the lack of explosives or armor to push past fortified positions inland. Red 2 was a hodgepodge of Marines from 1/2 and 2/2 who were fighting just to establish something like a coherent line, under the command of Kyle and Jordan, with Shoup in his command post at their center. At best, some small groups were 125 yards inland.

On Red 3, Crowe's continuing efforts to move 2/8 and those from 3/8 now under his direction past the most daunting of Betio's steel-reinforced concrete emplacements had made little headway. Crowe was the only battalion commander to have 37-mm anti-tank artillery available on D-Day, and although these guns helped ward off Japanese counterattacks, they were far too small to reduce the concrete positions that were proving most deadly. The 2d platoon of Crowe's F Company, for example, was nearly destroyed in an effort to encircle the deadliest of the concrete fortifications. To the far right of Red 3, 3/8 was inland near the airstrip, but constantly under fire and unable to establish a stable link to 2/2 to its immediate west.

But there was major progress on the extreme western portion of Betio, along and for about 150 yards to the east of Green Beach. With the aid of First Lieutenant Bale's two tanks, the Marines under Major Mike Ryan's impromptu leadership were able to neutralize Japanese fortified positions and move forward. They devised cooperative tank-infantry tactics on the spot, realizing that one element could not survive without the active support of the other. For the first time, at 1415, Ryan was able to notify Shoup that a cohesive Marine group was on and behind Green Beach and had moved 500 yards to the south, representing the only major movement of Marines on all of D-Day.

Whatever move might have been made to exploit these gains would have to wait. Shoup's unreliable

Julian C. Smith, on the night of D-Day at Tarawa

***PROCEEDINGS*, NOVEMBER 1953**

As the situation was viewed aboard the flagship, the night of D-day was the time for an enemy attack to roll up the left flank of our shallow beach head. This was the greatest danger to our landing forces. At night in the existing situation, support from the air was impractical, and effective support from ships' gunfire next to impossible because of the extreme difficulty of distinguishing our front lines, and the proximity of the enemy to them. Three-fourths of the Island was in enemy's hands, and even allowing for his losses, he should have had as many troops left as we had ashore. In fact it seemed that this was his one and only opportunity to annihilate or drive off the beach the bulk of our force on shore. I considered then, and still consider, that this was the crisis of the battle, and it was here the Japanese failed to avail themselves of their one opportunity to win.

communications with Julian Smith meant that no consideration would be given to using Green Beach to land more Marines on D-Day. By late afternoon, Ryan realized he was dangerously overextended given the approaching darkness, since he could not be sure that all Japanese positions he had passed were clear of enemy troops, nor could he prevent the positions from being reinfiltrated and reoccupied during the night. Ryan ordered his unit to give up hundreds of yards of territory they had won and to reconsolidate at the northwest tip of Betio in order to face a possible nighttime counterattack. As night fell, they held 300 yards to the south of the Bird's Beak and 150 yards inland from the western shore.

Sunset on D-Day took place at 1815, with nine and a half hours of total darkness (except for the moon) starting at 1929. There had been major Marine gains, but they were obscured then—and in later newspaper and historical accounts—by the slower than expected pace and the far higher than expected casualties. The Marines had landed approximately the same number with which the Japanese had started—5,000—of whom 1,500 were already casualties. The Marines held the pier, a long stretch of beach running from the Pocket to the Burns Philp wharf, and the northwest tip. Although their radio troubles prevented them from knowing it, on D+1 they would have the positions and the tactical advantages necessary to land several thousand more Marines quickly and begin the drive to the eastern tip, albeit two days later than they had originally hoped.

The Marines just had to withstand a Japanese nighttime counterattack, which experience in the Solomons had led them to expect. They were extremely vulnerable to such a Japanese threat, especially crowded together on Red 3—where plunging fire from grenade launchers could wipe out many Marines—and inland from Red 3 and Red 2, where, as Shoup put it, the lines looked like a "stock market graph." Holding their fire all night, the Marines were astonished and relieved to witness dawn break on D+1 with their lines intact. Shibazaki was dead, and no other Japanese officers had been able to organize or order a meaningful response to the Marines' vulnerabilities. Many Japanese may have assumed Shibazaki was still alive and just not communicating. Thus they had lost their last best hope of reversing the invasion and driving the Marines back into the lagoon.

Robert Sherrod, who lived out that night awake on Red 3, recalled, "I was quite certain that this was my last night on earth." He heard a sole Japanese plane making a weak bombing run close to dawn, but that was as dangerous as it got for most Marines that night. The Japanese had lost the battle by not attacking when they could, and that would become clear to all involved in the course of the next full day of battle.

D+1: SETTING THE STAGE FOR ULTIMATE VICTORY

1st Battalion, 8th Marines (1/8) (component of division reserve)

CO: Major Lawrence Coker Hays Jr.

Time Started Ashore: 0615

Target/Goal: Red 2, to reinforce 2/2's and 1/2's surviving units.

The most profound tragedy experienced by the 2d Marine Division on Tarawa may have been the landing of 1/8 at sunrise on D+1. Several factors contributed to the high casualties. Colonel Shoup's desire to have this final element of the division reserve arrive on Red 2 was not in and of itself excessively dangerous; he knew from personal experience and from watching others that arrival on Red 2 beside the pier would be the safest way in. But the communication difficulties that had plagued D-Day reached their most intense level during this episode, and instead of hugging the pier, 1/8 came ashore exactly as 2/2 and 1/2 had the day before—on a broad front, facing the full fury of Japanese fire from the Pocket and from behind Red 2.

The commander of 8th Marines, Colonel Elmer Hall, and his 1/8 battalion had spent the night bobbing in their landing craft beyond the reef. Hall's first orders from Julian Smith for D+1, after all the confusion about their whereabouts during the late afternoon and evening of D-Day had been clarified, were the same as before: Proceed to the northeastern tip of Betio guided by the *Pursuit*, which would mark a new line of departure for a landing at 0900.

Brigadier General Hermle was on board the *Ringgold* with the division's assistant D-3 officer, Major Rathvon Tompkins, who had been shuttling back and forth with messages between Shoup and Hermle. At 0513, Hermle reported to Smith regarding Tompkins' message from Shoup that the CT 2 commander wanted 1/8 to land on Red 2. But Shoup's additional, crucial qualification

to this request was that the site should be on Red 2, "close to the pier." Exactly what became of this last part of Shoup's message is unknown, because Smith did not include it when agreeing to Shoup's appeal. At 0522 Smith radioed 1/8 its new orders: Make an immediate landing on Red 2. Nothing was said about the pier.

The tide on D+1 was not much different than it had been on D-Day. It would rise all morning long to a height of around 4 feet after 12 noon, but at dawn, when 1/8 was sent ashore, it was at only 2 feet, with some areas actually drying completely in the early morning sun. The Marines of 1/8 would be wading or walking fully exposed for hundreds of yards.

First Lieutenant Deane Hawkins of the 2d Marines' scout and sniper platoon was one of thousands who were appalled at the spectacle of 1/8's landing. Unlike some others, Hawkins believed he personally was in a position to do something about it. Ashore on Red 2, he began to lead small unit assaults to the right against some of the guns situated just inland that were firing into the lagoon on the western edge of Red 2, near the Pocket. At 0630, he began his first attacks, running up to Japanese pillboxes and tossing in grenades. Hawkins was severely wounded when a Japanese soldier picked up one of his grenades and threw it back at him. He persisted, though, and refused to stop for medical care.

Grave marker of 1st Lt. William Deane Hawkins (pictured left), National Memorial Cemetery of the Pacific, Honolulu. (Naval History and Heritage Command; courtesy of the Author)

The landing operation began at 0615, in the first minutes after sunrise. The Japanese gunners who could see the lagoon off Red 2 had many slow-moving or even stationary targets for their artillery and machine gun fire. Marines in LCVPs approaching the reef's edge or already on foot were hit from the front and both sides in full view of their already landed comrades, who observed in frustrated horror. Sherrod thought he could count 200 Marine bodies from 1/8 lying motionless on the drying coral flats or shallow water off Red 2. It seemed much deadlier to him than what he had experienced and witnessed himself the day before.

Only half of battalion commander Major Lawrence Hays' men ultimately made it to Red 2 by 0800 in any condition to fight. Shoup put these Marines immediately on the right, to push against the Pocket. For the rest of the battle 1/8 would remain here, much frustrated like the Marines from 2/8 on Red 3 by a dense section of heavily fortified Japanese positions, impervious to anything except flamethrowers or dynamite.

Hawkins mounted the same sort of grenade attacks on more Japanese positions, but during the last of these was struck in the shoulder by a rifle round. It destroyed an artery that could not be repaired despite his immediate evacuation to a field aid station. The doctor and Hawkins' men could only watch as he quickly bled to death.

Hawkins and Bordelon had both died on Red 2 in order to make it possible for other Marines to land and move forward, and both would receive the Medal of Honor. Julian Smith, upon hearing accounts of the lieutenant's relentless bravery, asked the Navy to name the captured airfield on Betio Hawkins Field, an unusual tribute to an infantryman, since deceased Navy or Marine aviators had previously been the honorees when an airfield was captured or constructed.

On Green Beach, Major Mike Ryan's decision to pull back into defensible positions for the first night paid off. The minimal cohesion he had been establishing in his ad hoc unit, composed of

elements of his own 3/2, plus some from 2/2 and 1/2, allowed him to make plans to retake the ground he had conceded at dusk on D-Day and, this time, to hold onto it. In so doing, he and his Marines would open up a new landing area, mostly safe from Japanese fire, so that the corps reserve (the battalions of the 6th Marines) could land intact and cohesive and drive down the island from west to east, destroying remaining Japanese troops pushed into the southeast tail of Betio.

The advance of Ryan's men did not take long or go far. From about 1120 to 1235 on D+1, they moved only several hundred yards. Yet that was like miles on any other battlefield. For the attack to proceed so rapidly, two preconditions were essential so that riflemen could approach and then move past Japanese gun emplacements. First, a medium tank had to be ready to blast these spots, and second, the Navy had to be able to place supporting fire from destroyers offshore precisely where Ryan needed it.

The tank *China Gal*, taken by company commander First Lieutenant Edward Bale when his own *Cecilia* had been knocked out, used its 75-mm gun to silence Japanese positions in close coordination with the infantry who protected Bale from any Japanese on foot who might try to place magnetic mines on his tank or otherwise disable it. Meanwhile, naval gunnery spotter Lieutenant Thomas Greene coordinated 5-inch destroyer gunfire on emplacements at the southwest corner of Betio. With the way prepared by this naval fire, Ryan's carefully planned assault began at 1120, with the one tank and Ryan's infantry proceeding parallel to, but not actually on, Green Beach. Lieutenant Greene precisely directed naval fire just ahead of the Marines, sometimes as close as 50 yards, after Julian Smith approved firing so dangerously near the lead units. Meanwhile, the heavier ships enfiladed the south coast of Betio with large caliber high explosives that further dazed the defenders in that zone.

By 1225 it was over. At 1330, the destroyer USS *Anderson* (DD-411) engaged in semaphore communication with K Company, 2d Marines commander Captain James Crain on the southwest tip of Betio. The *Anderson* radioed to Admiral Hill a report from Crain that the bombardment had been "very effective," the area was secure, and drinking water was needed. Green Beach was now entirely in Marine hands. Ryan's men had assaulted and seized large caliber shore batteries and heavy and light machine gun positions. Julian Smith was now aware that an entire protected beach upon which the 6th Marines could land was at his disposal.

Although they were badly mauled, vastly understrength, and poorly equipped, 1/2 and 2/2 were in a position to help Shoup re-establish momentum on D+1. If they could be directed to race to the south, fully exposed, across the airfield and then dig in on the south coast, the Marines of 1/2 and 2/2 could begin the process of splitting Japanese forces on Betio into just two components: one in the Pocket and the other on the southeastern tail. Artillery, demolitions, flamethrowers, and naval/aerial support fire could then be concentrated on these areas, steadily wearing them down. But first, somebody had to dash across the machine-gun-swept center of the island at its widest. Of those from whom so much had already been demanded, Shoup would ask more.

Lieutenant Colonel Jordan still led the remnants of Amey's 2/2; Major Kyle had somewhat more cohesion within his 1/2. Kyle's Marines were within the triangle formed by the runway and taxiways, with some beyond to the right side, facing west. The Marines in the triangle were cut off from reinforcements and supplies by heavy Japanese fire that erupted anytime Marines moved across open ground. These companies were ordered, despite the manifest danger, to rise and race to the southern shore, in order to effect Shoup's plan for splitting the Japanese positions on Betio.

The combined units from 1/2 and 2/2 completed the run and held about 200 yards of abandoned Japanese positions just inland from Black Beach, at the south coast. Shoup ordered Jordan to join the Marines already there and take command in person, and thus Jordan followed them over the open ground. He took charge of the approximately 200 Marines there from 1/2 and 2/2.

Shoup's next mission for the 1/2 and 2/2 amalgam was to attack to the northeast toward 2/8 and establish a line with Crowe's battalion. But without the numbers and ammunition necessary, Jordan requested permission from Shoup, and received it, to wait until the morning of D+2 before attempting the move. Later that afternoon of D+1, Kyle himself reached this southern Marine pocket, and Jordan, the outside observer, relinquished command over the elements from Kyle's and Amey's battalions, ending his direct leadership role after richly earning the Silver Star he would be awarded for keeping 2/2's remnants in the fight after their devastation on D-Day.

Not much would change on D+1 for 2/8 and 3/8 on the left flank behind the cramped portion of Red 3 on which they had landed. Their way to the south and east was blocked by heavily fortified Japanese positions that would prove impervious to aerial attacks, naval fire, and infantry/engineer assaults. E Company of 2/8 had reached the airfield, only to have to pull back to avoid forming an isolated pocket. The Marines did occupy the Burns Philp wharf, site of heavy Japanese fire on D-Day and D+1, but the wharf was subjected to Japanese reinfiltration after dark on D+1, meaning neither side could truly be said to hold it securely yet. The mission of 2/8 and attached elements from 3/8 was thus reduced to protecting the left flank, keeping the Japanese troops there pinned down, and slugging away repeatedly at the fortified positions. Any Marine advance there was out of the question on D+1.

1st Battalion, 6th Marines (1/6) (component of corps reserve)

CO: Major William Kenefick Jones Sr.

Time of Arrival of All Elements: 1820, D+1

Target/Goal: Northern half of Green Beach, pass through Major Ryan's 3/2, prepare to move to pocket held by 1/2 and 2/2 on south coast.

In one sense, the entire Battle of Tarawa prior to twilight on D+1 had been preparation for what would now transpire on Betio's western coast: the landing of the 1st Battalion, 6th Marines in rubber boats on the northern portion of Green Beach. Major William K. Jones' battalion, like all the first battalions in each of the 2d Marine Division's regiments, had been given extra training in using rubber boats. Jones was known by his men, as a result, by the undesired nickname "Admiral of the Condom Fleet." By coming ashore in these boats over a brief period without losing many men, 1/6 was the first battalion to land on Tarawa essentially intact and, moreover, in a position to do immediate good by pushing hard and fast along the south coast.

Jones' battalion took all afternoon of D+1 to arrive on Green Beach. Shoup had wanted and expected it much earlier. Yet there were delays. Its attached medium tanks were stowed deep in the transports, requiring hours to extract past other supplies and equipment. The transport carrying 1/6, the USS *Feland* (APA-11), had to wait in the deeper water of Transport Area B, due west of Betio, as the minesweeper *Requisite* checked the waters off Green Beach for acoustic and magnetic mines. The *Requisite* completed this operation at 1515 without finding any mines in this deeper water, although it could not check over the reef.

The *Feland* lowered its LCVPs, older LCPLs (landing craft, personnel, large), and rubber boats (LCRs: landing craft, rubber) while it was waiting for the *Requisite* to finish. At 1515, two waves of the powered boats started for Green Beach from their rendezvous area, with rubber LCRs in tow, carrying 1/6's Marines. A third wave left at 1545, and the fourth and final wave at 1602. Fourteen LCVPs, 2 LCPLs, and 84 LCRs had been dispatched, each rubber boat carrying between 6 and 10 Marines who would paddle once the powered boats released the tow lines at the edge of the reef. It then took more than an hour to cover the final thousand yards, with the first waves coming ashore at 1820, just after sunset. The only two LVTs carried by the *Feland* followed at 1643. One struck a mine on the reef that the rubber boats had passed over safely, killing or wounding all its crew and destroying its supplies.

Once ashore, 1/6 was ready to assume its designated mission of passing through Ryan's lines and attacking toward the isolated area held by 1/2 and 2/2 along the shore to the immediate south of the airfield. Jones decided to attack at 2000, in full darkness. As he was preparing his battalion, a message arrived from Shoup that Smith had already approved Shoup's request to have 1/6 hold its ground until daylight on D+2. Jones thus deployed his men into defensive positions alongside Ryan's Marines, where they awaited the next day's orders. Meanwhile, the landing of the light tanks (M3A1 Stuarts) assigned to support 1/6 had gone badly. The surf and currents off Green Beach were too difficult. Only two of the tanks made it ashore there. The landing craft carrying the remainder of the Stuarts sought, and received, permission to circle around through the lagoon and land the tanks on Red 2, putting them far away from 1/6.

Another sign that the leadership of the 2d Marine Division had increased confidence in their position on Betio was their decision to send 2/6 to the next island to the east in the Tarawa Atoll chain, Bairiki. At low tide, Japanese wanting to escape might wade quickly to Bairiki and make the ultimate job of clearing the entire

atoll more difficult. Lieutenant Colonel Raymond L. Murray's battalion, originally slated to follow 1/6 onto Green Beach, instead would be diverted east to ensure the battle would not simply shift to other islands in the atoll. A day earlier, the Japanese would not have been fleeing, and the Marines would not have felt it a good use of their last reserves to block an escape rather than consolidate their shaky beachheads.

2d Battalion, 6th Marines (2/6) (component of corps reserve)

CO: Lieutenant Colonel Raymond Leroy Murray

Time of Arrival on Bairiki: 1655, D+1

Target/Goal: Neutralize any Japanese positions on Bairiki.

Originally, the 6th Marines' commander, Colonel Maurice Holmes, received orders at 1230 on D+1 to land 1/6 on Green Beach in rubber rafts that would be towed up to the reef, followed immediately by 2/6. This plan changed almost immediately. Shortly after 1300, reports of Japanese troops escaping to Bairiki spurred Julian Smith to order Holmes to land a battalion there. Holmes chose to alter 2/6's assignment and send it immediately to Bairiki. He put his final battalion, Lieutenant Colonel Kenneth F. McLeod's 3/6, into boats to be ready to move to either Bairiki or Green Beach in support of whichever landing team needed the assistance of 3/6 more. At 1428, the USS *J. Franklin Bell* (APA-16), the transport ship for 2/6, began lowering boats in Transport Area A, closest to the lagoon entrance. At 1520, the boats left the rendezvous area headed for Blue Beach, the designation for Bairiki.

Murray and his battalion landed on Bairiki at 1655 and faced some machine gun fire as they approached. Air attacks designed to suppress this Japanese fire ignited gasoline in the machine gun pillbox, killing all the Japanese there. Thus, 2/6 met no resistance at all upon coming ashore and, after thoroughly searching the entire island, found no living Japanese. This meant 2/6 could be immediately withdrawn and designated for another mission, which would not be long in coming. Later that night, the 2d Battalion, 10th Marines, an artillery unit, landed on Bairiki and prepared to fire upon the southeastern tail of Betio.

Meanwhile, the only rifle battalion of the 2d Marine Division yet to be landed at Tarawa, McLeod's 3/6, spent the night of D+1/D+2 on boats in the water, replicating the experience of 1/8 from 24 hours earlier.

Colonel Merritt Austin Edson Sr. (1897–1955), at Tarawa as Chief of Staff, 2d Marine Division

Born in Rutland, Vermont, Edson attended the University of Vermont. He left prior to obtaining a degree in order to serve in the National Guard at the border with Mexico, and then to accept a commission in the Marine Corps in 1917. He went to France during World War I, but did not see combat. He became a naval aviator in 1922, yet relinquished that qualification in 1927 in order to return to assignments on the ground. A skilled competitive marksman, Edson was assigned to Nicaragua, where he received the Navy Cross. Later assignments included China. He was promoted to colonel in May 1942 and led the 1st Marine Raider Battalion as it landed at Tulagi at the beginning of the Guadalcanal campaign in August 1942. He received the Medal of Honor for his leadership of the bloody battle at Lunga Ridge on Guadalcanal, henceforth known to Marines as Edson's Ridge. He was named chief of staff of the 2d Marine Division and assumed command from Colonel David Shoup of all landed troops on Betio on the evening of D+1 at Tarawa. Thereafter he was promoted to brigadier general and became assistant division commander of the 2d Marine Division. Edson retired from active duty in the Marine Corps as a major general in 1947. He went on to direct the Vermont State Police and serve as executive director of the National Rifle Association.

Vice Adm. Raymond Spruance (center) and Col. Merritt A. Edson, USMC (bottom), on Betio after the battle. (Naval History and Heritage Command)

David Shoup was never supposed to be in command of CT 2, not at the inception of Operation Galvanic, and not for the first full day and a half. Circumstances and Shoup's own resolve led Julian Smith to leave Shoup in charge of a collection of landed Marines who constituted a majority of the 2d Marine Division. Two regimental commanders (Hall and Holmes) who were senior to Shoup at the rank of colonel had landed with troops who would need firm direction. Hall had already deferred to Shoup upon his arrival, but the good order of the operation dictated that a more senior Marine officer from the division staff assume control on the ground. Instead of Hermle this time, Smith chose his chief of staff, Colonel Merritt Edson, Medal of Honor recipient from Guadalcanal and staff organizer and planner of the Tarawa assault. Edson left the *Maryland* at 1750, the setting sun at his back, and went to the pierhead. He arrived at Shoup's Red 2 command post at 2030, some 36 hours after the original H-Hour.

Shoup had overseen the arrival of seven battalion landing teams as well as 75-mm pack howitzer units that had proven crucial to maintaining pressure on the Pocket at the Red 1/Red 2 boundary. He had pushed 1/2 and 2/2 to the south coast, setting the stage for completely splitting the Japanese into just two strongholds. Even though he had expressed some concern on D+1 about the flow of battle prior to Ryan's success early that afternoon, by 1600 on D+1 he had composed a situation report that foresaw victory for the first time. It read:

> Our line runs generally from the Burns Philp pier across the east end of the triangle formed by the airfield to the south coast and along the coast intermittently to a place opposite the west end of the triangle; then from the revetments north of the west end of the main air strip on to the north; another line from west of the center of RED 1 across the end of the island to the south coast west of the end of the main strip. Some troops in 227 dishing out hell and catching hell. Pack howitzers in position and registered for shooting on tail. Casualties many; percentage dead not known; combat efficiency: We are winning. Shoup.

D+2: SPLITTING AND SQUEEZING THE JAPANESE ON BETIO

At sunrise on 22 November (D+2), the tactical situation of the Marines ashore had improved vastly from just 24 hours earlier. An entire reinforced infantry battalion—1/6, with some light tanks, flamethrowers, and demolition units—was on the west end of the island, ready to attack. Artillery batteries of the 10th Marines had been placed on Bairiki and would be able to pound away at the extensive Japanese redoubt on the southeastern tail of Betio. The division leadership had started landing. Supplies, equipment, weapons, and vehicles were coming ashore in vast quantities, although not always in the order and at the places desired or needed. There were two further entire battalions from the 6th Marines who could be landed on Betio and committed to combat. The only question seemed to be whether the Battle of Tarawa could be wrapped up before the Japanese navy made an appearance in force. On the afternoon of D+2, Julian Smith estimated that ending all Japanese resistance might take five more days. He made this assessment in person, having first waded ashore on Green Beach at 1155 that morning before moving back out into the water for a more harrowing landing on Red 2 near the division command post.

Three concentrations of Japanese troops remained as of dawn on D+2:

(1) the Pocket at the eastern edge of Red 1 and western edge of Red 2, facing 1/8 to the east and 3/2 to the west;
(2) along the south shore at either end of the isolated Marine positions held by 1/2 and 2/2;
(3) the southeastern tail, facing 2/8 and 3/8 along the airfield and south of the Burns Philp wharf.

On this third day of ground combat, small but important progress would be made by the battalions of the 8th Marines against the first and third of these. The most impressive gains of the entire battle to date, though, would be accomplished by 1/6 along and just inland from the southern coast against the second of these Japanese concentrations.

Command of the division ashore was Edson's, but he consulted closely with Shoup and allowed Shoup direct control of the forces in the center, south, and western portions of the island, while Hall directed the elements of his 8th Marines to the east. As for the Pocket, Edson and Shoup directed 1/8 to make an advance to the west along the beach and inland, hoping in vain to wipe out the Pocket on D+2. The attack by 1/8 commenced at 0700 and lasted all day. Its A and B Companies, operating just inland, made more progress than units along the beach. There, even

the heaviest fire from artillery, light tanks, and 75-mm self-propelled mounts (half-tracks) could not defeat the Japanese emplacements. Explosives placed by engineers directly into openings and flamethrowers were the only weapons capable of silencing the Japanese fire there and allowing Marine advances. Still, these Japanese holdout troops in the Pocket would be fully cut off from any support on D+2 due to Marine advances elsewhere.

To the southwest, Shoup ordered 1/6 to begin its attack at 0800. Its goal was to drive east and reach 1/2 and 2/2, end their isolation, and push beyond. This would be a narrow front: The entire action was squeezed into 100 yards between the south edge of the airfield runway and the southern coast. The runway itself was far too exposed to Japanese fire to allow continuous Marine operations on it.

C Company of 1/6 formed the vanguard of the infantry, moving about 50 yards behind the sole medium tank and the light tanks being used to protect it. The M4A2 Sherman tank's 75-mm main gun was the only one capable of dealing quickly with most Japanese fortifications at any distance. The light tanks and infantry would protect and support this valuable asset by ensuring no Japanese troops could approach it with explosives. Flamethrowers were also employed in this advance, since they had arrived over Green Beach the evening before.

By 1100, this first mission of the day had been accomplished. 1/6 reached the previously encircled units from 1/2 and 2/2. Major Jones was ordered back to see Edson and Shoup, where he was told to make 1/6 ready for an almost immediate second attack of the day, farther to the east along the south coast. The tanks would continue in support, but this time with more direct fire support from the Navy offshore and the artillery on Bairiki, which could pound the next Japanese concentrations in the way, those on the southeastern tail. Hall's two regiments in the east, 2/8 and 3/8, nearly at the end of their strength after battering the Japanese reinforced positions for 48 straight hours, would attack at the same time. If all went well, 1/6 would end up forming a continuous line with the 8th Marines' eastern battalions, and for the first time there would be a solid Marine wall running from north to south across all the central portion of Betio.

Before 2/8 and 3/8 could be of any assistance to the efforts on the southern coast, however, they had to finally overcome the most stubborn of reinforced positions south of the Burns Philp wharf that had stopped them for two days. Three in particular were blocking all movement: a steel pillbox, a firing position protected by coconut logs, and, most vexing of all, a sand-covered, steel-reinforced concrete blockhouse that had housed the Japanese power plant before the battle and now had firing positions both on top and inside. Success came against all three, but by different means in each case. The steel pillbox was eradicated by a direct hit from the only other operable medium tank on Betio (*Colorado*), which put several 75-mm rounds directly into the pillbox. The destruction of this Japanese position allowed F Company of 2/8 to move forward on the extreme left of the Marines' lines, closest to the Burns Philp wharf. Next, a mortar round plunged down into the coconut log position, setting off the Japanese ammunition in it.

But the concrete power-plant building was much more difficult, and any advance along a broad front that would allow the 8th Marines to link up with the 6th Marines would first have to neutralize or destroy it. It was impervious to naval, artillery, and tank fire. Through the efforts of First Lieutenant Alexander Bonnyman of the 18th Marines' shore party, a small contingent of volunteers covered by others began attempting to clamber up ladders and the piled-up sand to the top of the bunker, where grenades and flamethrowers might reach the Japanese on top. Then Bonnyman's plan was for Marines with explosives to throw them down the ventilation shafts, either killing the Japanese within or forcing them to flee the building entirely, so that waiting Marines could kill them as they ran.

Only after hours of probes, attacks, withdrawals, and renewed attacks were Bonnyman and the few men with him able to reach the top for the first time, to begin wiping out the Japanese guns there. Bonnyman would not survive the attack, however, as he was likely felled by some sort of shell fragments (demonstrated by the examination of his remains after their recovery in 2015). Follow-on groups of Marines continued the flamethrower and grenade attacks, clearing the roof and allowing Bonnyman's plan to be implemented after he fell. For his initiative, bravery, and leadership, he would receive the Medal of Honor.

Japanese troops trying to escape "Bonnyman's Bunker" were hit by Marine machine gun and canister fire from 37-mm antitank weapons pulled close. The entrances

Medical Care

The 2d Marine Division had a medical battalion that was staffed mostly by Navy physicians and corpsmen. It reported directly to the division's commanding general, but each infantry battalion was assigned surgeons and corpsmen for the battle itself. Along with every other element of the first assault waves, the medical staff suffered from casualties, confusion, lack of supplies, and disorganization. Early on, a physician remarked to correspondent Sherrod that it seemed all the corpsmen had been shot while aiding Marines. Under the circumstances, the medical staff did a heroic job despite logistical difficulties.

Like so many other vital supplies, the physicians' plasma and other essentials were subject to damage due to the lack of waterproof containers. Sometimes medical supplies were pilfered by Marines under the mistaken assumption that medicinal brandy could be found. Yet overall, enough of the most essential items—such as morphine, sulfa drugs, plasma, splints, and dressing materials—reached shore.

Even when the medical staff could get a battlefield aid station established in an area that was momentarily secure, they had difficulty getting casualties back to the treatment area once the wounded men had been stabilized; there had not been enough stretcher bearers designated for this essential task. If wounded Marines with a chance of survival required immediate evacuation to the lagoon and transport area for more extensive surgery, they had to be taken to the edge of the reef on rubber boats. Later, the few remaining LVTs that were bringing supplies ashore were used to carry out wounded on their return leg to the end of the pier, but they had not been designed for this purpose. There was no easy way to lift the stretchers over the gunwales, and no racks to support the stretchers once they were on board. The destroyers and minesweepers in the lagoon had to serve as a first evacuation point, a job for which they had not been designated or prepared (moreover, the destroyer *Ringgold*'s sick bay had been struck by a non-exploding Japanese shell and wrecked). Eventually, casualties would be carried by LCVP or other craft to the transports, where better treatment areas were ready. These facilities, too, however, were not up to the standard of specially designated hospital ships.

Two hospital ships had been assigned to stand by to treat and evacuate casualties from the Gilberts, but the USS *Solace* (AH-5) and USS *Relief* (AH-1) were not close at hand. Under international law governing the use of hospital ships in wartime, they were required to burn special lights at night, which would have given away the location of the transports to Japanese air and naval units. Instead, the hospital ships had arranged to meet the retiring transports after fighting had mostly died down in the Gilberts. The transports transferred the wounded in a rendezvous at Abemama on 24 November. The *Solace* continued on to Hawaii, arriving on 2 December at Pearl Harbor, where Admiral Nimitz and others came aboard to visit the wounded. The ship transferred 232 patients to the U.S. Naval Hospital at Aiea Heights that same afternoon, along with one Japanese prisoner of war (a submariner captured by the USS *Meade*). The *Relief*'s facilities turned out not to be needed, and she steamed from Abemama back to Funafuti.

In their recommendations for future operations, the division physicians recommended quicker access to hospital ships and the use of seaplanes as air ambulances.

The evacuation of the wounded out to the transports. (Hatch Collection, National Museum of the Pacific War)

were guarded closely until, as on so many spots on Betio, a bulldozer could arrive to bury remaining Japanese fighters and prevent any reinfiltration, especially after dark. Now 2/8 and 3/8 could make it to the eastern end of the airfield, where they waited for 1/6 to arrive and form a solid line, although they pulled back from their farthest advance so as to lessen the chances of friendly fire casualties. With this effort, the deadly and exhausting work of 2/8 begun on Red 3 on D-Day was largely complete. Its Marines would form a secondary line behind 1/6 to guard against significant penetrations during any Japanese counterattacks.

3d Battalion, 6th Marines (3/6)
(component of corps reserve)

CO: Lieutenant Colonel Kenneth Finley McLeod

Time of Arrival of All Elements: 1100, D+2

Target/Goal: Land on Green Beach and move along south coast to join 1/6 in the attack on the southeastern tail of Betio.

The final infantry battalion to be committed to the fight was 3/6. At 0850 on D+2, it was ordered to land on the northern end of Green Beach. By 1100, 3/6 was ashore intact and ready to be placed where needed most. While Ryan's 3/2 composite unit and 1/8 worked over the Pocket from two sides, 3/6 was needed more urgently for the final elimination of the Japanese in the east. At 1700 it was sent along the narrow strip between the runway and southern coast, behind 1/6. This fresh battalion stopped about 600 yards behind Jones's 1/6, forming, like 2/8 to its north, secondary lines ready to help 1/6 in the event of a counterattack. Later that evening, its I Company would be sent all the way forward to form part of the front line.

By the evening of D+2, Japanese soldiers were increasingly being discovered dead all over Betio in their fortified positions. Those who had not been killed by blasts from tanks, artillery fire, or demolition charges —or incinerated or suffocated by flamethrowers—had committed suicide. Usually they held a live grenade next to their chests or removed a shoe and used a bare big toe to pull the trigger of a rifle pointed at their head. Whatever the case, their sense of honor, pride, ideology, or religion deemed capture or even survival to be psychologically intolerable. Doubtless they were also running out of ammunition, due to the battle itself and their heavy air defense fire before the Marines had arrived.

While these Japanese suicides were the best sign the battle would soon be over, some Marines regarded the prospect of what they called a banzai charge as the truest omen of impending victory, an indication that the Japanese had forsaken all hope and were ready for a quick death en masse in battle. If such an attack occurred out in the open, as grisly and deadly as it might be for the Marines, it would have the effect of shortening the five days Julian Smith expected the battle to last to less than one. Yet Smith's lingering pessimism about a rapid conclusion was demonstrated by his decision to return 2/6 from its expedition to Bairiki and prepare it to engage in the final act on Betio. In Smith's thinking, that newly committed battalion would exchange roles with the exhausted and depleted 2/8 and 3/8, who would move over to Bairiki. But events and a shortage of landing craft would overtake his plan.

Major William Jones, battalion commander of 1/6, knew that a Japanese nighttime counterattack was likely, and on the afternoon of D+2, he began to coordinate artillery and naval gunfire in the area to the southeast of the Marines' front lines. The shore-based artillery could be registered at an unusually close and dangerous distance of only 75 yards ahead of the Marines' front lines. The naval fire, because it was less easy to control, would be saved for the areas 500 yards or more farther ahead.

The USS *Sigsbee*'s (DD-502) navigator determined the currents (2 knots from the west), noted the bearing of the target areas, and entered the information into the ship's fire control computer in order to launch its salvos toward Betio, as if it were engaging a ship. The Marines' artillery fired white phosphorous shells to indicate the precise targets for the naval fire. If the Japanese massed in the open, the shell fire would likely dispatch many of them, and the lines of 1/6, 3/6, and 2/8 would have to hold the rest in fighting at close quarters.

The counterattack did in fact materialize and took place in three phases on the evening of D+2 and early morning of D+3. True to expected form, the Japanese commanders began probing the Marine lines to determine their positions shortly after the onset of darkness on D+2. At 1930, about 50 Japanese

troops infiltrated between A and B Companies of 1/6, which were deployed between the south coast and the eastern end of runway. Jones' battalion reserve from his headquarters and weapons companies had to step forward and seal the gap. Jones asked Kyle's 1/2 to provide a company for a secondary line 100 yards back, which was later supplanted by I Company of 3/6. Jones requested, and received, Marine artillery and naval gunfire support in the prearranged locations to the east and southeast, to make Japanese coordination and massing of troops more difficult. The destroyers USS *Schroeder* (DD-501) and *Sigsbee* worked in concert with 75-mm pack howitzers from 1/10 and 2/10, both during this first probe and all night long. The destroyers also fired star shells to help illuminate the front and the Japanese-controlled areas.

The second phase of the Japanese counterattack began at 2300 on D+2. This time the Japanese facing A Company, 1st Battalion, 6th Marines, deliberately tried to call attention to themselves to draw fire and thereby reveal the Marines' dispositions and heavy weapons locations. They banged their canteens on their helmets and shouted out menacing taunts in English such as "Japanese drink Marines' blood!" As this was going on, a second Japanese detachment silently moved in to attack B Company of 1/6. The Marines had no choice this time but to fire and divulge their locations. This attack was also beaten back, but at the cost of making the third and final one all the more challenging since so much had been revealed to the Japanese in the meantime.

The third phase would begin at 0300 on D+3. The Japanese had moved 7.7-mm machine guns into abandoned trucks 50 yards ahead of the Marines. Only the efforts of a small group of Marine noncommissioned officers who crawled up to the trucks and threw grenades ended this serious threat. Then at 0400, 200–300 Japanese troops emerged together simultaneously, to again go at A and B Companies. Artillery and naval fire helped, but it was the efforts of Marines in hand-to-hand combat with rifles, bayonets, and anything else they could grab that defeated the assault. For a few moments, the new B Company commander, First Lieutenant Norman Thomas—who had assumed command from his position as executive officer when his company commander had been hit by sniper fire and paralyzed earlier on D+2—thought he did not have enough men for the job. He radioed Jones desperately for reinforcements. Jones could only tell him: "We haven't got them. You've got to hold." Thomas and his men did.

At the cost of 40 Marines killed in action and 100 more wounded, 1/6 had defeated the long-expected Japanese night attack. The east and southeast of Betio were now fully open to a final Marine push in daylight against the Japanese, who had destroyed whatever remained of their own cohesion by plunging forward into the melee after 0400. Marine howitzers and 5-inch naval guns had worked far longer and harder than their design specifications allowed, but they had held up and devastated the Japanese. The destroyers had fired so often that they had depleted their supply of 5-inch rounds. On land, the pack howitzers of 1/10 alone had fired 1,300 rounds. Two hundred Japanese soldiers were dead among and just beyond the Marine lines, and, farther back, 125 had fallen to the artillery and naval support fire. Now it truly would be a question of mopping up on Betio's tail, and of fully eradicating the last Japanese resistance in the Pocket—the final two tasks of a battle not yet even three days old.

D+3: THE END ON BETIO

Before D-Day, Marines had expected, or at least hoped, that the preliminary bombardments would make their job on Betio one of mopping up for a day. During the morning of D-Day, the Marines had discovered that any optimism had been overblown, and even defeat could not be ruled out. By the third afternoon of the battle (D+2), they had begun to believe they would win decisively, perhaps within a few more days to one week.

Yet on the morning of D+3, a Japanese collapse, which had in reality already occurred the night before, became obvious to all. By midday, suddenly, it was over except for enduring sniping from individual hidden rikusentai and sealing up or detonating bypassed emplacements. Betio could be declared secure, the Marines of the assault regiments could depart, and garrison forces and construction battalions could start the work for which the battle had been waged: making Tarawa into the westernmost threat to Japanese control of the Central Pacific and into a base for the next operation, already planned, into the Marshall Islands at the end of January 1944.

On D+3, the best organized, least battle-weary Marine battalion on Betio was 3/6. To it would be given the

Pictured right, Lt. Bill Kelly was the first Navy pilot to land on the captured airfield on Betio. (Hatch Collection, National Museum of the Pacific War)

final task, and honor, of completing the push to the southeast from the site of that morning's Japanese counterattack to the last bit of land, a mere 20 yards wide. Lieutenant Colonel McLeod's battalion commenced its attack at 0800 on D+3. Only on the north coast, just southeast of the eastern runway circle, did it encounter resistance it could not immediately overcome. McLeod opted not to pause to reduce the emplacements immediately. He left his I Company behind to isolate the position and continued forward with his K and L Companies. The entire width of Betio was now spanned by 3/6, although the island was a mere 700 feet wide here (compared to 1,800 feet at the base of the pier). The Marines' chief weapons were flamethrowers and the two remaining medium tanks, *China Gal* and *Colorado*, covered by light tanks that did not fire their main guns. The tanks and infantry moved along the same line, encountering minimal resistance by comparison with the previous days. At 1310 they reached the southeastern tail of Betio. The rikusentai who had been momentarily bypassed and left to I Company had also been blasted out or had committed suicide by then.

In a fitting symmetry to the battle, wrapping up at almost the same time was the other major action on D+3, the eradication of the deadly Pocket. That site had been the bane of 1/8—both as it waded ashore on D+1 and then as it moved west—and of all three regiments of the 2d Marines as they landed on D-Day. The flamethrowers of 2/8 had been moved over from Red 3, and Major Schoettel, now back in command of the surviving units of 3/2, pushed up toward the Pocket from the southwest. Demolition units and self-propelled 75-mm guns (half-tracks) assisted.

At 1000 on D+3, 1/8 and 3/2 linked up south of the cove on Red 1 at the western runway terminus. Sheer Marine tenacity combined with Japanese despondency and lack of ammunition resulted in the elimination of the Pocket in three hours, by 1305. At that time, Julian Smith and Harry Hill, who had landed at Smith's suggestion to see for himself what had taken so long, composed a message to Admiral Turner and Major General Holland Smith at Makin, informing them that all organized Japanese resistance on Betio had ceased. It had been 76 hours and 10 minutes since the scout and sniper platoon of the 2d Marines had jumped onto the pierhead and initiated the Marine attack.

Even before the last two Japanese redoubts were annihilated, the first Navy carrier plane, an F6F Hellcat fighter, landed at noon on Betio's quickly repaired airfield. The

pilot, Lieutenant William Wright Kelly from the USS *Bunker Hill* (CV-17) of the Southern Carrier Group, made a hard but safe landing and climbed down. He and his fellow fighter pilots had been in the air for an average of five hours per day, and were likely too weary to fight effectively had the Japanese fleet emerged to challenge them. Kelly was surrounded by grinning Marines and a motion picture camera, which filmed the happy moment for which thousands had already died. There was little for Kelly to do but take back off again for his carrier and report that the runway was available if needed.

Not all Japanese soldiers on Betio got the news that they had been defeated. Some emerged during the day and evening to issue their final statements. Marine casualties thus continued to climb even after 1305. Snipers made their presence known; pillboxes and holes had to be investigated, cleared, and sealed; and that night three Marines lost their lives to Japanese bayonets.

The main preoccupation for the Marines and Navy now was getting the transports and their screen of Navy warships loaded up and headed away before any more Japanese aircraft or submarines appeared. Marines from the designated garrison units could wade ashore unmolested, while their equipment was brought in at high tide and the island was made ready for handing over to its designated Navy commander. The transports reloaded the dirty, haggard, and hungry surviving Marines from Betio.

The 6th Marines were left to finish up at Tarawa, while the re-embarked 2d and 8th Marines steamed toward the Hawaiian Islands for about a week. To the disappointment of many—especially those with wives, fiancées, and girlfriends in New Zealand—they would be recovering and preparing for their next deployment on the island of Hawaii itself. Any return to New Zealand would have to be made on an individual basis after the war. Much more frequently, the women who had established such firm ties to these Marines would come to the United States when conditions allowed, sometimes years later.

The island of Hawaii was not Oahu—it was far less populated, and with fewer recreational opportunities of the type commonly available in urban environments. The 2d Marine Division was delivered to the Parker Ranch in a sparsely populated portion of the northwestern tip of the island. At an elevation of 2,650 feet, their new camp was dusty and cold. The climate was welcome to the men still suffering from their malarial days on Guadalcanal, and far more like New

Marines neutralize a Betio Island fortification by frontal assault, including a flamethrower, toward the end of the battle. (U.S. Naval Institute Photo Archive)

Members of the "Tarawa Press Club"—including then-1st Lt. Earl Wilson, 2d Marine Division public-relations officer (standing, fourth from left), and Marine Corps combat photographer Sgt. Larry Burns (kneeling)—are pictured at their headquarters on Betio. Associated Press's Frank Filan (far left) accompanied Wilson on his exploration of the island. (National Archives)

Waking up on Betio after the Battle

"SCENES FROM THE STORM" BY CAPTAIN EARL J. WILSON, U.S. MARINE CORPS RESERVE, *NAVAL HISTORY*, DECEMBER 2013

Dawn broke, and along with it came the familiar sound of a rooster crowing somewhere amid the ruins. The coconut trees, though blasted, were still beautiful in the early morning light, and for a while there was a vague uneasy quiet over the island disturbed by just a little sporadic firing.

A sergeant who had come ashore with me was nearby and suggested a walk. We started along the beach, and I was amazed at the thick coconut logs and the steel reinforcements that lined the beach and held masses of twisted, bloated, and burned enemy corpses. Because an overpowering stench was everywhere, I put my hand to my nose and picked my way along with the sergeant.

Equipment and battle gear was strewn about the ground in profusion. Grenades, bullets, bandoliers, weapons, papers, shells, shoes, kimonos, and books were all there. We pawed through a few of the papers. Also, there were songbooks, stationery, Japanese cigarettes, rations, all scattered like the material on a dump. Men were there too, picking over the stuff for souvenirs. I picked up a dozen clean handkerchiefs to wipe my carbine with, for it was a mess from the coral sand and the brief shower we had during the night.

Zealand than Tarawa had been. But it was miserable in its own way at first.

The Marines had little time to feel sorry for themselves or complain, because they had to take the material delivered for the construction of their tent city and start making a new home. Here the 2d Marine Division would stay, at a place they called Camp Tarawa, until they left for their next assault on Saipan in June 1944. The Hawaiian topography had the advantage of resembling what they would encounter in the Marianas, and thus made for more realistic training. Still, after the horrors of Tarawa, arrival back on U.S. soil in the most remote portion of the Territory of Hawaii was less of a distraction from the memories of combat than these Marines might have hoped for or dreamed of as they departed the Gilberts. They did as they were ordered, however, and prepared to train and receive replacements for the thousands who had died or been seriously wounded at Tarawa. Occasionally a diversion such as a rodeo with local ranch hands might be arranged, but the delights of Wellington, or even nearby Honolulu, could only be the subject of fantasy and envy.

Meanwhile, back on Betio, when it was relatively safe for top leadership to come ashore, they landed. Julian Smith had arrived on D+2 and Hill on D+3. Holland Smith was next, on D+4. He recalled the blank stares of the filthy and unshaven Marines he encountered as he made his way from the pier to Julian Smith's command post. Before his tour commenced, there was a double flag raising ceremony. The U.S. Stars and Stripes and the U.K.'s Union Jack were hoisted atop two adjacent coconut palm trees as the assembled Marines and sailors saluted.

The top Navy leadership was next to arrive. Spruance and Nimitz viewed Betio together on D+6, 26 November. Spruance had wanted Nimitz to remain at Funafuti because of the lingering danger from snipers, but Nimitz would not hear of it. His plane required more of the runway than was then available, and it had to circle while the Seabees made the landing strip ready. Nimitz was greeted by the same overwhelming stench that had plagued Marines and sailors in the equatorial sun since the first day of battle. The admiral responsible for the largest U.S. theater of warfare later noted, "It's the first time I've ever smelled death."

Flag raising ceremony on Betio, 24 November 1943. (National Archives)

NAVAL ACTION AND LOSSES IN THE GILBERTS

When more broadly considered as an operation spanning the entire Gilbert Islands chain, the Navy's losses of men were of roughly of the same magnitude as those of the Marines. Nimitz and Spruance's strategy of arriving without warning, attacking hard, and departing immediately had precluded any chance of the Japanese surface fleet's appearing in time. But Japanese submarines and aircraft were a different matter altogether.

The first major setback for the U.S. Navy involved the light aircraft carrier USS *Independence* (CVL-22). On 20 November, the Southern Carrier Group of which she was a part was engaged by 15 to 18 Japanese "Betty" bombers armed with torpedoes. The Bettys came in low and evaded detection until almost upon the carrier group. The bombers were highly vulnerable when making torpedo runs, and five were shot down by gunners on board the *Independence* alone. Yet one Betty dropped a torpedo that detonated on the *Independence*'s starboard quarter. Seventeen sailors were killed. "Seriously damaged, the *Independence* had to withdraw from the Tarawa area and head for Funafuti to make temporary repairs that would allow her to proceed to Pearl Harbor for more extensive, permanent refurbishment. It appeared to the crew of the *Independence* that they must have been stalked by Japanese submarines radioing back to the Marshall Islands to guide in the Betty bombers.

Two more serious losses by the Navy occurred near Makin, and a potentially far more serious Japanese air attack was endured near Makin after the battle on land had concluded. The first involved the battleship USS *Mississippi* (BB-41). At 0728 on D-Day, during a 15-minute squall that was the only weather-related disruption to the landings there, the *Mississippi* was participating in the preliminary bombardment of Butaritari Island. An explosion and fire occurred in her number 2 turret housing three 14-inch guns. The accident killed 43 sailors and wounded 19, although *Mississippi* continued firing other guns thereafter.

The second incident at Makin involved the greatest single loss of life by U.S. forces to occur other than on Betio. Before sunrise on 24 November, the escort carrier USS *Liscome Bay* (CVE-56) was patrolling 20 miles southwest of Butaritari. She was one of a class of vessels hurriedly conceived, designed, constructed, and introduced into combat in order to deploy aircraft for antisubmarine patrols and support of ground operations.

At 0510 that morning, the Japanese submarine *I-175* fired a torpedo that was spotted by a *Liscome Bay* lookout too late to give effective warning. It struck behind the engine room in an explosion that was followed immediately by a second one in which stored ammunition detonated. The entire aft portion of the *Liscome Bay* was demolished instantly. By 0533 the carrier had sunk, killing 644 sailors, including the skipper, Captain Irving D. Wiltsie; the commander of the Air Support Group at Makin (TG 52.3), Rear Admiral Henry M. Mullinnix; and Ship's Cook Third Class Doris Miller, winner of the Navy Cross at Pearl Harbor on board the USS *West Virginia* (BB-48). Only 272 of the *Liscome Bay*'s crew

Major U.S. Navy Ships at Tarawa (TF 53, Southern Attack Force)

ATTACK CARGO SHIPS

- ***BELLATRIX*** **(AKA-3)**
- ***THUBAN*** **(AKA-19)**
- ***VIRGO*** **(AKA-20)**

ATTACK TRANSPORT SHIPS

- ***ARTHUR MIDDLETON*** **(APA-25)**
- ***DOYEN*** **(APA-1)**
- ***FELAND*** **(APA-11)**
- ***HARRIS*** **(APA-2)**
- ***HARRY LEE*** **(APA-10)**
- ***HEYWOOD*** **(APA-6)**
- ***J. FRANKLIN BELL*** **(APA-16)**
- ***LA SALLE*** **(AP-102)**
- ***MONROVIA*** **(APA-31)**
- ***ORMSBY*** **(APA-49)**
- ***SHERIDAN*** **(APA-51)**
- ***WILLIAM P. BIDDLE*** **(APA-8)**
- ***ZEILIN*** **(APA-3)**

BATTLESHIPS

- ***COLORADO*** **(BB-45)**
- ***MARYLAND*** **(BB-46)**
- ***TENNESSEE*** **(BB-43)**

DESTROYERS

- ***ANDERSON*** **(DD-411)**
- ***AYLWIN*** **(DD-355)**
- ***BAILEY*** **(DD-492)**
- ***BANCROFT*** **(DD-598)**
- ***COTTEN*** **(DD-669)**
- ***COWELL*** **(DD-547)**
- ***DASHIELL*** **(DD-659)**
- ***FARRAGUT*** **(DD-348)**
- ***FRAZIER*** **(DD-607)**
- ***GANSEVOORT*** **(DD-608)**
- ***HARRISON*** **(DD-573)**

were rescued. If ever validation had been needed for the concerns of Nimitz or Holland Smith that the assault on Makin must move quickly, this was it: the *Liscome Bay* might have been steaming away by the time she was struck if the operation ashore had concluded a day earlier and the Northern Attack Force had begun its return journey to Hawaii.

But other Japanese naval counterstrikes failed completely. On 22 November at 1519, the destroyer USS *Meade* made sonar contact with the Japanese submarine *I-35* about ten miles southwest of Tarawa. The destroyer USS *Frazier* (DD-607) joined the hunt, and at 1705 began firing depth charges. By 1730, a large oil slick was obvious on the surface, and at 1749, the *I-35* surfaced 2,300 yards from the *Frazier* and only 1,200 yards from the *Meade*. The destroyers opened fire with 5-inch, 40-mm, and 20-mm guns, killing Japanese sailors who attempted to man the *I-35*'s deck gun. The *Frazier*'s captain decided not to chance the sub's escape and directed his destroyer to ram *I-35* at full speed.

After the impact at 1751, sailors from the *Frazier* fired their pistols to prevent Japanese sailors from emerging on deck with weapons. The *Frazier* backed off the *I-35*, and the submarine settled quickly by the stern, sinking at a 60-degree angle at 1754. A large underwater explosion was then noted. This Japanese attempt to pick off ships in the transport group had failed. Only three Japanese sailors were taken prisoner. The *Frazier*, badly damaged but the victor of the duel, would have to proceed slowly toward Hawaii in the week to come, her stem's lower 4 feet bent to the port side by 3 feet.

Japanese aircraft sortied against some of the Northern Attack Force's retiring ships during the evening of 25 November. Thirteen Bettys attacked Turner's battleships, cruisers, escort carriers, and destroyers as they were 60 miles east of Makin Atoll, steaming toward Hawaii. Employing sophisticated night fighting tactics such as parachute flares and beacon lights dropped into the water, the bombers attempted to hit the U.S. ships with torpedoes. Turner had practiced on the way to Makin for such an eventuality, and turned away from the planes just as the flares were at their brightest, since he guessed the torpedoes would soon be in the water. As a result, the U.S. ships presented smaller targets that the torpedoes missed. Turner continued the evasive maneuvers and spared his group even a single hit.

On the night of 26 November, another group of Japanese planes attempted to strike the Northern Carrier Group, including the USS *Enterprise* (CV-6), and for the first time in the war, a night air engagement involving U.S. carrier planes occurred. The Japanese, who had believed they could not be opposed effectively at night, were not ready for U.S. carrier aircraft that were able to fly and fight in darkness. Some Japanese aircraft were shot down, others fled upon being discovered aloft, and their entire attack failed. *Enterprise* fighter pilot Lieutenant Commander Edward "Butch" O'Hare, previously the recipient of the Medal of Honor for his heroics off New Ireland in 1942, went down in the engagement under unclear circumstances. The airfield constructed on just-captured Abemama would immediately be named for O'Hare; after the war, Chicago's new commercial airport would be named after him as well.

- ***HAZELWOOD*** **(DD-531)**
- ***HEERMANN*** **(DD-532)**
- ***JOHN RODGERS*** **(DD-574)**
- ***MCKEE*** **(DD-575)**
- ***MEADE*** **(DD-602)**
- ***MONAGHAN*** **(DD-354)**
- ***MURRAY*** **(DD-576)**
- ***RINGGOLD*** **(DD-500)**
- ***RUSSELL*** **(DD-414)**
- ***SCHROEDER*** **(DD-501)**
- ***SIGSBEE*** **(DD-502)**

LANDING SHIP, DOCK

- ***ASHLAND*** **(LSD-1)**

SUBMARINE (TARAWA AND ABEMAMA)

- ***NAUTILUS*** **(SS-168)**

ESCORT CARRIERS

- ***BARNES*** **(CVE-20)**
- ***CHENANGO*** **(CVE-28)**
- ***NASSAU*** **(CVE-16)**
- ***SANGAMON*** **(CVE-26)**
- ***SUWANNEE*** **(CVE-27)**

CRUISERS

- ***INDIANAPOLIS*** **(CA-35)**
- ***PORTLAND*** **(CA-33)**

LIGHT CRUISERS

- ***BIRMINGHAM*** **(CL-62)**
- ***MOBILE*** **(CL-63)**
- ***SANTA FE*** **(CL-60)**

MINESWEEPERS

- ***PURSUIT*** **(AM-108)**
- ***REQUISITE*** **(AM-109)**

LANDING SHIPS, TANK

- **LST 34**
- **LST 242**
- **LST 243**

GROUND OPERATIONS ELSEWHERE IN THE GILBERTS

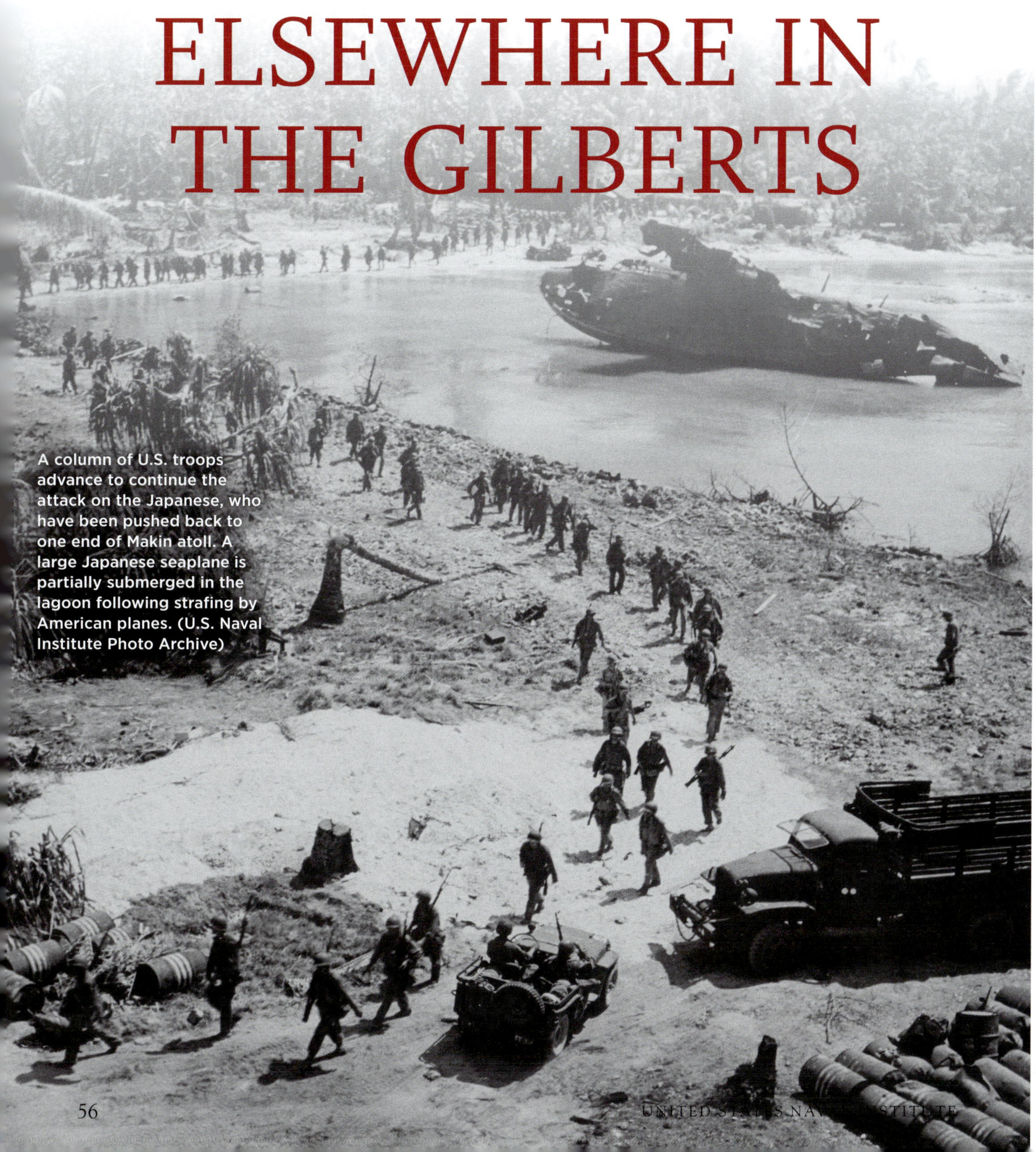

A column of U.S. troops advance to continue the attack on the Japanese, who have been pushed back to one end of Makin atoll. A large Japanese seaplane is partially submerged in the lagoon following strafing by American planes. (U.S. Naval Institute Photo Archive)

MAKIN

By many measures, Makin Atoll, about 100 miles north of Tarawa, should have been the most important objective of the Gilbert Island campaign. It was closer to the southernmost Japanese possessions in the Marshall Islands (a little more than 200 miles from Mili, and a little less than 300 miles from Jaluit). Furthermore, the Japanese had been developing Makin as a base longer than they had Tarawa.

Yet because the Japanese had elected to construct their main airfield in the Gilberts on Betio and had fortified it so heavily, it became the priority target of Operation Galvanic. Makin was added to the mix with Tarawa and Abemama only in September 1943, when it became obvious that Nauru Island, 440 miles south-southwest of Betio and originally one of the goals of Galvanic, would be too dangerous to assault with the men and ships then available.

Beginning with George Marshall's compromise proposal at the Casablanca Conference in January 1943 that U.S. offensives in the Pacific would be accomplished with the forces already available in the theater, U.S. planners faced a Goldilocks dilemma: they needed to locate just the right Japanese positions to invade and seize with the forces available. If they proceeded too cautiously, they risked allowing the Japanese the space and time to fortify their existing holdings. If they went forward too abruptly, they might suffer the morale blow of heavy losses or even a failed amphibious assault.

Thinking that Makin was precisely the right size, it had been substituted for Nauru. But in reality, the Goldilocks solution had remained elusive. Instead of hitting Makin with too few men, the U.S. hit with too many—the U.S. Army regimental combat team there would outnumber the Japanese on Makin by a factor of 10 to 1. The result was, unfortunately, not a lightning assault, quick handover of Makin to garrison forces, and the immediate withdrawal of the attacking elements to Hawaii, or to Betio in order to assist the Marines. Securing Makin took almost exactly as long as taking Betio, notwithstanding the vastly increased ratio of U.S. attackers to Japanese defenders.

There was nothing obviously wrong with the Army's plan for attacking Butaritari Island at Makin. It was, to be sure, slightly more complex than the 2d Marine Division's landings through the lagoon at Tarawa, in that it would occur in two distinct phases on two widely separated beaches, one on the ocean and the other in the lagoon. It counted on a reaction by the Japanese that did not occur, however. The defenders did not fall for the bait and rush to the site of the first landing, which would have left their core positions exposed to the second landing. U.S. Army planners had counted on this.

Even so, the landings themselves were so successful when compared with those on Betio that determined commanders leading well-trained and highly spirited troops could have pushed down the entire length of Butaritari in a day. Neither the commanders nor their troops evidenced such qualities, nor did they feel themselves to be in a hurry. As a result, the U.S. Navy would pay a grievously high price for the operation at Makin when its ships lingered nearby for what turned out to be a day too long.

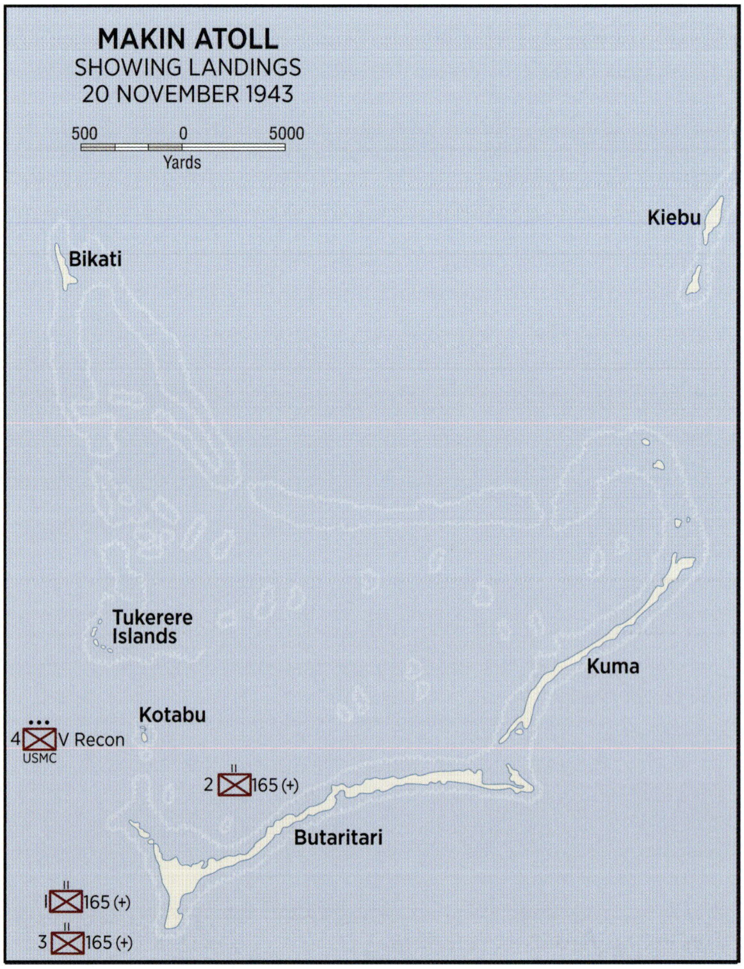

V Amphibious Corps commanding general Holland Smith reluctantly approved the intricate plan that the Army's 27th Division had devised for the Makin landings. This division, formed from the New York National Guard, had thus far in the war been used to guard California and the Hawaiian Islands against the threat of attack or invasion. To prepare for its role in the Gilberts, in summer and fall 1943, the 27th had required accelerated training and an introduction to amphibious attack doctrine and procedures.

The 27th Division's commander, Major General Ralph Smith, faced Japanese units who had dug into the middle of Butaritari and constructed two long antitank trenches running the entire width of the island, from northern lagoon to southern coast. The central portion of the island between the two trenches, containing most of the Japanese defenses and structures, was referred to among U.S. forces as the Citadel. Ralph Smith needed a way to attack it without bogging down in trying to bypass or overcome the antitank trenches.

He split his attacking force. Two battalion landing teams of the 165th Regimental Combat Team would land on beaches designated Red 1 and Red 2 on the western end of Butaritari at 0830 on D-Day, 20 November. Two hours later a second landing, taking place at the time designated as W-Hour, would occur inside the lagoon on beaches Yellow 1 and 2, and would be conducted by another battalion of the 165th and one from the 105th. The Army's hope and expectation was to catch the Japanese units scattering to defend the approach of the first landing forces on the western beaches. The western tank barrier would then be caught in a vise from east and west.

The preliminary bombardments at Makin were likely somewhat more effective than those on Betio, but only because the Japanese forces had constructed far fewer concrete, steel, and coconut log positions (having far fewer men to place in them). The timing of the bombardments worked somewhat better, because the Navy planes' dawn bombardment came when expected here, unlike at Tarawa, and because the first assault waves to hit the Red Beaches were more or less on time. Yet the core element of Smith's plan did not work, since the Japanese held fast to their positions in the Citadel and prepared to defend it against an assault across the western antitank ditch rather than trying to meet the Americans on the western beaches.

The Makin assault would have already been slowing down by dint of the unexpected Japanese response to the Red Beach landings, but further unforeseen factors added still more complexity. The western beaches were rocky, leaving only very narrow areas on which LVTs could land, or to which LCVPs could pull up in order to allow the disembarkation of their troops and supplies. Nonetheless, the Japanese did a favor to the 165th's two landing teams on the Red Beaches by not resisting the U.S. landing, which the Japanese might have disrupted or defeated if they had been willing

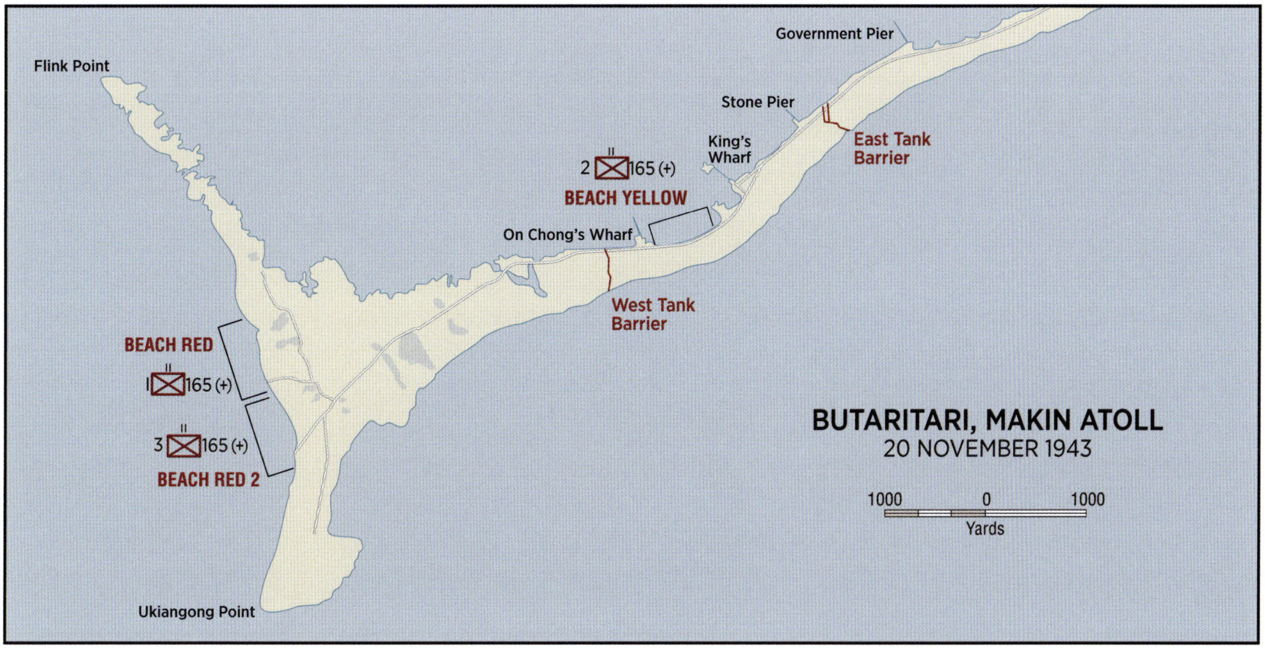

to meet the Americans maneuvering slowly on the boulder-strewn beaches.

Even though the elements of the Army's 105th and 165th Regiments now faced more Japanese organized resistance in the Citadel than they had been prepared for, they still landed effectively and began to execute their plan of moving to the east and west immediately. Once these troops began to move inland, along with those on the western end of Butaritari who had landed on the Red Beaches, they faced challenges from the vegetation, topography, and their own inexperience in combat. The pace slackened dramatically.

The U.S. troops moved deliberately, determined not to fall victim to snipers hidden in trees or elsewhere. Sometimes the sniper threat was real enough. At 1455 on D-Day, the 165th's regimental commander, Colonel James Gardiner Conroy, strode ahead just west of the western tank trap to try to get his troops moving. He was shot in the head and died on the spot. For the moment at least, this validated the concern about snipers that was slowing down the Army. Meanwhile, the troops that had landed from the lagoon into the Citadel stalled when their follow-on waves were delayed by Japanese fire from wrecked ships in the lagoon.

By sunset on D-Day (shortly after 1800), the troops in the west had established a line at the western tank barrier, just across from U.S. soldiers who had landed in the Citadel. In that central portion of Butaritari, not only was the area around the western tank barrier in U.S. hands, but large pockets of the Citadel were also held by U.S. infantry and armored units. To be sure, a small pocket of Japanese holdouts had been bypassed near the lagoon just west of the western tank barrier. But otherwise there was a firm U.S. presence in the west and center of Makin's main island. Five thousand U.S. troops had landed on D-Day to face 700–800 Japanese (soldiers and otherwise), and 25 U.S. soldiers were dead so far. For D+1, there appeared to remain only the linking up of all U.S. forces and driving to the northeastern tip of Butaritari early in the day.

Taking this step would require the next 48 hours, a delay that would bring Holland Smith blustering ashore to find out what was wrong. The Japanese commander, who had assumed the position because the base commander, Lieutenant Seizo Ishikawa, had likely been killed on D-Day, learned how to communicate effectively and move his men around, stalling the U.S. advance on D+1.

Major U.S. Navy Ships at Makin (TF 52, Northern Attack Force)

ATTACK CARGO SHIP

- *ALCYONE* (AKA-7)

ATTACK TRANSPORT SHIPS

- *CALVERT* (APA-32)
- *LEONARD WOOD* (APA-12)
- *NEVILLE* (APA-9)
- *PIERCE* (APA-50)

BATTLESHIPS

- *IDAHO* (BB-42)
- *MISSISSIPPI* (BB-41)
- *NEW MEXICO* (BB-40)
- *PENNSYLVANIA* (BB-38)

DESTROYERS

- *BURNS* (DD-588)
- *DALE* (DD-353)
- *DEWEY* (DD-349)
- *FRANKS* (DD-554)
- *GRIDLEY* (DD-380)
- *HOEL* (DD-533)
- *HUGHES* (DD-410)
- *HULL* (DD-350)
- *KIMBERLY* (DD-521)
- *MACDONOUGH* (DD-351)
- *MAURY* (DD-401)
- *MORRIS* (DD-417)
- *MUSTIN* (DD-413)
- *PHELPS* (DD-360)

LANDING SHIP, DOCK

- *BELLE GROVE* (LSD-2)

ESCORT CARRIERS

- *CORAL SEA* (CVE-57)
- *CORREGIDOR* (CVE-58)
- *LISCOME BAY* (CVE-56)

CRUISERS

- *BALTIMORE* (CA-68)
- *MINNEAPOLIS* (CA-36)
- *NEW ORLEANS* (CA-32)
- *SAN FRANCISCO* (CA-38)

MINESWEEPER

- *REVENGE* (AM-110)

LANDING SHIPS, TANK

- *LST-31*
- *LST-78*
- *LST-179*

Wreckage of on Chong's Wharf on Butaritari Island, Makin Atoll, from pre-invasion bombardment, circa 20 November 1943. Note bomb crater at edge of wharf in center of photograph. Cleared area in upper right is the western tank trap on the island. (U.S. Naval Institute Photo Archive)

Soldiers of the U.S. Army's 2d Battalion, 165th Infantry Division, move through the water toward the shores on Yellow Beach on Butaritari. Japanese are firing machine guns from the two wrecked ships at (right), 800 yards away. The assault barge (right) where Japanese machine gun fire is strafed and hit the operator and gun crew is grounded on the coral reef. Smoke rising on the island is from oil dumps hit by naval gunfire. Medium tanks (left center) are mopping up any Japanese machine gun emplacements in the area.
(U.S. Naval Institute Photo Archive)

When Holland Smith landed, he found what he later recalled as "undisciplined, trigger-happy Army troops." With the eastern end of Butaritari still in Japanese hands on the night of D+1, Smith said he had "one of the worst nights I ever spent in the Pacific." Jittery U.S. sentries fired all night long, sometimes "drilling holes in the command post tent," as Smith remembered it. Holland Smith, regarded as a "sadist and a bully" by U.S. Army historian S. L. A. Marshall, who was observing from the scene, held 27th Division commander Ralph Smith in low regard then and later: Smith later remembered in his memoir, *Coral and Brass*: "I was anxious to go to Tarawa and here he [Ralph Smith] was fiddling around with an operation that should have been ended long before in my opinion. His communications with his regiment were extremely poor and he showed little enterprise in improving them. He didn't know where his battalions were, and insisted on sitting by the phone, where he couldn't get any information because the phone didn't work."

With plodding persistence and overwhelming superiority in firepower and numbers, Ralph Smith's units pushed to the northeast. Only at 1000 on D+3 did the 27th Infantry Division commander feel confident in communicating to his superior, Admiral Turner, a terse rhyming victory proclamation: "Makin taken." Smith had lost 66 men killed in action and 218 wounded, as opposed to an estimated 445 Japanese killed, with 104 Korean laborers and 1 Japanese soldier taken prisoner. It had been clear from the outset, when the Red Beach landings went unopposed, that Makin would be subdued, but the battle revealed training deficiencies and a lack of leadership coordination that would remain to be worked out in coming Army and Marine joint amphibious efforts in the Central Pacific.

ABEMAMA, TARAWA'S OTHER ISLANDS, NAURU, AND NEW AIR BASES

Abemama

The least elaborate of the three Gilbert Island assaults occurred at Abemama Atoll and was codenamed Operation Boxcloth. Abemama was included because it made an ideal setting for an air base. Its northernmost island had more than enough solid land at the proper east-west orientation to allow for the construction of an airfield on which heavy bombers could be stationed. Although it was 85 miles southeast of Betio and almost 200 miles south-southeast of Makin, meaning that it was farther away from the Marshalls, it was still more than close enough for bombers. Preliminary reconnaissance had not established for certain whether the Japanese had manned and fortified the atoll.

Boxcloth was a deliberately small-scale endeavor. After conducting last-minute observations of Tarawa just prior to D-Day there, the submarine USS *Nautilus* proceeded directly to Abemama with the V Amphibious Corps Reconnaissance Company, under the command of Marine Captain James L. Jones, the brother of 1/6 battalion commander Major William Jones. The company reported directly to Major General Holland Smith, but would be dependent on assistance from Harry Hill's Southern Attack Force. James Jones' unit had been formed in 1942 and was trained, among many other things, in rubber boat landings.

Their orders were to land and detect any Japanese presence, but not to engage the enemy if the Japanese were present in force. That would be left to units that would follow from Tarawa once Betio was secure. However, as previously described, the *Nautilus* was hit by fire from the USS *Ringgold* near Tarawa and barely managed to escape. The episode delayed the reconnaissance company's arrival off Abemama, but not the success of the mission.

The landing did not go according to plan, like many other things during Boxcloth. Early on 21 November,

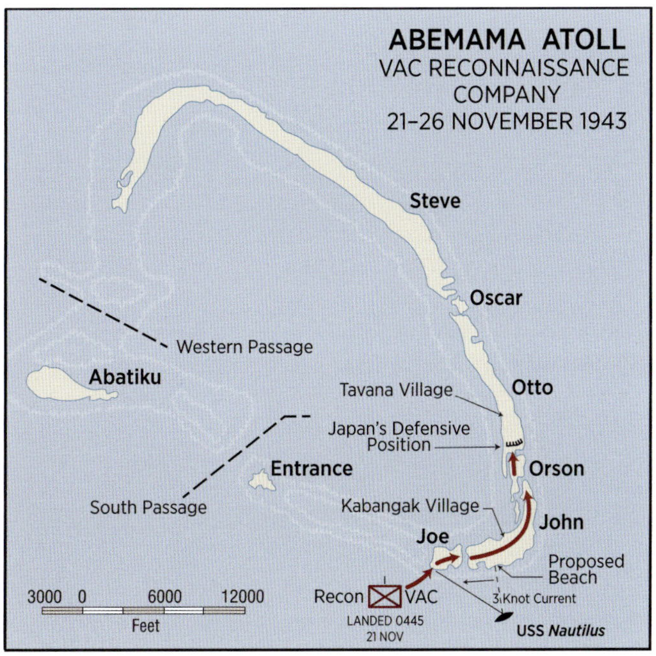

the Marines embarked on their boats. But not all the boats' motors functioned properly, and the currents pushed the reconnaissance units one island to the west of their intended landing site. Still, they were ashore and ready to perform their mission. They encountered a small Japanese force along with some island natives who proved to be reliable informants about the enemy. The Japanese then withdrew to prepared positions on the eastern atoll island that the Marines had codenamed Otto.

Jones and his men approached the Japanese, but the Marines realized they had reached the limits of their capabilities. Jones went back to the *Nautilus* to discuss options with the submarine's captain, Commander William D. Irwin. Jones and Irwin decided to use the *Nautilus*'s 6-inch deck guns to shell Japanese positions and to move forward offshore, parallel to the Marines, in order to enable and assist their advance. The fire was not accurate or helpful, however, and Jones broke off his assault. In the interim, the Japanese had opened up machine gun fire and mortally wounded the sole Marine to die in this operation.

Hill had dispatched the USS *Gansevoort* (DD-608) to assist in the operations, and in the evening twilight of 24 November, the destroyer fired 48 rounds quickly after receiving guidance from Marine Lieutenant Merwin H. Silverthorn, Jones' executive officer, who had arrived on board the *Gansevoort* by rubber raft. While Jones was pondering whether the fire had achieved the desired effect, a native arrived with word that the Japanese had all committed suicide. Jones sent a small unit to confirm their deaths, and then the Marines occupied Otto.

By 25 November, Abemama was in U.S. hands, captured by only a company of reconnaissance Marines and one submarine. Hill arrived shortly with Brigadier General Hermle and battalion 3/6 to handle the expected resistance, but instead took grateful possession of the entire atoll from Captain Jones.

Tarawa's Other Islands

Southern Attack Force commander Hill had left Tarawa for Abemama because he had expected a contested landing there for 3/6 and likewise believed the main task left at Tarawa was entirely on the ground, against a small number of disorganized and poorly supplied Japanese troops who could be chased around the atoll until they ran out of land. Julian Smith had

USMC Weapons in November 1943

INFANTRY, INDIVIDUAL

- M1 GARAND RIFLE, .30-06 CALIBER, 8-ROUND CLIP
- M1918A2 BROWNING AUTOMATIC RIFLE (BAR), .30 CALIBER, 20-ROUND MAGAZINES
- M1 BAYONET
- KA-BAR KNIFE
- MK IIA1 FRAGMENTATION GRENADE
- M1A1 THOMPSON SUBMACHINE GUN, .45 CALIBER, 30-ROUND BOX
- M1 CARBINE, .30 CALIBER, 15 ROUNDS
- M1912, 12-GAUGE SHOTGUN, 20-INCH BARREL, 6-ROUND MAGAZINE
- M1911A1, .45-CALIBER PISTOL, 7-ROUND MAGAZINE

INFANTRY, CREW-SERVICED

- M1919A4, .30-CALIBER AIR-COOLED MACHINE GUN
- M1917A1, .30-CALIBER WATER-COOLED MACHINE GUN
- M2, .50-CALIBER AIR-COOLED MACHINE GUN
- M2 60-MM MORTAR
- M1 81-MM MORTAR
- M1A1 FLAMETHROWER

ARTILLERY

- M3A1 37-MM ANTI-TANK
- M1A1 75-MM PACK HOWITZER
- M3 75-MM SELF-PROPELLED GUN ("HALF-TRACK")
- M2A1 105-MM HOWITZER

ARMOR

- M3A1 STUART TANK, 37 MM, PLUS MACHINE GUNS
- M4A2 SHERMAN TANK, 75 MM, PLUS MACHINE GUNS

already been concerned about disparate Japanese units roaming the atoll and had landed division scouts on the outer islands as early as 21 November (D+1).

The job of securing the outer islands at Tarawa was given to Lieutenant Colonel Murray's 2/6. The battalion came ashore east of Bairiki on the islet of Eita on 24 November. Artillery from 3/10 had preceded 2/6 to Eita and could be used to assist a rapid and violent advance around the atoll. When 2/6's Marines came to a break between islands, if the tide was high they had to wade across. They pushed on as hard as they could, the freshest of any remaining Marines from the 2d Division.

The thick vegetation on these islands resembled that of Butaritari at Makin more than that of Betio, which meant Murray's Marines faced rooting out the Japanese from many more hiding places, despite the lack of prepared defenses such as those on Betio. The final battle occurred on one of the northernmost islets of the atoll, Buariki, on 27 November. Murray pushed his men forward despite the hidden dangers. He was unwilling to wait for more artillery support, as the Army had waited on Butaritari. As for tanks, Murray had none. The Japanese fired from behind bushes, trees, and logs as the Marines came very close. The Japanese grenade launchers, "knee mortars," killed and wounded many

Major U.S. Navy Ships in Carrier Force (TF 50)

Carrier Intercept Group

BATTLESHIPS

- *ALABAMA* (BB-60)
- *SOUTH DAKOTA* (BB-57)
- *WASHINGTON* (BB-56)

CARRIERS

- *LEXINGTON* (CV-16)
- *YORKTOWN* (CV-10)

LIGHT CARRIER

- *COWPENS* (CVL-25)

DESTROYERS

- *CHARRETTE* (DD-581)
- *CONNER* (DD-582)
- *IZARD* (DD-589)
- *LA VALLETTE* (DD-448)
- *NICHOLAS* (DD-449)
- *TAYLOR* (DD-468)

Northern Carrier Group

CARRIER

- *ENTERPRISE* (CV-6)

LIGHT CARRIERS

- *BELLEAU WOOD* (CVL-24)
- *MONTEREY* (CVL-26)

BATTLESHIPS

- *INDIANA* (BB-58)
- *MASSACHUSETTS* (BB-59)
- *NORTH CAROLINA* (BB-55)

DESTROYERS

- *BOYD* (DD-544)
- *BRADFORD* (DD-545)
- *BROWN* (DD-546)
- *FLETCHER* (DD-445)
- *JENKINS* (DD-447)
- *RADFORD* (DD-446)

Southern Carrier Group

CARRIERS

- *BUNKER HILL* (CV-17)
- *ESSEX* (CV-9)

LIGHT CARRIER

- *INDEPENDENCE* (CVL-22)

CRUISERS

- *CHESTER* (CA-27)
- *PENSACOLA* (CA-24)
- *SALT LAKE CITY* (CA-25)

LIGHT CRUISER

- *OAKLAND* (CL-95)

DESTROYERS

- *BULLARD* (DD-660)
- *CHAUNCEY* (DD-667)
- *ERBEN* (DD-631)
- *HALE* (DD-642)
- *KIDD* (DD-661)

Relief Carrier Group

CARRIER

- *SARATOGA* (CV-3)

LIGHT CARRIER

- *PRINCETON* (CVL-23)

LIGHT CRUISERS

- *SAN DIEGO* (CL-53)
- *SAN JUAN* (CL-54)

DESTROYERS

- *EDWARDS* (DD-619)
- *STACK* (DD-406)
- *STERETT* (DD-407)
- *WILSON* (DD-408)

CONTENTS

Bow-on view of the USS *Massachusetts* (BB-59) as she moves beneath the Braga Bridge at Fall River, Massachusetts, with tugs on either side, 12 June 1965.

Library of Congress Control Number: 2021946729

INTRODUCTION

THIS IS THE BIOGRAPHY OF A BATTLESHIP.

The USS *Massachusetts* (BB-59) was the third vessel in the *South Dakota* class. Her massive 16-inch guns were the first of their type to fire in anger during World War II, and they also held the distinction of discharging the last 16-inch salvos of the war. Her shells fell on targets from Casablanca to Tokyo, reflecting her great range and flexibility as a weapon system. She engaged an enemy battleship and protected the most important American amphibious operation of the war, but she spent the majority of her career shepherding the fast carriers of the U.S. Navy from one strike to the next, from one landing operation to the next. In this role, she participated in most major operations of the Pacific War from mid-1943 on. She earned 11 battle stars, and her story is the story of the U.S. Navy's unprecedented triumph in World War II.

This work is based mainly on the *Massachusetts*'s war diary and the reports filed by her captain or executive officer after major actions. It is supplemented by the reports of the ships she protected, and in certain cases by the reports filed by the enemies she fought. Color has been provided by the oral histories recorded by her crew members and preserved by the Battleship Cove Museum in Fall River, Massachusetts, where the historic ship continues her career as an ambassador of education and peace. Portions of articles or sections of works from the U.S. Naval Institute's *Proceedings* and *Naval History* magazines and from books published by the Naval Institute Press have been selectively incorporated as sidebars to further illustrate the *Massachusetts*'s career or to give context to her actions. As this is a popular work, no attempt has been made to source the various quotes used throughout; with very few exceptions they come from the sources mentioned above.

The USS *Massachusetts* on the slip. The workers seen looking down from the stern are seven stories high. (U.S. Navy)

A SHIP IS BORN

WORKERS AT THE BETHLEHEM FORE RIVER SHIPYARD IN QUINCY, Massachusetts, laid the keel of battleship number 59, the third ship in the South Dakota class, on 20 July 1939—barely a month before the German invasion of Poland started what would become World War II. The task of assembling the material for this project was enormous, but working with a sense of urgency caused by the perilous international scene, the shipyard completed the hull, the basic superstructure, and the engine and boiler arrangements in just over two years. Battleship 59, the USS *Massachusetts*, was launched on 23 September 1941, two and a half months before the Japanese attack on Pearl Harbor propelled the United States into the war.

The United States was building its next generation of fast battleships literally just in time.

On 21 May 1942, the U.S. Navy took delivery of the new ship and commissioned the *Massachusetts* at the South Boston Navy Yard Annex, with Francis E. M. Whiting as her first captain and Commander Edward M. Thompson as executive officer. She continued fitting out, uncompleted items were worked through, and the ship reported for duty to the Atlantic Fleet on 10 July. She commenced her first voyage to Casco Bay, Maine, on the 12th.

It is a long process to take a completed ship fresh from the builders and ready her for active service. Such a complicated machine always will have items that require adjustment, repair, or modification, but even more important is the crew. Men must be gathered, trained, and grown accustomed to their new assignment. Competence and teamwork do not happen overnight, especially in a vessel as massive as a battleship. In the case of the *Massachusetts*, the crew had a mix of veterans and reservists, but 70 percent were draftees. Of the ship's 113 officers, only 19 had more than two years' service and 22 had never been to sea. Captain Whiting established a routine whereby his crew stood at general quarters for an hour each day and spent the rest of the day, from before sunrise to 2200, in gunnery drills and exercising damage control, abandon ship, and other tasks. After her run up to Maine, the *Massachusetts* returned to the yard on 21 July for post-trial inspections and more work. Finally, on 2 August, according to her war diary, she sailed from Boston for the Chesapeake Bay for "training, deperming and degaussing calibration, compass and radio direction finder work."

Between 3 August and 28 September the *Massachusetts* made short training cruises and spent ten days in dry dock before reporting for duty in Task Group 21.3 at Hampton Roads, Virginia. She stopped in Annapolis the first weekend in October so the U.S. Naval Academy's midshipmen could visit the fleet's newest battleship. From there she returned to Casco Bay, and then on the 16th, back to Boston to load oil, stores, and ammunition, a process that took three days. She anchored in Casco Bay on 20 October and the next day, Rear Admiral Robert C. Giffen transferred to the *Massachusetts* along with his staff and formed Task Group 34.1. Big events were afoot. In July the United States had determined to invade French North Africa and allocated the brand-new *Massachusetts* to this operation. She would be the big muscle for Task Force 34, an amphibious assault force, poised to strike Morocco in a

The *Massachusetts* being nudged alongside the fitting-out dock by five tugs shortly after launch. (U.S. Navy)

transoceanic thrust across the submarine-infested waters of the central Atlantic. The *Massachusetts* would lead American's first offensive operation in the European-African theater of operations.

On 25 October, a rainy Sunday morning, the *Massachusetts* weighed anchor in patchy fog and proceeded with Cruiser Division 7 (Crudiv), the heavy cruisers *Tuscaloosa* (CA-37) and *Wichita* (CA-45), and Destroyer Division 8 (Desdiv), the *Wainwright* (DD-419), *Mayrant* (DD-402), *Rhind* (DD-404), and *Jenkins* (DD-407). The squadron proceeded south at 15 knots to rendezvous with the loaded transports coming from Hampton Roads. This vitally important operation of war would serve as the battleship's shakedown cruise.

New crewmen practicing ammunition drill. The majority of the ship's crew were teenagers brand new to the Navy and had to learn their jobs from scratch. (U.S. Navy)

Captain Francis Whiting on the quarterdeck. Whiting was promoted to rear admiral shortly after the *Massachusetts*'s successful deployment to Africa. (U.S. Navy)

The *Massachusetts* passing through the Fore River Bridge for her first underway trials. The crew can be seen clustered topside, apparently appreciating the stately progress of their new vessel. (U.S. Navy)

The *South Dakota* Design

From the launching of HMS *Dreadnought* in 1906, battleships were the world's single most powerful and expensive weapon. A navy's strength, even its significance, was measured by the number of battleships it possessed. After the Great War, the major naval powers acted to avoid another crushingly expensive battleship building race, which some perceived as being responsible for the war, by agreeing to restrict the construction of battleships. The new construction that was allowed under the Washington Naval Treaty limited the size of battleships to 35,000 tons standard displacement and their guns to a caliber of 16 inches (406-mm). The art of ship design involves compromise, and in the case of battleships the tradeoffs between characteristics, armament, speed, and protection on the one

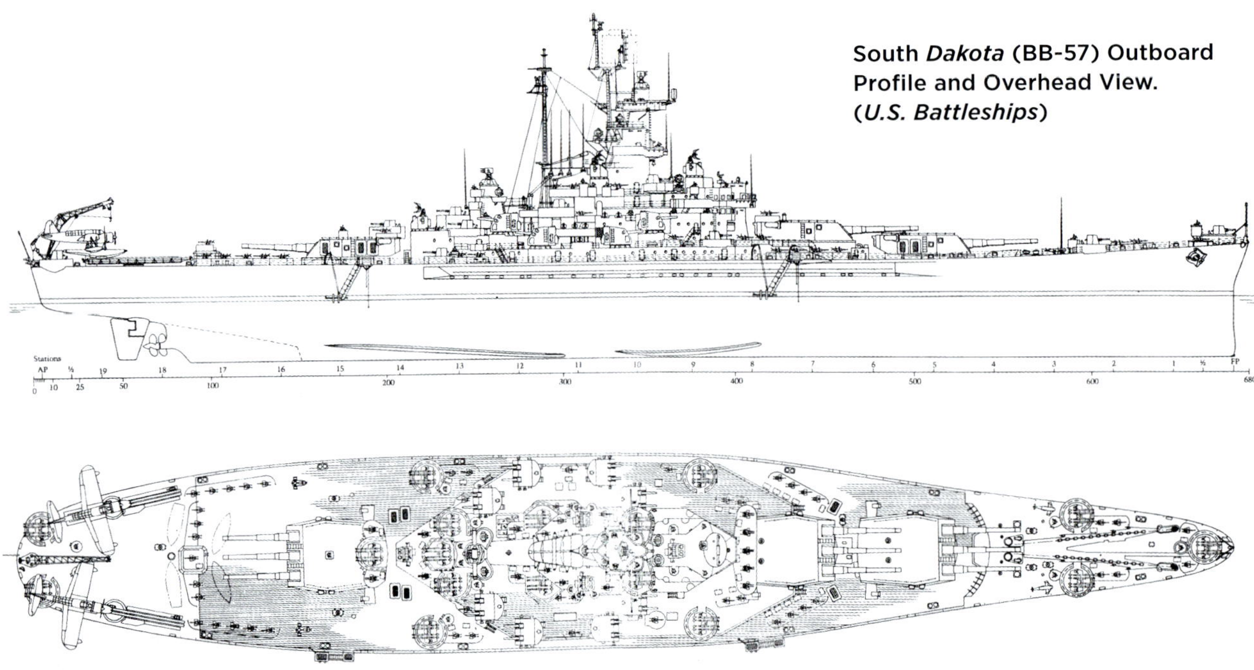

South *Dakota* (BB-57) Outboard Profile and Overhead View. (*U.S. Battleships*)

hand and weight on the other really becomes a juggling act. It was impossible to design a ship with high speed, heavy armor, and the most powerful guns all within a limit of 35,000 tons. Some signatory nations, such as Italy, cheated and constructed the *Littorio* class, a 35,000-ton ship with a good mix of speed, armor, and armament, but an actual displacement of 41,000 tons. The British built the *King George* class, a ship with good armor and speed, but a main armament of only 14-inch guns compared with the U.S. standard of 16-inch and the French, German, and Italian 15-inch armed battleships. This difference is more than it seems, as a 14-inch shell is 1,590 pounds compared to 1,764 for the German 15-inch, and 2,700 pounds for the shell fired by the *Massachusetts's* 16-inch guns. The French *Richelieu* had good speed and decent armor on 35,000 tons, but saved weight by squeezing its main battery forward with eight guns in only two turrets. The *South Dakota*'s design allowed for superior firepower and armor compared to the British, French, German, and Italian "fast battleships" but at the cost of several knots in speed. She had other design compromises; being shorter than the *North Carolina* (BB-55) that preceded her, she was cramped. Habitability was relatively poor, at least by U.S. standards, and she was very wet forward. However, she was handy for a ship of her size and did not suffer from the vibration problems that plagued the *North Carolina*.

(ADAPTED FROM DULIN AND GARZKE, *BATTLESHIPS*, 1985 - NAVAL INSTITUTE PRESS, AND FRIEDMAN, *US BATTLESHIPS*, 1985 - NAVAL INSTITUTE PRESS)

Massachusetts **Inboard Profile. (Dulin and Garzke)**

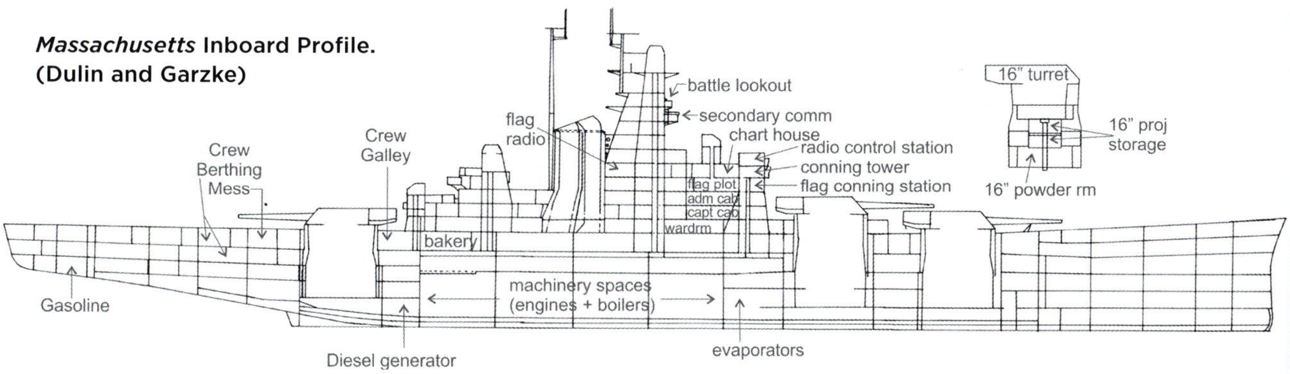

Armament

The *South Dakota* class mounted the new 16-inch/45-caliber Mark 6 gun in three triple turrets, each of which weighed 1,437 tons. Guns were mounted in separate sleeves allowing individual elevation and depression.

The basic characteristics were:

Training gear rate:	4°/second
Elevation rate:	12°/second
Maximum elevation:	45°
Firing cycle:	30 seconds
Designed capacity:	1,280 rounds
Shell weight (lbs/kg):	2,700/1,225
Muzzle Velocity (fps/ms):	2,300/701
Maximum range (yds/m):	36,900/33,741

1. Range finder
2. Breech block (open)
3. Chain rammer
4. Pan floor
5. Center projectile hoist
6. Left projectile hoist
7. Roller path
8. Powder hoist
9. Powder car
10. Electric deck
11. Elevating cylinder

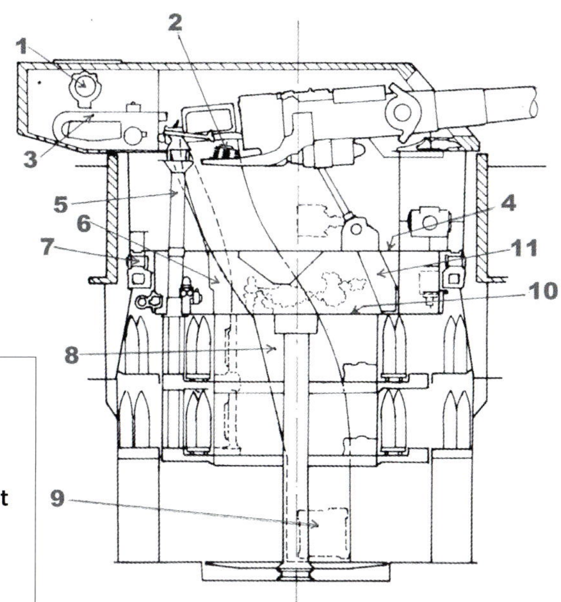

MK 6 16-inch turret. (*Naval Weapons*)

(ADAPTED FROM DULIN AND GARZKE, *BATTLESHIPS*, 1985 - NAVAL INSTITUTE PRESS, AND CAMPBELL, *NAVAL WEAPONS OF WWII*, 1985 - NAVAL INSTITUTE PRESS)

The secondary armament consisted of ten twin mounted 5-inch/38 Mark 12 dual-purpose guns. The Pacific Fleet Ordnance Board described the Mark 12 as "outstandingly accurate, fast-firing and easy to maintain, with a long barrel life."

5-inch gun. (*Naval Weapons*)

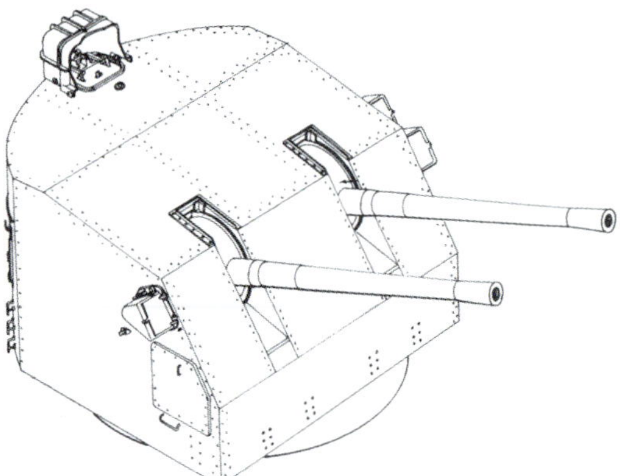

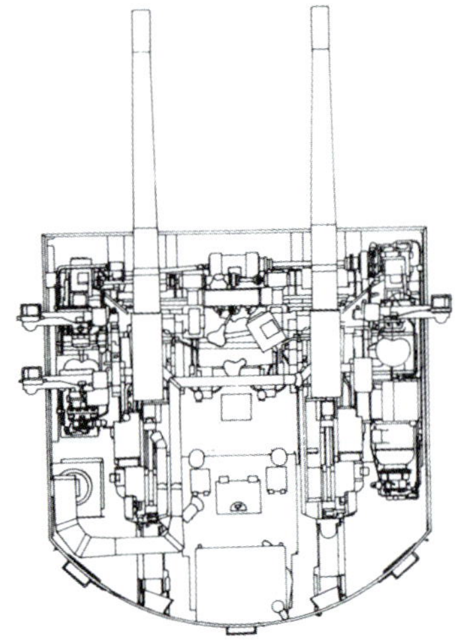

Its basic characteristics were:

Training speed:	25°/second
Elevation rate:	15°/second
Maximum elevation:	85°
Firing cycle:	3 seconds
Ammunition carried:	9,600 rounds or 480 rounds/gun
Shell weight (lbs/kg):	53.85/24.43
Muzzle Velocity (fps/ms):	2,600/792
Maximum range (yds/m):	17,575/16,070

The antiaircraft battery was designed without the benefit of wartime experience, and by 1940 the Navy recognized the inadequacy of the short-range batteries in the original design. These consisted of three quad 1.1-inch mountings and a dozen 0.50-caliber machine guns. Fortunately, there was time to improve these arrangements. As constructed, the *Massachusetts* had six quadruple 40-mm mounts and 35 single 20-mm guns. She added four more quadruple 40-mm mounts after her return from Africa and two more in February 1943 for a total of a dozen mounts and 48 barrels. By this date the *Massachusetts* had added another 26 20-mm guns for a total of 61 barrels. She went to the Pacific with this outfit. War experience led to further modifications, and by late 1944 she possessed 18 quadruple 40-mm mounts (72 barrels) and 38 20-mm barrels.

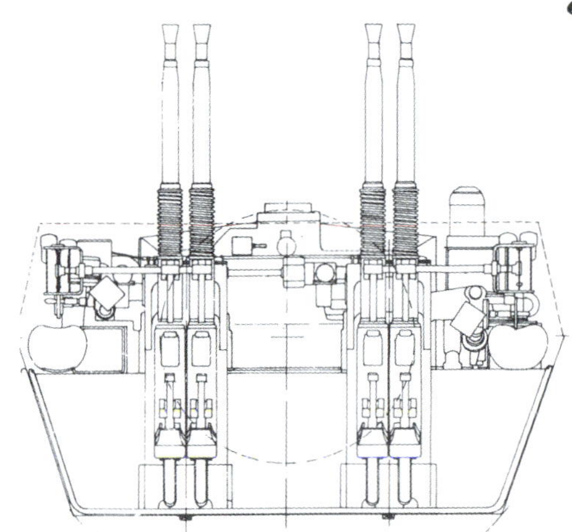

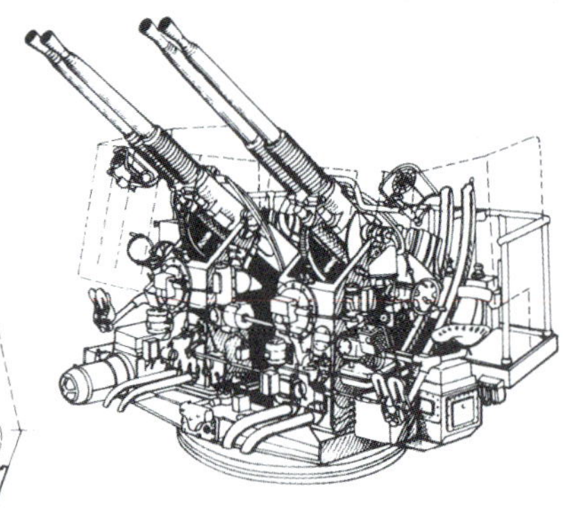

40-mm gun. (*Naval Weapons*)

Characteristics 40-mm:

Shell weight (lbs/kg):	1.985/0.9
Muzzle Velocity (fps/ms):	2,890/881
Ceiling at (ft/m):	22,800/10,060
Maximum range (yds/m):	11,000/10,058

The 20-mm Oerlikon was a popular Swedish design used by the Americans, the British, the Italians, and the Germans, among others.

As the war wore on, many considered the Oerlikon too light to meet the needs of fleet air defense—especially in the face of the Kamikaze threat. There was a saying that "When the 20-mm opens fire it's time to hit the deck." Nonetheless, the gun remained in use throughout the war.

In U.S. service its characteristics were:

Shell weight (lbs/kg):	.2714/0.1231
Muzzle Velocity (fps/ms):	2,740/835
Rate of Fire:	450 rounds/minute
Ceiling at (ft/m):	10,000/3,050
Maximum range (yds/m):	4,800/4,390

Armor

The reason the U.S. Navy Bureau of Ships (BuShips) designed the *South Dakotas* in the first place and did not build more *North Carolinas* was to improve the armor protection. They accomplished this with no sacrifice in speed or firepower, and the design, in this respect, must be considered successful although the gains came, as always, at a cost. The design's biggest innovation was the placement of the boilers above the engines. This reduced the ship's overall length, at no sacrifice in speed, and reduced the area that required protection—another weight savings.

The protection scheme was designed to withstand 16-inch shellfire. Against the older 2,240-pound shell the immunity zone was calculated as from 17,700 to 30,900 yards. Against the newer 2,700-pound shell this became 20,500 to 26,400 yards.

ADAPTED FROM DULIN AND GARZKE, *BATTLESHIPS*, 1985 - NAVAL INSTITUTE PRESS.

The armor characteristics were:

Side armor: 12.2 inches with 19 degree inclination from the vertical. The lower belt extended down through the underwater protective system, tapering from 12.2 inches at the top to 1 inch at the bottom to protect against large shells hitting below the waterline.

Main deck:	1.5 inches
Second deck:	5.75 inches
Splinter deck:	0.625 inches
Third deck:	0.3 inches
Steering gear third deck armor:	6.2 inches
Turrets:	18-inch face plates, 9.5-inch sides, 12-inch backs, and 7.25-inch tops
Barbette:	17.3 to 11.6 inches
Conning tower sides and communications tube:	16 inches
Conning tower roof:	7.25 inches

Machinery

Design studies established that a 30-knot maximum speed would require more than 200,000-shaft horsepower and a hull appreciably longer than that of the *North Carolina* class. This was not possible at a displacement of 35,000 tons given the requirements of nine 16-inch guns and enhanced armor. Thus, the Navy accepted 27.5 knots as a design goal.

The class was equipped with four sets of geared turbines and eight Somers-type boilers. These employed stream pressure of 600 psi at a temperature of 850° F. The propulsion plant arrangement had four main machinery spaces with two air-encased boilers, one set of geared turbines, and auxiliary equipment in each compartment. This allowed the main propulsion

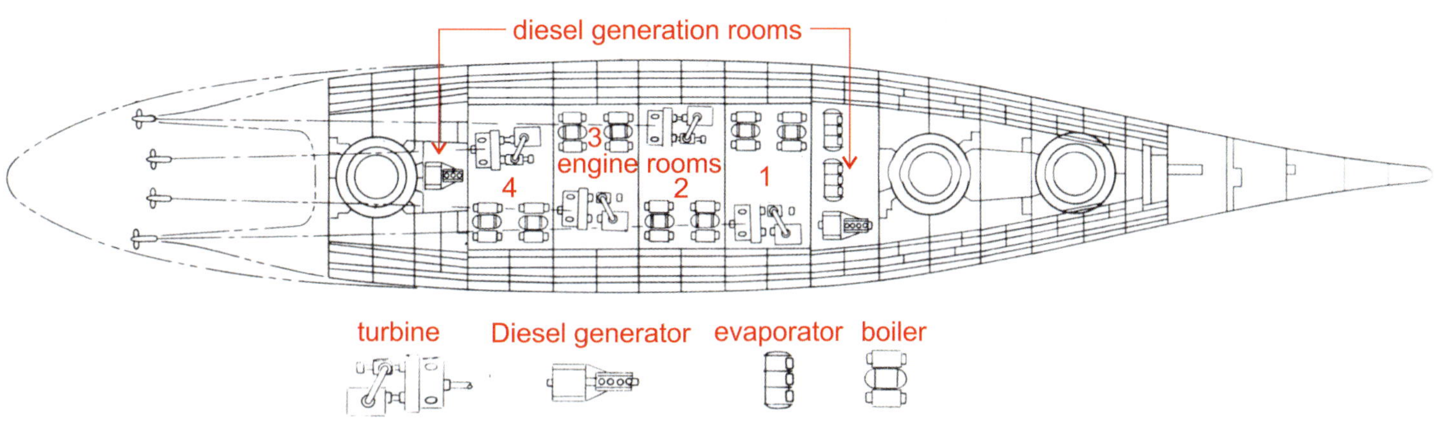

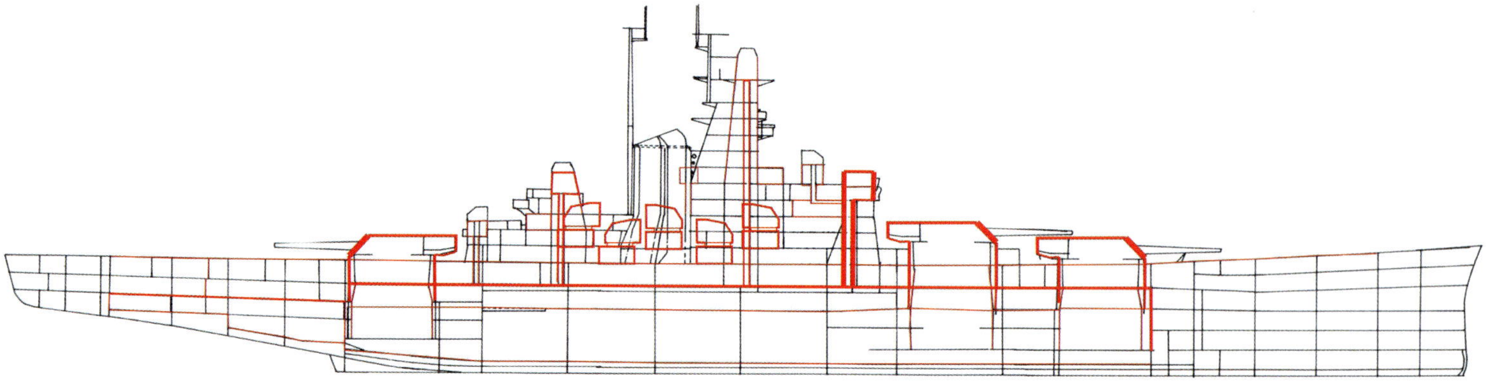

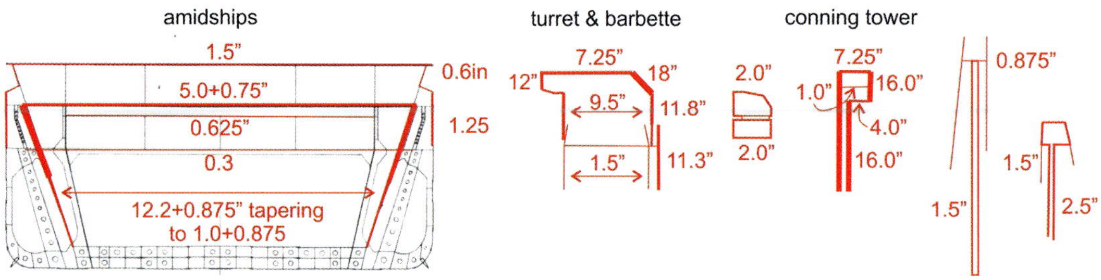

The designers considered the *Massachusetts*'s side protection better than that of the *North Carolina* class. It consisted of four bulkheads parallel to the side shell. The two outboard compartments normally were liquid loaded at all times, while the two inboard compartments were void. The internal sloping armor of the side belt was expected to reduce the deflection of the holding bulkhead. This allowed the number of bulkheads to be reduced by one with a corresponding reduction in the system's breadth. With tanks outboard of the armor belt, the gas jet from an underwater detonation could be somewhat vented upward, thus moderating the forces on the inboard bulkheads. The side protection of this class was never tested in action.

machinery to be completely isolated and consequently improved overall resistance to damage. The boilers in machinery rooms 1 and 3 were to port with the turbines to starboard. Rooms 2 and 4 had the opposite arrangement. The boilers were elevated sufficiently above the inner bottom to provide for better shaft clearances than in the *North Carolina* class. The evaporators were located forward of machinery room 1.

The high-pressure, high-temperature steam cycle made it possible to increase normal maximum shaft horsepower. The close proximity of the forward tower and the uptakes permitted mutual structural support and protection, a feature repeated in subsequent designs.

Shaft horsepower:	**135,000 (136,872 mhp)**
Weight:	**3,580 (3,637 metric tons)**
Pounds per horsepower:	**59.4 (26.57 kg/mhp)**

Radar

The *South Dakota* class was designed before the development of practical shipborne radar and the Navy first specified installation of radar in the summer of 1941. Initially the *Massachusetts* was equipped with an SC air search on the mainmast, and an SG surface search radar on a platform ahead of the forward main battery director and a second SG on the mainmast. The main and secondary batteries also used radar for fire control with a pair of F.D. Mark 3 radars for the Mk 38 Main Battery Director and four F.C. Mark 4s for the Mark 37 Secondary Battery Directors. The *Massachusetts* went to war in Africa with this outfit, but the Mark 3s were replaced by the F.C. Mark 8 before her Pacific deployment. Whereas the Mark 3 could return an accurate range, it had a broad spread and could not give useful bearings. This required optical input to determine and correct. The Mark 8's improvement was a "B" scope presentation of targets in a plot of range versus bearing. Thus, this system promised accurate surface fire under

complete radar control during night engagements. In her only surface action against enemy warships the *Massachusetts* experienced failures or inaccuracies in all fire control radars. Her success in hitting the French warships *Jean Bart* at 25,000 yards and *Milan*, which was under way, at 28,000 yards was attained using optical systems in conditions of intermittent to poor visibility. Radar problems continued to plague the *Massachusetts* even during shore bombardment missions later in the war.

Captain Whiting's comments after the bombardment of Casablanca and the subsequent naval battle are telling: "It is recommended that these fire control sets be shock tested and vibration tested, to determine the cause of the numerous failures in the 10 ampere fuses. Nearly every set had these fuses blow during the firing. Under normal conditions they seem satisfactory, but under gun fire (own ship's) they seem to fail very easily. These fire control sets are still too complicated and touchy for the concussion and shock they are subjected to. Whenever something goes out, too much time is lost in finding the failure. One thing such as loss of the ranges notch can be caused by at least three different tube failures, with the consequent testing of three different circuits, to find the failures."

(ADAPTED FROM FRIEDMAN, *US BATTLESHIPS*, 1985 - NAVAL INSTITUTE PRESS)

Counting Beans

Construction of a ship such as the *Massachusetts* was not only a marvel of engineering and organization, it required mighty feats of accounting by both the Bureau of Ships and Bethlehem Steel, the company constructing the vessel. Payment was made in monthly installments, with Bethlehem submitting a voucher that BuShips carefully scrutinized and then passed along to the Judge Advocate General of the Navy for payment. The November 1940 voucher, for example, was for $498,150. This voucher included material and labor for 40 line items such as drawings, piping, pumps, and compressed air system, giving the total estimated cost and the amount expended to date. The total cost of drawings, for example, was $450,000 for materials and $450,000 for labor, of which, by November 1940, $97,500 had been charged. Pumps were $381,500 for material but only $19,900 for labor. The entire amount was still outstanding in November. The ship's machinery cost was nearly $15 million, and the estimated total cost $77 million.

The Navy, it should be noted, was a good customer. Bethlehem Steel submitted the November 1940 voucher on 10 December 1940. BuShips completed its review and approved payment in less than a week. Considering that in November 1940 the Navy had 8 battleships, 1 aircraft carrier, 4 cruisers, and more than 20 destroyers under construction, this speaks of a bureaucracy that could get things done.

Accounting included more than just finances: More important for the ship's ultimate purpose of engaging in successful operations was keeping track of all the many construction defects or improvements that the ship required. Many of these items only could be discovered once the ship was complete and the crew was engaged in readying the vessel for active operations. For example, on 20 July Captain Whiting wrote to BuShips requesting permission to cut 6 inches off the armored splinter deck next to Hatch 2-102 because when going through this hatch "the head must be ducked in order to pass the splinter deck without hitting it. To date several men have received head injuries in hurrying down the hatch to their battle stations." This request generated a work order to the Commandant of the Boston Navy Yard on 8 August with copies to the other ships in the class, which presumably were experiencing a similar problem. In early June 1942 hot weather in New England revealed a more serious problem. ". . . the inadequacy of sheathing and ventilation in living spaces has come to attention. The temperature has been sufficient to trip the magazine fire alarms which functions at 105° F." In this case Captain Whiting only could throw the problem at BuShips and request that immediate remedial steps be taken.

Through 16 July, when the *Massachusetts* was recommended for acceptance, the contractor had accomplished 90 of 115 such improvements, "undertaking work not a part of the contract but which could be accomplished at the building rather than the outfitting yard." Of course, every change order and every job undertaken, no matter how trivial, generated an invoice.

Expanding the Fleet

One of the Navy's great accomplishments during the war was the way it rose to the challenge of manning its vastly expanded fleet with competent officers and quality crews.

The Navy traditionally filled its ranks with volunteers. During the Great Depression of the 1930s, there was a surplus of young men seeking to join, and the Navy could accept only those candidates who had a high school diploma or equivalent. This led to a highly trained cadre of recruits, giving the service some of the most capable enlisted men in its history. The available surplus facilitated the Navy's rapid increase in size during the last years of peace. In 1939 the authorized strength was increased to 145,000 men; by the time of Pearl Harbor the number in service had grown to 337,000. On V-J Day, 2 September 1945, the Navy had 2.995 million men. When the *Massachusetts* was laid down, there were 178 surface warships in the navy and 380 total active vessels. On 14 August the count was 833 surface warships and 6,768 total active vessels.

The situation with officers was far different. The primary source of new officers was the U.S. Naval Academy, and although graduating classes were larger than the number of officers retiring, there were not enough officers to meet peacetime demands, let alone those of war. This problem was particularly acute at higher grades. The number of officers that could be promoted to higher ranks was based on a percentage of officers available, not the number of open positions.

In 1935 the authorized strength of the officer corps was 6,531, but only 6,320 were in service. Nearly 8,000 would be needed to meet the requirements of new construction. The number of authorized officers was increased again in 1938, but as the size of the fleet continued to grow, the officer count lagged behind. The dramatic increase in the size of the Navy authorized in 1940 invalidated all prior approaches to resolving the issue and forced the temporary augmentation of the regular officer corps with reserve, retired, and fitted officers. This measure, however, was still insufficient to meet the needs of wartime expansion. Reserve officers were provided through the Naval Reserve Officers Training Corps (NROTC). Established in 1925, the program grew from humble beginnings to a large program during the war. There were nine civilian universities participating in 1940, which produced about 200 reserve ensigns a year. By 1945, 52 universities participated and the number of graduating officers had increased tenfold. There were 35,760 officers on active duty on 7 December 1941 and, at the peak in June 1945, 198,383 officers.

(ADAPTED FROM *O'HARA ET AL, ON SEAS CONTESTED*, 215, 2010 - NAVAL INSTITUTE PRESS)

New recruits drill at the San Diego Naval Training Center. At the start of the war the Navy operated training centers in San Diego, California; Great Lakes, Illinois; Bainbridge, Maryland; and Newport, Rhode Island. During the war the Navy opened three more centers at Norfolk, Virginia; Sampson, New York; and Farragut, Idaho. These centers met the Navy's tremendous personnel needs by transforming civilians into sailors in roughly six weeks. (U.S. Naval Institute Photo Archive)

The USS *Massachusetts* in an official wartime photograph. (U.S. Navy)

USS *Massachusetts* as Completed

- Launched 23 September 1941
- Commissioned 20 March 1942/ Operational August 1942
- 680′ 10″ overall length
- 666′ 0″ waterline length
- 108′ 2.25″ maximum beam
- 28′ 7" mean draft @ 35,000 tons
- 36′ 9" maximum draft @ 47,000 tons
- 35,113 tons light
- 43,884 tons optimum battle load
- 45,216 tons full load
- Nine 16-inch/45-caliber Mark 6 in three turrets
- 20 5-inch/38-caliber Mark 12 in ten mounts
- 24 40-mm/56-caliber in six mounts (by December 1944 72 guns in 18 mounts)
- 35 20-mm/70-caliber in 35 mounts (by December 1944 38 guns)
- Fuel oil 6,876 tons; diesel 157.1 tons; gasoline 23.8 tons
- Speed 27.5 knots at 130,000 mph
- Endurance: 17,000 nm @ 15 knots; 6,400 nm @ 25 knots

A rogue wave upended one of the *Massachusetts*'s Kingfisher floatplanes, forcing her to enter her first combat with just two aircraft. (U.S. Navy)

TORCH

IN JULY 1942 THE UNITED STATES AGREED TO INVADE FRENCH NORTH AFRICA in conjunction with British forces. Dubbed Operation Torch by British Prime Minister Winston Churchill, this venture, launched from bases in the United States and Great Britain, included an audacious transoceanic landing on the shores of Morocco. The invasion force, commanded by Rear Admiral H. Kent Hewitt, was named Task Force 34. The elements of TF 34 included amphibious task groups 34.8 and 34.10, which departed Hampton Roads, Virginia, on 23 October and headed southeast. The next day another amphibious force, TG 34.9, left Hampton Roads as if bound for Great Britain. The *Massachusetts*, flagship of Rear Admiral Robert C. Giffen, led Task Group 34.1, including two heavy cruisers and four destroyers, from Casco Bay, Maine, the same day. These task groups—along with a carrier group, TG 34.2, with the *Ranger* (CV-4), three escort carriers, a light cruiser, and nine destroyers—rendezvoused in the east central Atlantic on the 28th. The three amphibious groups embarked the U.S. 3rd Division for landings at Fédala, near Casablanca; the 9th Division's 60th Regimental Combat Team (RCT) for landings at Port Lyautey north of Rabat; and the 47th RCT with Combat Command B of the 2nd Armored Division for landings at Safi, southwest of Casablanca. Major General George C. Patton commanded the ground forces.

The planners had worried about submarines, but the American force never came within a thousand miles of a U-boat attack. The biggest concern turned out to be weather. Rough seas made refueling impossible, and by mid-ocean the bunkers on some of the small vessels were nearing empty. Even the *Massachusetts*, normally the most stable platform in any sea, suffered a mishap when a rogue wave broke over the fantail and upended one of the ship's Kingfishers.

Fortunately, the weather moderated as the Americans neared Africa. The smaller ships were able to fuel, and at 0700 on 7 November Hewett made the flag signal "proceed on service assigned," and the Central Group turned toward Casablanca. Fifteen transports would land troops of the 3rd Division at Fédala under the *Massachusetts*'s protection.

The battleship's crew went to breakfast at 0400 hours on the morning of 8 November and then proceeded to battle stations. A general mood of anxiety pervaded the ship. From Rear Admiral Giffen down to the youngest of the new recruits (who was just 15, having used forged papers to join the Navy), no one knew if the French would resist.

The Americans based their hopes of a peaceful operation on a French dissident group, which included military and civilian elements, that wanted to rejoin the war on the American side. As it happened, this group had little support in Morocco, and all its attempted putsch accomplished was to alert the French command that something was up. When French naval headquarters in Casablanca began receiving reports of strange events offshore, such as the sound of

motorboats, it leapt to the assumption that the allies were conducting a commando attack in conjunction with the suppressed coup d'état. It had no idea that an American armada was just offshore waiting for dawn, nor that thousands of troops were even at that moment motoring to landing beaches at three widely separated locations in Morocco.

As the *Massachusetts*'s crew assembled to general quarters and the ship's two Kingfishers waited on the catapults ready to be launched (and to scout for the white flags the pilots had been told to look for), the port of Casablanca was crowded with civilian and military shipping. On the evening of 7 November a major convoy had just arrived from the French West African base at Dakar, and three more were expected. Civilians, largely women and children, evacuated from Dakar, were disembarking from the large liner *Protros*, which was docked at the end of the Quai Delinde, just yards from the French battleship *Jean Bart*. This powerful ship had been towed to Casablanca following the collapse of France in June 1940. She could not get under way, but had modern fire control and a turret of four 15-inch guns in service, making her a very powerful shore battery. Other French naval forces in Casablanca consisted of a light cruiser, 3 large destroyers (1 under repair), 7 fleet destroyers, 1 large and 2 small sloops, and 11 submarines.

At 0530, as civilian ships unloaded, French Vice Admiral François Michelier ordered five submarines to sea to determine what was happening offshore. An hour later, one of the subs reported the blinding flashes of large naval guns off Fédala, a fishing port 12 miles up the coast. At 0630, as more reports began flooding French headquarters, Michelier ordered his surface forces to raise steam and attack the intruders, whoever they might be. Dawn was still 20 minutes away, and a thick haze smothered the shoreline.

As French warships prepared for sea, Task Group 34.1 was 15 miles off Casablanca with the *Massachusetts* in the van followed by the *Tuscaloosa* and *Wichita*. The destroyers *Wainwright* and *Mayrant* screened to starboard and the *Rhind* and *Jenkins* to port. The carrier fighters and bombers commenced roaring off flight decks at 0615, but even before that TG 34.1 started launching its own aircraft. The *Tuscaloosa* and *Wichita* catapulted seven Curtiss SOC Seagulls for spotting and antisubmarine patrol. The *Massachusetts* launched her two Kingfishers at 0618 and 0620.

The planes arrived over the city, and several radioed that enemy submarines and destroyers were standing out to sea. They had hardly delivered this surprising news when French fighters appeared. Robert Etheridge, flying as a Kingfisher radioman, recalled, "We circled the *Jean Bart* at 5,000 feet when the war started. We had only been over our target for five or ten minutes when enemy fighters approached, so we started evasive action. Tom [Thomas Doherty, the ship's senior aviator] was a super pilot. He could slip to the side and get down to a lower level and sometimes the fighters couldn't get down that low. Anyway, the fighters missed twice. I think it was the third time when he hit us with a lot of shells, and at that time Tom knew we had to take

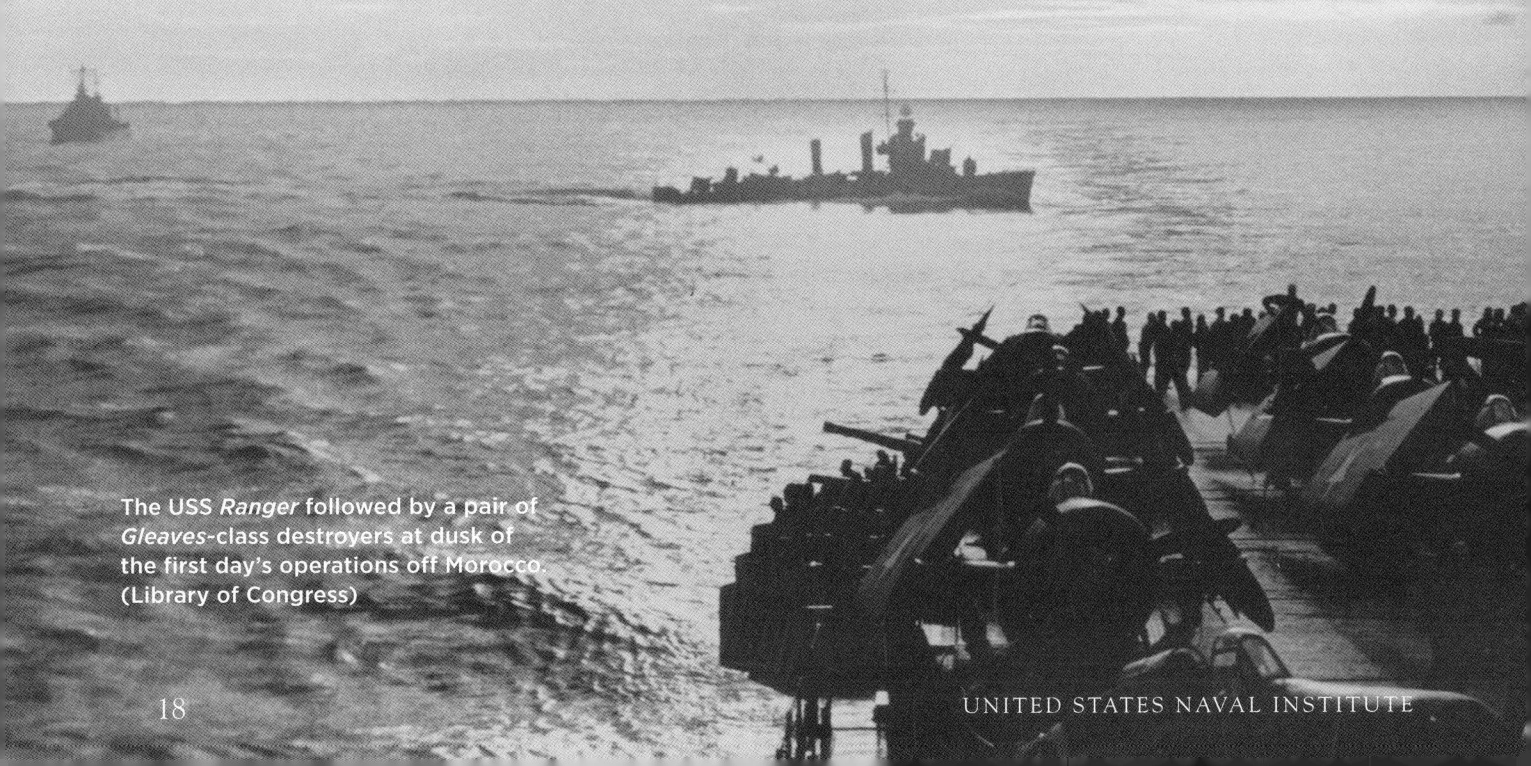

The USS *Ranger* followed by a pair of *Gleaves*-class destroyers at dusk of the first day's operations off Morocco. (Library of Congress)

Casablanca Harbor, crowded with shipping. This photo shows the French destroyer *Tempête* with a patrol vessel alongside moored along the harbor's outer jetty. The El Hank light and battery are visible in the background. (U.S. Navy)

evasive action and find a place to land before we were gonna crash. So he spotted this beach not too far, just up north of town. It looked like a good clean beach, but as we were approaching there the engine quit and we crashed. . . . we were probably 100 yards off the beach." Etheridge was wounded in the hard landing. French soldiers helped the two aviators ashore and took them prisoner.

The battleship's other Kingfisher also had a close call. At 0659 it radioed the battleship: "Am coming in on starboard bow with couple hostile aircraft on my tail. Pick them off—I am the one in front." The *Massachusetts* obliged with 35 5-inch rounds, and other ships joined in.

At 0705 the major shore battery just south of Casablanca, El Hank, loosed a four 7.64-inch gun salvo at the *Massachusetts* from 27,000 yards. These events made it clear that the French were going to resist. This caught most crewmen by surprise. "We were standing there behind the 16-inch guns, all a sudden I looked up I saw sprays. Purple colors, red colors, orange colors, so I said to the bosun's mate, 'What's the cause of that?' And he said, 'Hit the deck, the French are shooting at us.'" The French used dye to color the geysers thrown up by their shells. The technique assisted spotting, especially in cases where more than one ship was firing at the same target.

As colored gouts of water splashed nearby, the *Massachusetts* turned 40 degrees away and a minute later opened fire on the *Jean Bart* from 24,400 yards. With this salvo, the *Massachusetts* fired the very first 16-inch shells by an American warship at an enemy target. At 0708 the *Jean Bart* answered. Her first two-round salvo raised giant yellow splashes 600 yards off the *Massachusetts*'s starboard bow. The next, fired at 0711, fell close to port. El Hank's aim was also good. The battleship's chronology recorded "very large" yellow and green splashes falling "close aboard" to starboard at 0711 and to port at 0713. However, the French could barely discern their targets, and the *Jean Bart* only fired two more salvos for the rest of the day, one of two rounds at 0716 and the last of one round at 0719.

The Americans had targeting problems of their own. Smoke enveloped the harbor, and after the third salvo a vacuum tube failure caused the *Massachusetts*'s Fire Control Mk 3 radar to blink out. It was not fixed until that afternoon. Next the massive concussion from the second nine-gun 16-inch salvo blew the fuses on two Mk 4 FD (antiaircraft fire control) radars. Air spot was initially unavailable due to the action of French fighters. For the first 15 minutes the battleship used indirect fire and her gunnery was ineffective. When her surviving Kingfisher did begin to spot, smoke over the harbor affected its observations; it reported range accurately but not deflection. The battleship did not hit until 0725 when a 2,700-pound shell bashed the *Jean Bart* aft on the shelter deck, slicing through two armored decks before exploding in an empty magazine.

The French destroyer squadron was berthed in the line of fire, but remarkably, as they raised steam and recalled men and officers, the operational vessels escaped damage. They masked their movement with smoke as they started to file out of the harbor, but aircraft repeatedly warned the *Massachusetts* that destroyers were getting under way. The flotilla included the large destroyers *Milan* and *Albatros* and the fleet destroyers *Brestois*, *Boulonnais*, *Fougueux*, *Frondeur*, and *L'Alcyon*. The *Tempête* and *Simoun* were repairing hull damage suffered in a collision and could not immediately sail. The large destroyer *Malin*, which had come up from Dakar for a refit, likewise could not get under way. At 0806 a 16-inch shell landed between the *Malin* and the jetty. Enormous splinters riddled the vessel, killing seven. The projectile's cap tore a destructive path 80 feet long, flooding the boiler and engine rooms. The light cruiser *Primauguet* sailed later.

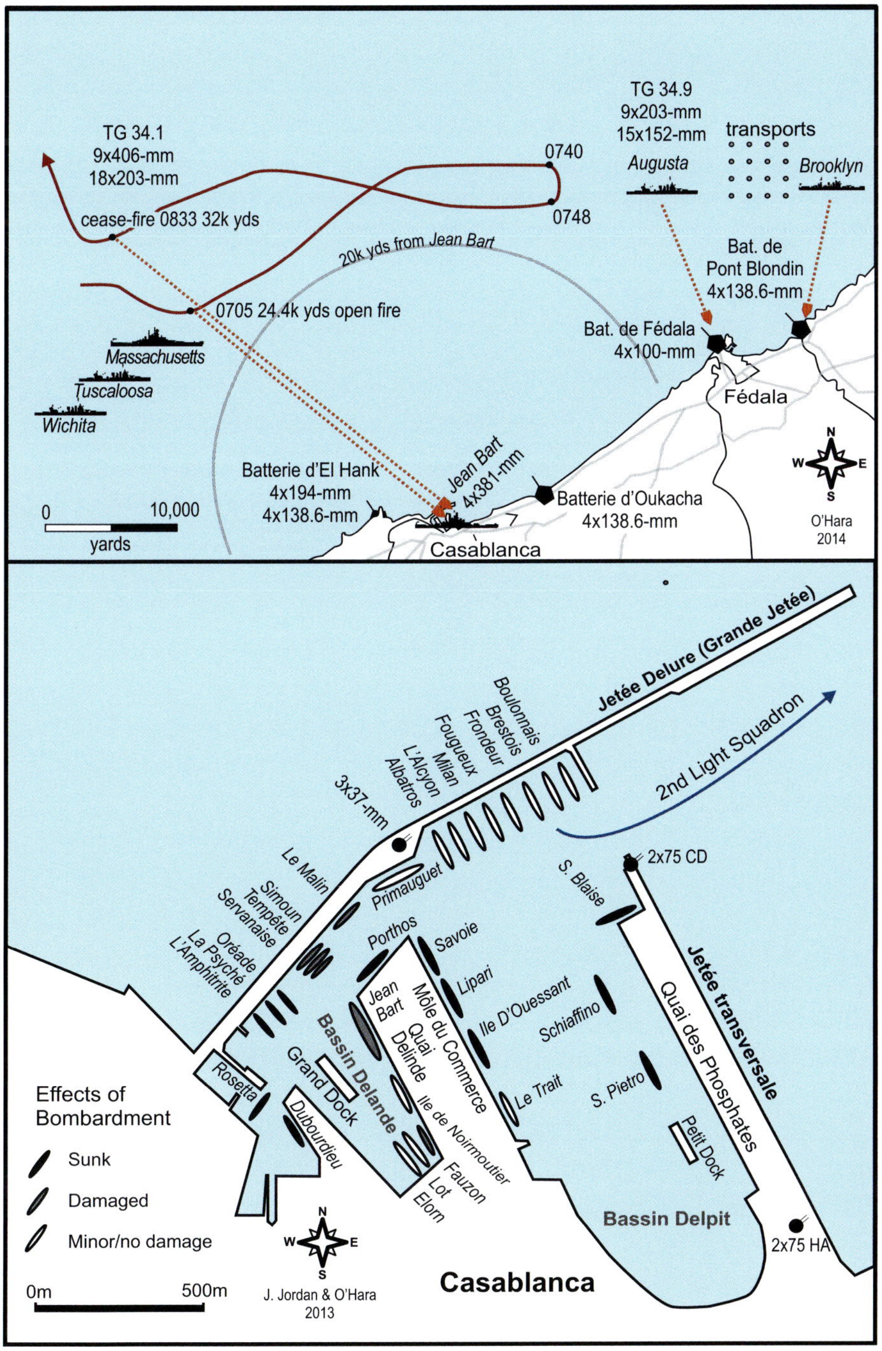

As the French destroyers hastened to sea, the *Massachusetts* started to hit the *Jean Bart* consistently. At 0735 a 16-inch projectile clipped the French battleship's bow, and a minute later another struck the quay, showering the French ship's deck with stone fragments. A minute after that a round punched through the *Jean Bart*'s funnel and angled down into the hull before exiting at the main armored deck; another plowed through the quay wall and hit the main armor belt. The belt deflected the shell down and it exited without exploding.

The bombardment destroyed or damaged much of the commercial

Kingfisher on the catapult. These aircraft served as jacks-of-all-trade, performing reconnaissance, gunnery spotting, rescue work, antisubmarine patrol; providing practice targets for the ships' antiaircraft crews; and even carrying out bombing missions. (U.S. Naval Institute Photo Archive)

shipping in the harbor as well. The newly arrived passenger ships *Porthos*, *Savoie*, and *Lipari* were still crowded with civilian evacuees. They had started disembarking at 0545, and when the first shells came screaming into the harbor the final 400 passengers fled at a run. At 0736 a 16-inch shell smacked the *Porthos*, which was tied to the head of the mole. She capsized, suffering 24 dead. A pair of 16-inch rounds smashed the tanker *Île d'Ouessant* at 0755 and she sank rapidly. The *Fauzon* and *Île de Noirmoutier* were moored behind the *Jean Bart*. Sixteen-inch shells passed through the *Fauzon* at 0800 and 0815, but the ship remained afloat. Another ripped *Île de Noirmoutier* at 0810 and caused major flooding.

At 0806 a 16-inch round ricocheted off *Jean Bart*'s operational turret, carrying away a 90-mm gun mounted alongside; the shell did not explode, but it pushed the glacis plate down and jammed the turret in place. Another shell from the same salvo struck turret No. 2's barbette and broke up. It ricocheted off the main armored deck and penetrated several compartments before coming to rest. Four minutes later a projectile pierced the *Jean Bart*'s quarterdeck forward of the starboard catapult. After ripping through a 100-mm armored deck, the shell exploded in a ballast tank beneath the steering gear. Fragments punched through the ship's bottom.

The El Hank and the smaller Table d'Oukacha battery to the east of the harbor remained fully operational despite being targeted by 69 8-inch and 19 16-inch salvos. The ships were using armor-piercing rather than high-explosive type ammunition, which reduced their effectiveness against such targets. A subsequent analysis called the results disappointing and complained that many of the *Massachusetts*'s rounds were duds (although the Naval Inspector General later disputed this). El Hank targeted mostly the *Massachusetts*. From the battleship's decks it seemed to one participant that "Throughout this action, heavy stuff was whizzing over . . . and splashing in the water close aboard."

At 0830 Rear Admiral Giffen overheard a TBS message that there was no resistance ashore and that the bombardment was killing townspeople. He ordered cease-fire at 0833. This came at a good time for the *Massachusetts*, inasmuch as with salvo 45, fired at 0812, a shell being loaded into Turret 1 tipped and fell through the hoist, jamming the turret, which was training to port at the time. It took 35 minutes to clear. Minor problems with shell supply or mechanics caused one or more guns to misfire during 16 of the 50 salvos discharged during the bombardment.

The Naval Battle of Casablanca

The naval battle of Casablanca was the largest surface, air, and subsurface naval action fought in the Atlantic Ocean during World War II. From first shot to last the battle lasted more than six hours and during that time the U.S. Navy deployed the *Massachusetts*, three heavy cruisers, one light cruiser, and ten destroyers supplemented by carrier fighters, bombers, and a minesweeper (which got accidentally involved); the French had one immobile battleship, three shore batteries, a light cruiser, two large destroyers, seven fleet destroyers, two sloops, a patrol boat, and three submarines. During the battle the French flotilla repeatedly threatened the transports and even broke up a landing with gunfire. Both sides suffered damage during this prolonged action, but the French suffered the most by far. French gunfire from warships and shore batteries moderately damaged the destroyer *Ludlow* and heavy cruiser *Wichita* and did minor damage to the minesweeper *Palmer*, the cruiser *Brooklyn*, and the *Massachusetts*. The French had two destroyers sunk and one light cruiser, two large destroyers, and two destroyers heavily damaged. The other ships engaged all suffered at least minor damage.

Antiaircraft fire chases four French fighters away from an American spotting plane during the early morning hours of the Battle of Casablanca. (U.S. Navy)

Casablanca Harbor, showing the *Jean Bart* and the Lafonde Basin to port of the battleship and the capsized hulk of the *Prothos*, victim of the *Massachusetts*'s heavy guns, bottom left. (U.S. Navy)

The French liner *Prothus*, hit by a 16-inch shell intended for the *Jean Bart*, is capsized at dock. She had arrived in Casablanca early that morning carrying refugees from Dakar. (U.S. Navy)

Shell falling just short of the *Massachusetts* during the battle. The size of the geyser suggests it was fired by El Hank. French guns hit the battleship twice during the action but inflicted only minor damage. (U.S. Naval Institute Photo Archive)

At 0815 the French squadron, two large and five fleet destroyers, started up the coast at 18 knots. Aircraft reported their presence, but the information did not reach Rear Admiral Giffen even though he was responsible for their containment. He was 15 miles away sailing in the opposite direction, trading slow salvos with El Hank. The *Massachusetts*'s chronology notes that at 0817 two submarines were observed leaving Casablanca but says nothing about destroyers. Giffen's report does not address this failure to contain the French squadron. Perhaps the intensity of the bombardment and the smoke roiling up from the harbor made him believe the surface threat had been eliminated. What is certain is that the battleship's absence gave the French a golden opportunity. Their plan was to head up the coast with the rising sun behind them and strike enemy transports reported off Fédala. It was just a 30-minute sail.

At first, the only response to the French intrusion was a group of F4Fs orbiting Fédala waiting a call to action. They spotted the French warships and dropped one-by-one to strafe the enemy column while radioing frantic alerts. In the meantime, the *Milan* spotted unknown destroyers off her port bow. The French formed up and attacked. The ships the *Milan* spotted were the *Wilkes* (DD-441), *Swanson* (DD-443), and *Ludlow* (DD-438). At 0825 the French opened fire from 16,000 yards. The *Wilkes* and *Swanson* retreated north at flank speed. The *Ludlow* zigzagged after them as pink, green, blue, and uncolored geysers spouted around her and a few splinters rattled aboard. Then one of the *Milan*'s 138-mm rounds hit the *Ludlow* and knocked her from the fight.

At 0825 Admiral Hewitt's flagship, the *Augusta* (CA-31), which had been bombarding shore batteries near the landing beaches, turned to engage the French ships. The admiral also jumped on the radio and informed Giffen that enemy warships were off Casablanca. At 0830 the *Milan* trained her battery on landing craft loaded with troops of the 7th Regiment's Company L off Fédala Yellow Beach. She sank one boat and damaged others. This was the only occasion during World War II when loaded American landing craft came under direct fire from a major enemy warship. At this point the *Milan* was just five miles from the *Leonard Wood* (APA-12), the flag transport. Fortunately for the Americans, thick black smoke from a burning oil tank screened her and the other transports from French view. The fact that the strafing aircraft had wounded the French admiral and most of the lookouts may have contributed to the failure to seize such an opportunity. Then, when the *Augusta* and *Brooklyn* (CL-40, the other

cruiser supporting the landings) came up, the French reversed course, hoping to lure the Americans toward the big guns of the *Jean Bart* and El Hank.

At 0845, with still no word from Giffen, Hewitt radioed his subordinate: "French Cruisers standing up coast from Casablanca to Fedala. Cover Transports." In fact, Giffen had just ordered cease fire thinking that he had overcome resistance in the city. At 0834 the *Massachusetts* turned north by northwest, still sailing in the wrong direction. At 0848 Giffen radioed Hewitt asking if he desired assistance after observing "what appeared to be two destroyers standing out of Casablanca harbor." Because he was beyond sight of the harbor at this time, he was likely responding to radio chatter about the French sortie. In any case, this was the first indication in any report produced by Giffen or the *Massachusetts* that French warships were in action. Shortly thereafter, Hewitt's 0845 order arrived. It answered Giffen's question, and at 0855 the *Massachusetts* swung her bow toward the east and headed at top speed for Fédala, 35 miles away.

At 0916, after sailing east-southeast for 21 minutes (covering 19,000 yards) the *Massachusetts* spotted enemy ships making heavy smoke off the starboard bow. Her report noted that "it was difficult to ascertain the exact number . . . or to identify them accurately." Nonetheless, she opened fire two minutes later, range 19,400 yards. ". . . more than one or two ships were rarely visible . . . consequently it was necessary to shift [fire] from ship to ship as they emerged from the smoke." The *Massachusetts* was shooting first at destroyers and then at the French light cruiser *Primauguet*, which joined the battle at 0900. The battleship noted return fire at 0921 and reported that enemy "fire control was excellent and numerous splashes of various colors were observed, many within 50 yards of various ships of this group."

Poor visibility and equipment failures affected American gunnery. The *Massachusetts* relied on optical spotting because the main battery director's Fire Control Radar 1 had blown a fuse, and Fire Control Radar 2's ranges varied so greatly from optical spots that the gunners discounted its output. At 0930 the concussion from a main battery salvo jumped a circuit breaker and all four FD Mk 4 and FC Mk 3 radars lost power "with a consequent loss of target pips." "Shooting was 'from the hip' with application of spots in range and deflection when salvo landed." Nonetheless, the French situation was dire and, as the battleship and her attendant cruisers and destroyers closed, it grew worse. Rear Admiral Hewitt, who had General Patton pacing beside him anxious to get ashore, withdrew because it seemed Giffen had taken control and the French were retreating. However, at 0935, having reached a point ten miles north of Casablanca and just 11,500 yards

The *Massachusetts* received two significant hits during the action. A 155-mm round fired by the French light cruiser *Primauguet* ricocheted off battleship's starboard quarterdeck at 1057 and burst over a 20-mm mount, igniting small fires. This photograph shows the splinter damage that resulted. (USS *Massachusetts* Memorial Committee Inc.)

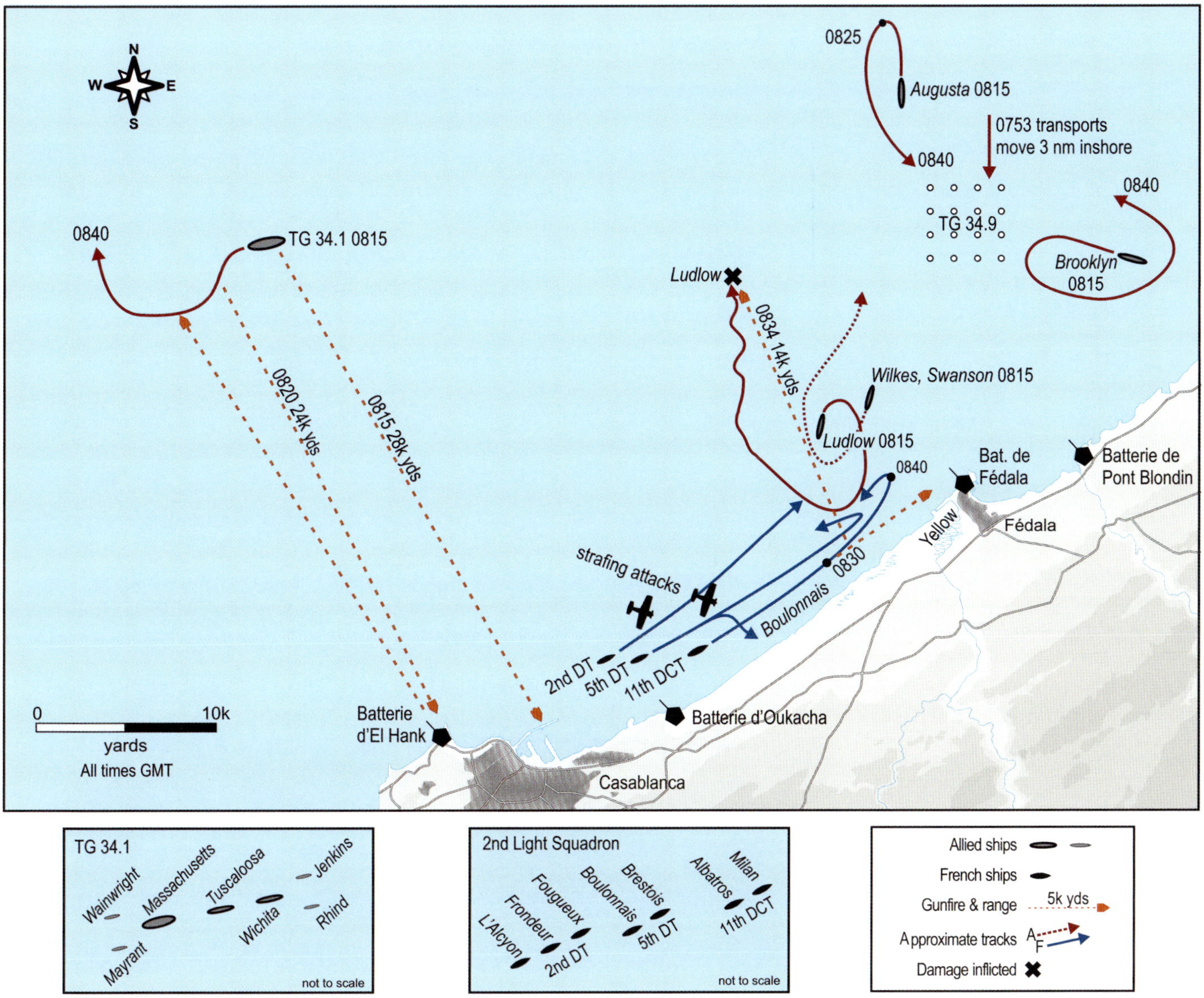

from the nearest enemy ship, the *Massachusetts* came about. The battleship's log records that this was done to avoid "restricted waters." Giffen's report only notes that "range varied from 11,500 yards at 0935 to 30,000 yards at 1016." This perplexing maneuver gave the *Primauguet* and the large destroyers another opportunity to make for the transports and now, with Hewitt's withdrawal, only destroyers opposed them.

As American destroyers assigned to supporting the landings skirmished with French warships northwest of Fédala, the *Massachusetts* steamed west, her aft turret engaging the *Fougueux*, *Frondeur*, and *L'Alcyon* to the south. At 0940 a 16-inch round fired from 12,000 yards crashed into the *Fougueux*. This, the first direct hit obtained by the Americans on the French flotilla, crumpled the destroyer's bow up to the quarterdeck, drove the stem underwater, and set the bridge on fire. The *Fougueux* rapidly flooded. Despite her radar difficulties and the poor visibility, the battleship scored again at 0956. The *Milan* was 2,700 yards north-northwest of Oukacha steaming southwest when she disappeared in a giant geyser. A 16-inch shell fired from 28,000 yards rumbled through the large destroyer, igniting fires and rupturing the hull. Splinters wreaked havoc and cut down more than a hundred men. This extraordinary blow was the longest-range hit obtained by one warship on another warship while under way during the entire war. The *Milan* turned into the wind to contain the flames and slowly drifted toward shore while survivors jettisoned ammunition and torpedoes. Because the *Massachusetts* continued to withdraw, however, the *Primauguet* and *Albatros* came about and headed back toward the transports.

As TG 34.1 passed to the north, El Hank opened an intense fire. Rear Admiral Giffen remarked that "there were many instances of enemy overs landing

within 50 feet of the disengaged side, in some cases as close as 10 or 15 feet." The stately progress of the *Massachusetts* and her attendant cruisers across the battle zone also had attracted French submarines. One just missed the *Tuscaloosa*. Two sailors on the signal bridge simultaneously reported tracks off the cruiser's port bow, and the captain immediately ordered a hard turn to port. Minutes later the *Massachusetts* was 28,000 yards northwest of El Hank heading west at 27 knots when "a shower of wooden splinters so stunned [her] executive officer . . . that it took him a few seconds to realize the ship had been hit." One of the lookouts recorded, "you could see [the] shells and [one] went flashing by and down into the deck and exploded; it detonated in the Marine storage room, into all those nice, full dress Marine uniforms." In fact, a 194-mm projectile struck opposite No. 2 turret on the port side, penetrated a deck and detonated against the second, five-inch thick protective deck gouging an inch-deep hole. The main deck planking caught fire. There were no casualties, although one sailor's "locker yielded thirty shell fragments varying from the size of a pea to that of a match box." Then the same officer, who was conning the battleship from a catwalk, spotted torpedo wakes. Overriding Captain Whiting's orders he turned the *Massachusetts*, seeking to maneuver between a spread of four torpedoes launched by the *Méduse* at 1003 from a range of 4,000 yards. One sailor recalled, "We made a turn and I know no battleship has probably ever listed that much. We had things like the chief engineer's director's chair sliding down across those checker plates and the rag hands sliding across the checker plates and everyone's holding on to keep from sliding across the checker plates. We said what's going on topside because we didn't know and the guy who was on the phones up on the smoke watch, called down and said that three torpedoes passed on one side and one passed on the other side." Another sailor identified this as his most frightening moment in three years of war. "I was on watch in #2 boiler room. Now that's about frame 29 on the configuration of the ship. Well, right over the intercom, it says, 'standby to receive a torpedo on frame 26' and everybody froze, but thanks to the quartermaster, it didn't hit us." This torpedo reportedly passed five yards down the battleship's starboard side.

In 100 minutes of action the French warships had circled between Casablanca and Cape Fédala. They had moderately damaged the *Ludlow* and foiled a minor landing but had failed to seize two opportunities to attack the transports. They had been subjected to sustained fire from a vastly superior naval force as well as dive-bombing and strafing attacks. Nonetheless, with the effective use of smoke they had suffered the loss of only the *Fougueux*, the crippling of the *Milan*, and

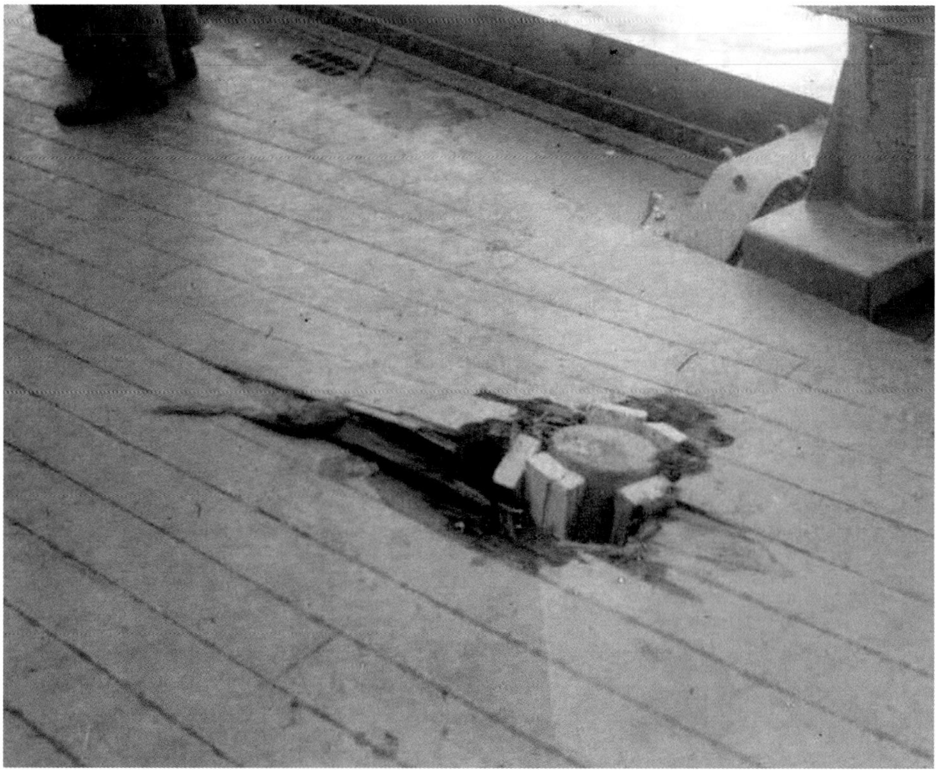

***Massachusetts* was 28,000 yards northwest of El Hank when she took a 194-mm round fired by the battery. This struck opposite No. 2 turret on the port side, penetrated a deck and detonated against the second, 5-inch thick protective deck gouging an inch-deep hole. The main deck planking caught fire. (USS *Massachusetts* Memorial Committee Inc.)**

The U.S. Navy's ability to refuel smaller warships from larger ones while under way was critical to the Navy's ability to project power over oceanic distances, as in Operation Torch. Here the *Massachusetts* is refueling the *Gleaves*-class destroyer USS *Hambleton* (DD-455) on the day before the landings. *Hambleton* was torpedoed and severely damaged by *U-173* on 11 November. She was patched up in Casablanca and went on to participate in the Normandy and Okinawa invasions. (USS *Massachusetts* Memorial Committee Inc.)

moderate damage to the *Frondeur*. One cruiser, one large destroyer, and three fleet destroyers remained effective.

By 1000 Hewitt had returned to supporting transports and Giffen to his duel with El Hank. Giffen wrote: "It is believed that severe losses were suffered by the enemy during this phase." In fact, both admirals exaggerated the damage caused by their gunnery. This was understandable; it was their first surface combat and spotters and lookouts tended to see a hit in every puff of smoke, or ships rolling over and bows projecting from the water. Consequently, they embraced victory prematurely. Moreover, in just two and a half hours of combat the battleship had expended 580 16-inch rounds. There was another French battleship, the *Richelieu*, stationed 1,500 miles down the coast at Dakar, and Rear Admiral Giffen wanted to preserve ammunition in the (very unlikely) event the *Richelieu*'s squadron suddenly should appear.

The French admiral, on the other hand, refused to embrace defeat. By prolonging the action he gave his potential equalizers—shore batteries and submarines—opportunities to inflict a telling blow on the American force. The French remembered how, two years before, the British attack on Dakar had been foiled on the operation's third day when a submarine torpedoed the battleship *Resolution*. While the hope of repeating such a victory off Casablanca was slim, it was the second-best hope the French had. The best hope was to sink transports and at 1000, with the *Boulonnais* and *Brestois* forming up for an attack, the Americans were allowing French warships another opportunity to do exactly that.

The *Massachusetts* had vanished over the western horizon when the two destroyers appeared, nearing Fédala. At 0951 Hewitt once again had to interrupt his prime mission, which was supporting the landings. The *Brooklyn*, rushing to the action, barely dodged a spread of five torpedoes fired by the *Amazone*. At the same moment the *Boulonnais* and *Brestois* opened fire and straddled the light cruiser. The *Augusta* was north of the transports, refueling a plane and preparing to land Patton, but the general had to wait.

At 1010, an 8-inch shell plunged into the *Brestois*' forecastle. The *Wichita*, which was targeting "whichever of 3 DD's or *Primauguet* could best be seen in the smoke," likely was the source of this blow, which, if so, was delivered from near 27,000 yards. Two minutes later, the *Brooklyn*'s rapid-firing 6-inch guns staggered the *Boulonnais* with a crippling broadside that landed six shells on target. The *Boulonnais* shuddered to a stop and started to sink. Meanwhile, the *Primauguet* remained pressed against the coast zigzagging at high speed in an area 4,000 yards wide. The *Massachusetts* ceased fire at 1016 when she was 18 miles west-northwest of El Hank. She started back toward Casablanca at 1018. After nearly ten minutes her lookouts could observe "4 cruisers and 4 destroyers at the entrance to the harbor" with "2 cruisers badly afire." Big Mamie engaged this

collection of French ships at 1030 from a range of 30,000 yards. She went to rapid fire five minutes later at a destroyer and claimed four hits even though her gunners complained of the smoke and difficulty in acquiring targets. In fact, she was shelling the immobile *Boulonnais*. At 1036 the *Albatros* tagged the *Brooklyn* on the No. 1 five-inch mount. The 138.6-mm round wounded five men before bouncing over the starboard side without exploding.

At 1052 the *Massachusetts*, steaming north-northwest at 27 knots with ranges to the *Primauguet* at 22,000 yards, reported shells splashing 25 yards off the starboard beam. As long-range salvos crisscrossed the smoky sky a plunging 155-mm round ricocheted off the battleship's starboard quarterdeck at 1057 and burst over a 20-mm mount igniting small fires. At 1103, after shooting 23 six- to nine-gun salvos over the previous half hour, the *Massachusetts* ceased fire. Giffen explained that the battleship "had expended 60% of her 16" ammunition and the preservation of the remainder was considered essential against a possible sortie of the *Richelieu*." At 1105 the *Augusta*'s guns also fell silent and she headed east toward the transports.

The *Boulonnais* sank by the stern at 1110, four miles northeast of the harbor entrance. At 1125 an 8-inch shell struck the *Frondeur* astern. She dropped out of formation with a heavy list and anchored at noon 1,800 meters off the port's entrance. At 1128 a round from El Hank punched through the *Wichita*, detonating on the starboard side and blowing a hole in the deck. It wounded 14 men, and fires filled several compartments with smoke and fumes. These were quickly extinguished

View looking forward from the ship's afterdeck during a lull in the Battle of Casablanca. Note: 16/45 guns of her after turret; 20-mm gun at left with "Lead, Dammit, Lead" printed on its shield; FC and FD radar antennas atop her gun directors; two large National Ensigns flying from her masts; and two destroyers screening ahead to port and starboard. (Collection of Rear Admiral Clifford Van Hook, 1972. U.S. Naval History and Heritage Command photograph)

and the ship's fighting ability remained intact.

By 1146 all ships had ceased fire, although the *Ranger*'s aircraft continued to harry the French, landing bombs on the *Primauguet*, *Brestois*, and *Albatros*. They so damaged the *Albatros* she had to limp toward the coast on one engine, and at 1155 anchored outside the port. The *Primauguet* and *Brestois* anchored nearby shortly thereafter. The *Milan* was still burning in the outer harbor, and the *Frondeur* was slowly flooding.

Task Force 34 had expended huge amounts of ammunition considering the operation was still in its first day. Hewitt had expected Giffen to contain the French flotilla, but fear of the *Richelieu* and a focus on El Hank had distracted TG 34.1 all day. For example, even though she had withdrawn from the surface battle to preserve ammunition should *Richelieu* appear, the *Massachusetts* exchanged fire with El Hank from 1345 to 1351, firing seven nine-gun salvos. The battery fired back, and as one participant recorded, "Every few seconds, intermingled between the shocking blast from our own guns, could be heard the ominous rumble of the approaching French shells and their sharp whine as they splashed a few feet on either side of the big ship or directly ahead or astern. . . . Why we were not hit dozens of times no one will ever know." Plainly running short on patience, Hewitt radioed Giffen again at 1340, "Light forces Casa Blanca making reported sorties. Destroy them before nightfall." Giffen sent the *Wichita* and *Tuscaloosa* to do the job, although their magazines were nearly depleted. In fact, the French fleet already was neutralized. After a dangerous long-range exchange with El Hank, the cruisers began opening range at 1450. With this the battle ended.

Throughout this long and confused action, the *Massachusetts* expended 798 16-inch rounds. She was hit twice with minor consequences, and a third shell passed through her battle ensign. The blast effect of her own guns caused far more trouble than enemy fire. Her after-action report listed the damage: "Heavy steel fixtures were torn loose from their fastenings . . . Steel doors in some cases stood swinging idly on their hinges, bent and useless."

Generally shooting at ranges beyond 15,000 yards and hampered by the enemy's use of smoke, the *Massachusetts* nonetheless disabled the *Jean Bart*'s sole turret early

Casablanca Harbor after the battle. The *Primauguet* is anchored top center left. The *Frondeur* (T-22) is capsized inside the harbor while the *Tempête* (T-52) is alongside. (U.S. Navy)

The transport fleet was anchored off Fedala, as seen here, waiting to unload when German submarines struck and, on 11 November, sank the large transport *Joseph Hewes*. The next day submarines picked off *Edward Rutledge*, *Hugh L. Scott*, and *Tasker H. Bliss* from the same fleet, accounting for nearly 54,000 gross tons of shipping over the two days. Not by coincidence, *Massachusetts* left for the United States that same day. (USS *Massachusetts* Memorial Committee Inc.)

in the action. She also sank the *Fougueux*, severely damaged the *Milan*, and hit the docked destroyer *Le Malin*. She turned in an impressive performance for a new ship in her first combat. The same was true of the cruisers and destroyers of Task Force 34. On the other hand, American tactics led to some needlessly dangerous moments. The U.S. task group commanders had conflicting priorities and failed to coordinate their activities. Hewitt had overall responsibility for all three landings, but the command arrangements put him in the middle of a battle on the bridge of a heavy cruiser while the army commander hovered impatiently at his side. The transport commander, even though he was on board a transport, had tactical responsibility for the *Augusta*, *Brooklyn*, and a destroyer division as shore bombardment vessels. He needed to secure the beachhead and get his transports unloaded, and his main concerns were the shore batteries, although that would have changed in a hurry had French destroyers burst through the smoke to confront him. Giffen was tasked with suppressing the *Jean Bart* and El Hank, watching for the *Richelieu*, and containing the French warships at Casablanca. These proved too many jobs. The fact that a battleship based 1,500 miles away received consideration while a French squadron sneaked out of port and attacked transports 15 miles away spoke to the deep respect battleships inspired in those with the job of potentially facing them, but reflected poorly on Giffen's sense of priority. Had the French warships reached the transports, had their submarines disabled the *Massachusetts* or one or more of the cruisers, the consequences could have materially affected the outcome of the landings.

On 12 November, once the landings had succeeded and an armistice was agreed upon, the *Massachusetts* turned back for the United States. The main danger in African waters was now German submarines, and against that threat the battleship was nothing more than a large and attractive target. Few ships received such a dangerous and important working-up period as the *Massachusetts* had in supporting Operation Torch. She acquitted herself remarkably well.

Her destination was the South Boston Naval Yard where she was taken in hand to repair defects and damage experienced in her brief but intense period of combat.

The *Massachusetts* remained in Boston until 11 December when she went to Casco Bay. The next day Robert Ogden Glover replaced Captain Whiting, who was promoted to rear admiral and sent to command Cruiser Division 14 in the Pacific. The month was a quiet one with training exercises on the 17th and the 22nd–23rd. On 29 December the *Massachusetts* returned to the Boston Navy Yard, in the words of her log, to "complete alterations and repairs to improve the military efficiency of the ship." On 5 January 1943 it was back to Casco Bay for more training and working up, and then on the 10th back to Boston where she "conducted such exercises and drills as Navy Yard work would permit." The work was tested with another run up to Casco Bay on 30 January. All the work proved satisfactory, and on 6 February, the *Massachusetts* raised anchor for what would be her longest voyage yet.

TO THE PACIFIC
March–October 1943

ON 6 FEBRUARY 1943 THE *MASSACHUSETTS*'S, ESCORTED BY THE *PHILIP* (DD-498), *Eaton* (DD-510), and *Renshaw* (DD-499), left Casco Bay for the last time and shaped course for Panama.

The first day out Big Mamie ran through heavy seas that tore off a gangway, caused a life raft to break away, and inflicted structural damage topside, but after that, she enjoyed smooth sailing at 18 knots on four boilers. She crossed the Tropic of Cancer on her third day out and arrived at Cristobal Harbor, Panama, on the afternoon of the 11th. One seaman remembered, "Then we got to Panama and everyone took off their shirts. We had about 350 guys with sunburns, but bad ones. I mean bad. One week you're freezing and the next week you're out in the

The *Massachusetts* seen from the afterdeck of the USS *Alabama* (BB-60), in Casco Bay, Maine, January 1943. The muzzles of the *Alabama* after 16/45 guns are in the foreground. (U.S. Navy)

The *Massachusetts* in transit through the Panama Canal. Her men, in dress whites, are lined up observing the tight squeeze as the ship moves through the lock with just inches to spare. (U.S. Navy Cruise Book)

beautiful sun." They passed the British aircraft *Victorious* on her way to the South Pacific as well. The *Massachusetts* serenaded the *Victorious* with "God Save the King" to which the carrier replied with "The Star-Spangled Banner."

After fueling, the *Massachusetts* began the tricky task of transiting the canal's locks—tricky because the width of the locks was 110 feet and the battleship's beam of 108.2 feet, less than a foot's clearance on either side. While clearing the Pedro Miguel Locks her starboard propeller caught on a safety chain, and the giant ship had to stop engines and go astern to clear the foul. She then continued on to Balboa where work parties repaired the damage. This allowed for a short period of shore leave. A sailor recalled that "they gave us one hour liberty in Balboa. They had about 300 guys that had captain's mast, being an hour late or a half hour late or something."

By the 15th the *Massachusetts* was under way for the South Pacific, escorted by the same trio of destroyers. Once at sea she conducted radar and rangefinder calibrations and drilled her antiaircraft and gun crews. On the morning of the 17th, for example, the ship expended 23 5-inch rounds, 899 20-mm rounds, and 240 rounds of 40-mm ammunition, firing at sleeves towed by her Kingfishers. That evening, according to the ship's log, "Davey Jones and messenger boarded the USS *Massachusetts*, emissaries of His Majesty King Neptune, to present His Majesty's compliments to the Captain, Officers, and Crew. They were very much displeased to find so many pollywogs on board. They informed the Captain that King Neptune and his Royal Party would board the ship at 00° 00' 00''." However, at the moment the battleship crossed the equator, the *Philip* was alongside taking on fuel oil. Work had priority, and even King Neptune had to wait. When the crossing ceremony did go forward, more than three quarters of the crew were pollywogs, that is sailors who had never crossed the equator. The pollywogs who got

the worst of the initiation were those who had joined the ship after her return from Africa. One crewman recalled, "there were always a bunch of transfers on the ship and they were rough. They had the planes tow sleeve, you know. They threw all kinds of garbage in [the sleeves] and they had to go through there and they were beating them or hosing them down in there and everything, and then you gotta kiss the guy's belly and all that."

battleship, 1,400 nautical miles out from Balboa, provided 725 tons of fuel oil to her consorts in about five hours. On the 21st it was the *Massachusetts*'s turn, and between 0907 and 1258 she received 590,268 gallons of fuel (2,420 tons) from the oiler USS *Sepulga* (AO-20). On the 24th she dispensed 875 tons to the three destroyers, having come 2,800 nautical miles since the last fueling. The ability to routinely perform such a complicated maneuver was one other fleets lacked.

The *Massachusetts* refueling two of her escorting destroyers. One of the great strengths of the U.S. Navy in World War II was its ability to routinely refuel warships while under way. Note the turbulent waters between the ships. The ship's power and majesty also stand out in this image. (U.S. Navy Cruise Book)

One of the key elements of the U.S. Navy's ability to project power across oceanic spans was its ability to refuel ships while under way. The *Massachusetts* demonstrated this on the 18th after launching her three Kingfishers to patrol for submarines. The *Philip* came alongside at 1306. In less than two hours she received 55,713 gallons of fuel oil from the battleship. Simultaneously, the *Renshaw* received 63,059 gallons between 1325 and 1457. The *Eaton* got her share of 58,731 gallons between 1536 and 1711. Thus the

Major German warships could refuel from astern while under way but only from specially adapted tankers. The Japanese first tested underway replenishment during their voyage to Pearl Harbor in December 1941, and the British, except in extraordinary circumstances, did not practice underway replenishment until 1944. The battleships pursuing the *Bismarck* in 1941, for example, came near to breaking off the chase because they had to maintain a fuel reserve sufficient to get them back to base.

During her long transit, Big Mamie conducted gunnery drills and her Kingfishers swooped every day to make mock attacks. On 26 February her diary records that she carried out a "special exercise to determine arbitrary correction to hit for main battery, USS *Renshaw* acting as target, 16"/45 caliber battery firing 3 shot salvoes, 2 salvos at each range of 5,000, 10,000, 15,000, 20,000, and 25,000 yards."

On Thursday, 4 March, the *Massachusetts* was back in French territory, arriving at Noumea, New Caledonia. She had come 9,000 nautical miles from Maine in 26 days. This was roughly equivalent to the miles steamed by the ship from commissioning to her return from Operation Torch. By way of comparison, the Italian battleship *Vittorio Veneto* steamed 13,409 nautical miles during her entire career from June 1940 to September 1943, admittedly under far different conditions and under fuel restrictions such as the U.S. Navy scarcely could imagine.

At Noumea the *Massachusetts* was assigned to Task Force 64, consisting of the *Washington* (BB-56); flagship of Vice Admiral Willis Lee; *North Carolina* (BB-55); and *Indiana* (BB-58). After a few brief training cruises, on 7 April the *Massachusetts* finally got under way on her first Pacific combat mission, in company with the *Washington* and *Indiana*, escorting the large carrier *Saratoga* (CV-3) into the central Coral Sea. Nothing happened and the *Massachusetts* was back in Noumea by the 29th of the month. In May she ventured once again into the Coral Sea with the *Saratoga* and the battleships but again stayed more than 300 miles from enemy air bases. Lieutenant (j.g.) Douglas Butler, who joined Big Mamie in Noumea, remembered that "when I was notified the ship was coming in that day I checked out of the receiving station and went down to the waterfront and went to the pier . . . and so I had the thrill of watching this giant ship come into the harbor and tie up there to the pier in Noumea and then shortly after I went aboard and saluted the officer of the deck and told him I was reporting aboard for duty so they sent me around to the various places in the ship . . . My first impression of the *Massachusetts*: I was struck with the size and strength of the vessel."

June was spent at anchor, engaged in upkeep and training. On 27 June, Task Force 36.3, the *Saratoga* and *Victorious* protected by the *Massachusetts* (flagship of Rear Admiral Davis), *Indiana*, and *North Carolina* with the cruisers *San Diego* (CL-53) and *San Juan* (CL-54), and 13 destroyers proceeded north, once again into the Coral Sea, in support of Operation Cartwheel—the 30 June landings of the 43rd Infantry Division at New Georgia in the central Solomons. The *Saratoga*/*Massachusetts* group's assignment was to stand by in case the Japanese fleet at Truk intervened.

In conjunction with this operation, U.S. cruisers and destroyers fought three surface actions: Vila on 5 July, Kula Gulf on 5/6 July, and Kolombangara on 12/13 July. Vice Admiral William Halsey, the Navy's commander in the Southwest Pacific, rightfully held the fast battleships well away from these confused night melees in constricted waters. In fact, the *Massachusetts* never came closer than 240 miles to New Georgia. On 23 July Task Force 36.3 began heading south, and on the evening of Sunday the 25th the *Massachusetts* was moored in Noumea once again. On her three

Range and Endurance

A ship's range, that is the number of miles it could travel on one load of fuel, was a function of three things: fuel capacity, engine efficiency, and speed. In the 1930s, when the U.S. Navy began designing a new fleet to replace its World War I vessels, it identified Japan as its most likely enemy. It envisioned fighting across oceanic distances, so range and endurance were necessary qualities. The *Massachusetts's* range was 15,000 nautical miles at 15 knots or 10,610 nautical miles at 20 knots. She could carry 6,959 tons of oil as a normal load and more if required. In contrast, her foreign cousins had the following characteristics:

Class	Bunkerage	Range
King George V	3,770 tons	5,400 nm at 18 knots
Littorio	4,140 tons	4,580 nm at 16 knots
Yamato	6,300 tons	7,200 nm at 16 knots
Richelieu	6,796 tons	5,500 nm at 18 knots

Oil consumption increased dramatically as speed increased. As can be seen, however, the *Massachusetts* could go farther, faster than any of her foreign contemporaries.

major excursions into the Coral Sea the battleship had encountered nothing of the enemy—not even an air or submarine alert. On 1 August TF 36.3 was at sea once again with the *Saratoga* (but not the *Victorious*) making for Efate Island in the New Hebrides, which she entered on the afternoon of the 5th. There she remained for a week.

The *Massachusetts* stayed near Efate until 30 August when, as part of Task Force 38, she accompanied the *Saratoga* on another support mission toward the central Solomons, operating this time roughly 300 miles northeast by east of Guadalcanal. This excursion lasted until 5 September, when the task force returned to Efate. Through the end of October Big Mamie remained in the vicinity of Efate going to sea for training on 21–22 September, 7–10 October, and 20–21 October. The fast battleships were available should the Japanese fleet choose to intervene against the American offensive into the upper Solomons, but they were not needed otherwise. The dangers from mines and torpedoes were too great to risk the great ships in the narrow waters of the long island chain. In November, the U.S. Navy capped the drive by landing on Bougainville. By this time the United States, rightly dissatisfied by the time and blood spent conquering the Solomons, was looking to jump-start the advance toward Tokyo, still 3,000 miles away, with a leap into the Central Pacific.

Getting Under Way

The process of getting 40,000 tons of ship under way is much more than a matter of raising anchor. The ship's eight boilers generated the steam that was necessary to spin the turbines that provided motive power to the ship's shafts. Generally, one boiler would be kept lit when the ship was at anchor, providing steam to power the generators for electricity. The ship's diary for 12 August gives an idea of the process involved. "Boiler #5 steaming for auxiliary purposes . . . ready to get underway on 6 hours notice. 0347 Lighted fires under Boiler #6. 0443 Cut in Boiler #6 on main steam line. 0444 Secured Boiler #5. 0531 Lighted fires under Boiler #4. 0534 Lighted fires under Boiler #2. 0630 Cut in Boiler #7 on main steam line. 0635 Cut in boiler #4 on main steam line. 0655 Cut in Boiler #2 on main steam line. 0700 Made all preparations for getting underway. 0729 Underway."

A Kingfisher landing. This image shows the plane's crew arrangements with the wide separation between pilot and radioman. (U.S. Navy Cruise Book)

Vought-Sikorsky OS2U Kingfisher

The *Massachusetts* was equipped with three Vought-Sikorsky OS2U "Kingfisher" floatplanes. The aircraft handling arrangements consisted of two catapults upon which the aircraft were stored and from which they were launched. A crane positioned on the fantail lifted the aircraft from the water when they were being retrieved.

The Kingfisher was the U.S. Navy's primary ship-launched scout and observation aircraft during World War II. The first model flew in 1938 and over the course of the war more than 1,500 were built. The plane could carry two 100-pound bombs or two 325-pound depth charges. Its top speed was 165 mph and its range 800 miles. The ceiling was 13,000 feet. The pilot and a rear-facing gunner/radioman each had a .30-caliber machine gun. One of the ship's observers recalled that the aircraft was very rugged, a "good airplane but very slow. You were lucky to get over a hundred knots. It seemed like you weren't moving." As for being catapulted: "That was a thrill."

An aerial side view of three U.S. Navy OS2U Kingfisher observation-scout aircraft flying in formation. (U.S. Naval Institute Photo Archive)

Manning the ship

The full wartime complement of the *Massachusetts* was 2,354 men; in practice, however, this number was generally 10 percent less. The crew was organized into a hierarchal system designed, in the words of the Navy wartime publication *Seamanship*, to "implement the primary function of the ship—effectiveness in battle." The captain held ultimate authority over his ship and all that happened on board. His chief assistant was the executive officer. "He is thoroughly informed as to the policies of the Commanding Officer and sees that these are carried out by his subordinates in such a way as to insure the military and general efficiency of the ship." The entire ship's complement was organized into nine departments:

- Executive
- Navigation
- Gunnery
- Hull
- Communication
- Engineering
- Medical
- Supply
- Chaplain corps

Each department was headed by a commander or lieutenant commander. The ship was further subdivided into 28 divisions, one or more divisions in each of the nine departments. The numbers of crewmen assigned to each division that are given below should be considered approximate.

EXECUTIVE

The Executive Department consisted of the executive officer, the personnel officer, and two divisions:

- EX-1: in charge of personnel, correspondence, administration, and the band, with 31 men including the personnel officer, yeomen, buglers, photographers, and musicians.
- EX-2 (Police): with the chief master at arms and ten masters at arms.

NAVIGATION

The Navigation Department was headed by the navigator and had one division with 34 men including quartermasters, boatswain's mates, yeomen, and seamen.

Navigator works on charts in his office on bridge of USS *Yorktown* (CV-10). October 1943. (U.S. Naval Institute Photo Archive)

GUNNERY

The Gunnery Department was headed by the gunnery officer and had six gunnery divisions and four additional units: Combat Information Unit, Aviation Unit, Drone Unit, and the Marine Detachment:

Gunnery Divisions

- 01: approximately 130 men manning 16-inch turret 1 and including boatswain's mates, gunner's mates, turret captains, and seamen.
- 02: manning turret 2 and otherwise the same as Division 01.
- 03: manning turret 3 and otherwise the same as Division 01.
- 04: approximately 130 men manning the 12 quad 40-mm mounts and including boatswain's mates, gunner's mates, and seamen.
- 05: approximately 130 men manning the five twin 5-inch mounts on the starboard side.
- 06: manning the five twin 5-inch mounts on the port side and otherwise the same as Division 05.
- 07: Marine detachment with 80 men. They also manned 20-mm guns when at battle stations.
- TDD: with seven men, was in charge of the drone planes used to tow target sleeves.
- FA: with 50 men, was in charge of antiaircraft fire control.
- FM: with 65 men, was in charge of main battery fire control.
- CIU (Combat Information Unit): with 60 men by late 1944.
- L (Lookouts): with 65 men. They also manned 20-mm guns when at battle stations.
- V (Aviation Unit): with 20 men, included aviation machinist's mates, aviation radiomen, aviation ordnance men, and aerographers.

Crew levels fluctuated as additional weapons were added or capabilities, such as the combat information center, were refined and expanded. According to her quarterly personnel lists, the fewest number of enlisted men to man the ship was 1,817 on September 1943, and the most was 2,170 in the quarters ending on 30 September and 31 December 1944. To this should be added approximately 120 officers. The average number of crew throughout the battleship's career was 2,130 officers and men living in a completely self-contained world.

HULL

The Hull Department was headed by the first lieutenant and had one division:

- **R (Repair): with approximately 90 men, including shipfitters, carpenter's mates, painters, boatswain's mates, patternmakers, sailmakers, and seamen.**

COMMUNICATION

The Communication Department was headed by the communications officer and had three divisions:

- **CR (Radio): with 66 men, including radiomen and radio technicians.**
- **CS (Signals): with 44 men, including signalmen and seamen.**
- **CY (Captain's office): with 23 men, including yeomen, printers, boatswain's mates, and seamen.**

ENGINEERING

The Engineering Department was headed by the engineering officer and had four divisions:

- **A (Auxiliaries): with 82 men, including machinist's mates, water tenders, metalsmiths, molders, and firemen.**
- **E (Electrical): with 110 men, including electrician's mates and firemen.**
- **PA (Machinery space 1 and 2): with about 100 men, including machinist's mates, water tenders, boilermakers, and firemen.**
- **PF (Machinery space 3 and 4): the same as PA.**

Firemen man their stations in the fire room aboard the USS *Jouett* (DD-396). (U.S. Naval Institute Photo Archive)

MEDICAL

The Medical Department was headed by the medical officer and had one division:

- **H (hospital): with 35 men, including pharmacist's mates and hospital apprentices.**

SUPPLY

The Supply Department was headed by the supply officer and had three divisions:

- **S: with 85 men, including storekeepers, chief commissary stewards, ship's cooks, bakers, steward's mates, cooks, and stewards.**
- **SO: with 37 men.**
- **SS: with 35 men.**

CHAPLAIN CORPS

The Chaplain Corps consisted of a Roman Catholic priest and a Protestant minister.

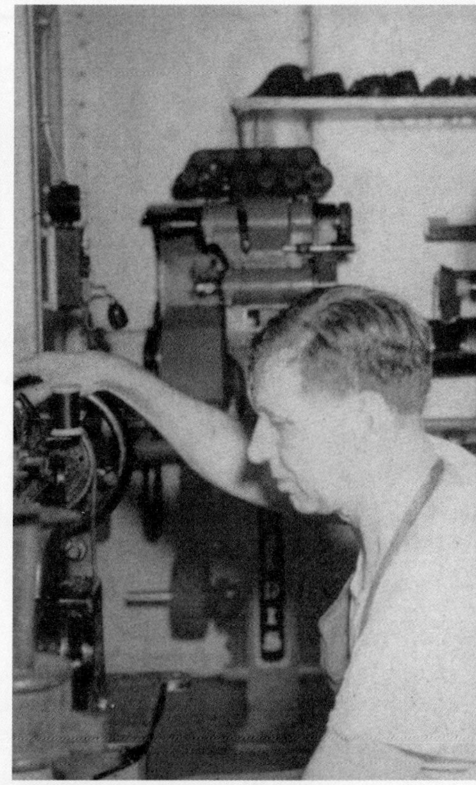

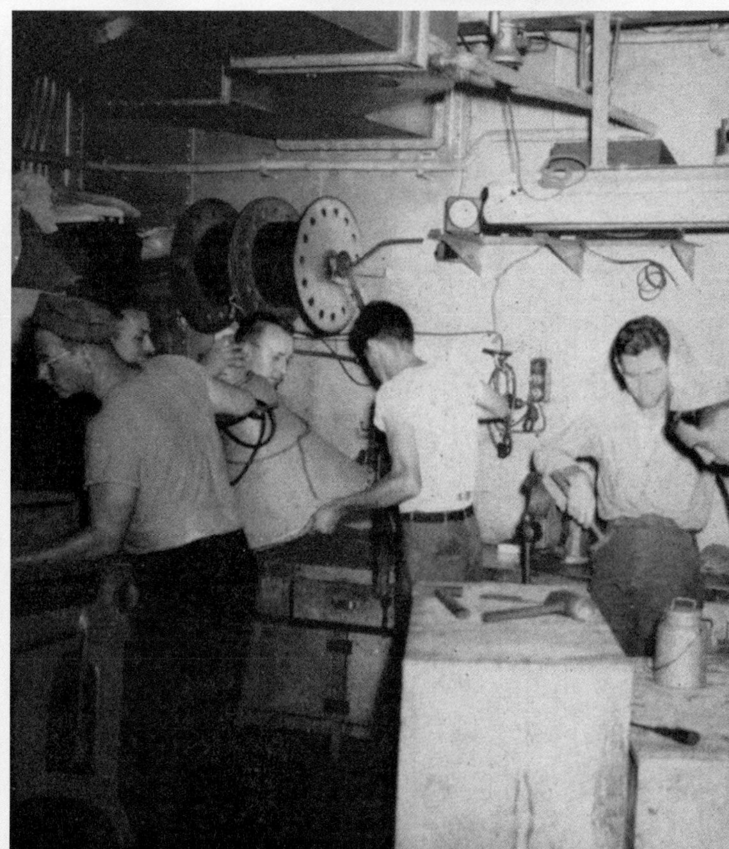

(top left) Ship's bakers inspecting a tray of freshly baked bread. The recipe for 300 biscuits called for 15 pounds of flour, 15 ounces of baking powder, three ounces of salt, nearly four pounds of shortening, and five quarts of milk. This was considered enough to feed 100 men. Thus, to serve the entire crew a portion of biscuits would require 300 pounds of flour and 26 gallons of milk. (U.S. Navy Cruise Book); (top right) The ship provided all the routine necessities of its crew. This is the ship's cobbler at work. (U.S. Navy Cruise Book); (bottom left) Three crewmen working in the ship's laundry. Their attire suggests a warm work environment. (U.S. Navy Cruise Book); (bottom right) The Machine Shop. Three jobs are under way in this photograph, with a hood or shield being fabricated (U.S. Navy Cruise Book)

The Daily Routine

The ship's day was organized into six four-hour watches. The first watch started at midnight and ran till 0400. The second was from 0400 to 0800, and so on. Generally, a crewman served one watch on duty and two off, although in times of danger or potential action the routine would be quickened to one watch on and one off, which made it difficult to get more than an hour or two of sleep in any one sitting. When at general quarters, the entire crew would be at battle stations. Moreover, when in enemy waters, the entire ship would go to general quarters during the half hours before and after dawn and before and after sunset, the reason being these were the times when the ship was most vulnerable and enemy aircraft were most likely to strike.

Every crew member had two stations: his duty station and his battle station. For example, a laundry man on duty would be a fireman when at battle stations. The Marines manned the 20-mm guns. Sailors who swabbed the deck while on duty were loading 16-inch projectiles in combat. As one sailor remembered, "You had to work. Ours was the 4th Division. We had the quarterdeck on the port side aft. . . . We scrubbed the decks down, cleaned and washed the bulkheads. They had something for you to do all the time. Get up in the morning, get a cup of coffee. Do a little washing the decks. Seven o'clock, go down for breakfast. Come back up about eight o'clock. Back on deck. Always something to be done. Clean this, clean that. It was monotonous . . . but when things got hot, it got pretty exciting." Another officer recalled, "An awful lot of free time, if you had any, was devoted to sleeping. I remember one time, I never went topside for over a week. It was just mainly going from the watch to the bunk and I never even looked out at the sea for an entire week." Or another officer: "In dangerous waters where we were going to dawn to dusk stand to and working four on and eight off, we were tired. And sleeping was something that took priority."

The *Massachusetts* at sunset. She is protected by an antitorpedo net. (U.S. Navy Cruise Book)

OPERATION GALVANIC: November–December 1943

ON 11 NOVEMBER 1943, THE 25TH ANNIVERSARY OF THE END OF WORLD War I, "the war to end all wars," the *Massachusetts* departed Nandi Bay, Fiji, to participate in Operation Galvanic, the invasion of the Gilbert Islands. The battleship flew the flag of Rear Admiral G. B. Davis, ComBatdiv 8, which included the *Indiana* and *North Carolina*. The screen consisted of the six destroyers of Desdiv 42. She sailed in company with Batdiv 6: the *Washington*, *Alabama*, and *South Dakota* and another six destroyers. Collectively, they formed Task Group 50.2.3.

From Operation Galvanic until the end of the war *Massachusetts* escorted the fast carriers as they supported a series of amphibious assaults. Here a bomb delivered by a Navy Grumman Avenger torpedo bomber drops toward a burning target on Makin Island during the first phase of the assault on the former British possession. The Japanese seized the Gilberts just days after Pearl Harbor. U.S. forces liberated Makin on 23 November 1943 after 72 hours of fighting. (U.S. Naval Institute Photo Archive)

The *Massachusetts* crossed the equator heading north on the 14th. Her diary does not mention any visits by King Neptune; presumably the ship had been purged of pollywogs. By that afternoon she was 30 miles west by north of Makin Atoll (Butaritari Island) in the Gilberts. She continued north, and the next day Task Group 50.2.3 rendezvoused 135 miles north of Makin with the nine carriers of Task Force 50, which had sailed from Pearl Harbor. Rear Admiral Charles Pownall in the *Yorktown* (CV-10) assumed tactical command. Task Force 50 then split into three groups, each based on a trio of aircraft carriers, to strike individual targets before the landings.

On 19 November TG 50.2, commanded by Rear Admiral A. W. Radford, with the carriers *Enterprise* (CV-6), *Belleau Wood* (CVL-24), and *Monterey* (CVL-26), Batdiv 8, and six destroyers operated 70 miles southeast of Makin while the carrier air groups repeatedly plastered the island. The battleships treaded water as the air strikes continued on the 20th in support of the 6,472 troops from the 27th Infantry Division that assaulted Makin starting at 0840 that day. Batdiv 8 did not have to concern itself with shore bombardment duties; the *Pennsylvania* (BB-38), *New Mexico* (BB-40), and *Mississippi* (BB-41) were on hand to take care of that, although with only 740 defenders, of whom maybe 300 were combat troops, the amount of force applied was surely excessive (in contrast with the famous and deadly landings on Tarawa that took place simultaneously to the south). Coincidentally, the *Leonard Wood*, one of the transports involved in the landing, had been with the *Massachusetts* a year earlier off Africa.

Rear Admiral Glenn Benson Davis, ComBatdiv 8. Davis spent many months on the bridge of the *Massachusetts*. He was an experienced battleship man, having been captain of the USS *Washington* (BB-56) and successfully fighting that ship at the Second Battle of Guadalcanal. He commanded BATDIV 8 from April 1943 through February 1945. (U.S. Navy Cruise Book)

Repeated reports of bogies disturbed the predawn hours of the 21st, but no attacks developed. At 0602 that morning a fighter shot down an Emily flying boat about ten miles from the force. On the 21st the *Massachusetts* refueled the *Boyd* (DD-544), *Brown* (DD-546), and *Bradford* (DD-545) as the fleet stood ready to defend against Japanese air strikes or a sortie by the Combined Fleet from Truk, a thousand miles to the west. On the 23rd the *Massachusetts* refueled from the oiler USS *Platte* (AO-24). The load of oil increased the ship's mean draft by 18 inches.

Multiple bandit reports enlivened sunset on the 24th. A squall was blowing up, and the *Massachusetts* maneuvered to stay within the bad weather. On the 25th flares started dropping around the battleship shortly after sunset as two dozen Japanese Bettys orbited the task group. The crew found this unnerving. "They would circle

Captain Robert Ogden Glover, center, being relieved by Captain Theodore Davis Ruddock Jr., in dark pants, on 27 September 1942. Ruddock had come from the Bureau of Ordnance; the *Massachusetts* was his first major command. Glover went on to command the 7th Fleet's Service Force as a rear admiral. (U.S. Navy Cruise Book)

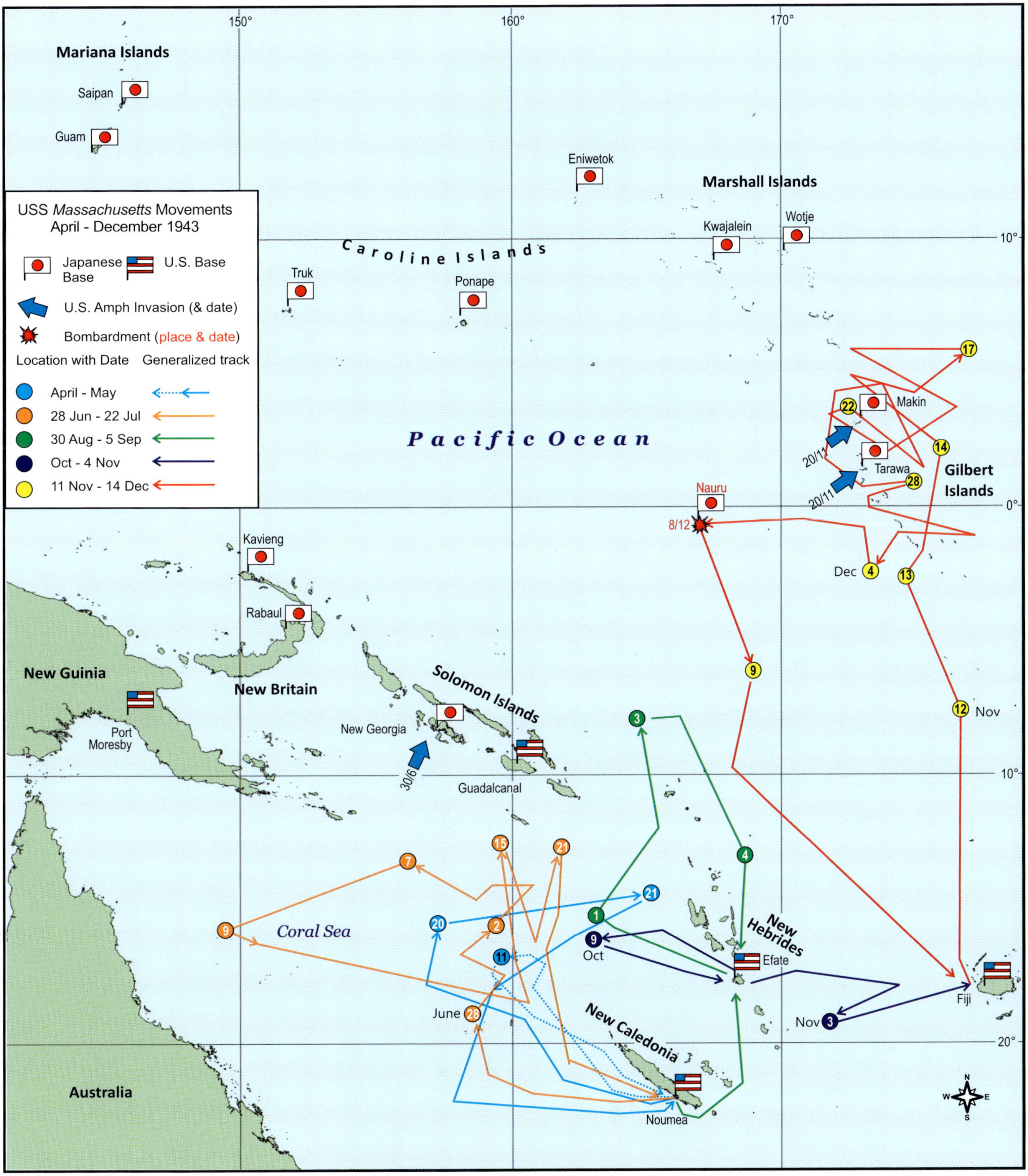

This chart shows the movements of the *Massachusetts* from the time of her arrival in New Caledonia in March 1943 through her return to Fiji on 14 December after Operation Galvanic. On this and subsequent charts the battleships' movements are indicated by colored lines with a different color for different operations. The circles show the noon-time position and the numbers inside the circles indicate the date. The month is generally clear from the context, but if not, it is indicated. The *Massachusetts* supported U.S. landings on New Georgia and in the Gilberts during this period and she bombarded Nauru on her way back to Fiji after the Gilbert landings.

around us and drop their flares, so they could see us. Most flares lasted too long; it seemed it was like it was hours before those damned things would go out." Another man remembered: "Just been aboard for a little while and they announced thirty-five planes coming in at us and I thought man, I just got out here and I'm gonna be killed already."

In fact, 18 minutes later a group made a "really determined approach" toward the *Massachusetts*. The battleship held fire until the raiders had closed to 4,000 yards, according to radar, and then her starboard 5-inch battery opened up. This was the first time since Africa, more than a year earlier, that Big Mamie had fired her guns in anger. The action lasted just 90 seconds, and she only expended 18 rounds. Nonetheless, lookouts reported that "a plane crashed off the ship's starboard quarter with its tail sticking up out of the water." The 40-mm guns held fire because they lacked radar control, and Captain Ruddick was concerned that if he used the 20-mm battery the flashes would merely illuminate the ship and make her an easier target.

Japanese Night Air Attacks. From Morison, *Aleutians, Gilberts and Marshalls*

"A little before sunset, one or more snoopers trailed the formation, waiting for darkness when they dropped a string of float lights marking the direction from which the striking planes would approach. These lights also served to mark the point of rendezvous. When the striking planes arrived, the snooper flew ahead of them high over the ships and dropped bright parachute flares. As the target became illuminated, groups of three or four "Kates" or "Bettys" armed with torpedoes launched attacks from favorable positions, one after the other, over a period of 30 to 45 minutes. Japanese night tactics were economical, as they required no fighter escort, and they were far more effective than the German Luftwaffe's night attacks on Mediterranean convoys in the spring of 1944."

The next night the Japanese aircraft again gathered along the fringes of the task group. At 1907 the *Massachusetts* fired a 30-second barrage of 5-inch shells (30 shells in total) at an aircraft coming in "low and fast." The plane veered off, although the gunners claimed a possible hit. Then at 1920 the lookouts observed a torpedo passing on the port quarter, and the ship surged ahead at emergency flank speed. The 5-inch guns erupted flame and smoke, this time at 7,000 yards, and the batteries expended 147 rounds over the course of 23 minutes, claiming one sure and one probable plane shot down. The battleship's report noted that "The attacks on night of 26 November 1943 were made by an estimated 20 to 30 planes. These attacks were much more vigorously made than the previous evening and appeared to have been well planned, though not executed with great coordination." Three night fighters from the *Enterprise* were one reason the Japanese attack lacked coordination. They harried the enemy, but lost one aircraft in the process.

A TBF Avenger flying antisubmarine and combat air patrol over columns of transports. This gives a good image of how convoys were arranged in columns and the spacing of individual vessels. (U.S. Naval Institute Photo Archive)

The Japanese deployed 27 aircraft, including six fighters and 17 bombers out of Roi, on the evening of 25 November. They named the engagement the Second Air Battle off the Gilbert Islands and claimed the destruction of an aircraft carrier for the loss of two bombers. The affair the next night earned the name of the Third Air Battle off the Gilbert Islands. It involved 31 bombers from Roi and claimed the destruction of two aircraft carriers and one cruiser at the cost of eight aircraft.

Japanese submarines presented another threat to the American forces attacking the Gilberts. Ten submarines had hurried to the area in response to the invasion, and two days earlier *I-175* had registered a major success when she sank the carrier *Liscome Bay* (CVE-56), which exploded and sank with the loss of 644 men. This tragedy confirmed that the longer amphibious forces stay tied to a beachhead, the greater the risk they ran. It was the same lesson the Germans taught the Americans off Morocco when their U-boats, arriving after the landings, sank five large transports. At 2256, only an hour after securing from general quarters, the *Boyd*, one of *Massachusetts*'s screening tin cans, picked up a surface contact nearly ten miles away. Admiral Radford ordered her "to go get it." She closed the target and, according to radar, surprised the submarine on the surface although haze defeated her attempt to illuminate. When the radar pip disappeared, the *Boyd* dropped several depth charge barrages at 0006 on the 27th and another at 0016 in response to "an excellent sound contact." After losing contact the *Boyd* remained in the area until dawn, when carrier planes joined to assist in the search. They found an oil slick 15 miles from the point of attack but nothing else. The *Boyd*'s captain, Lieutenant Commander U. S. G. Sharp, concluded there was no evidence of a kill "but it seems certain that the submarine was damaged." In fact, he had sunk the Japanese submarine *I-39*, probably in his second attack. In addition to *I-39*, the Japanese lost *I-17*, *-19*, *-21*, *-35*, and *-40*, as well as *RO-38*. The only survivors, *I-169*, *-174*, and *-175*, returned to Truk in December with slight damage from depth charge attacks. Task groups heavily defended by destroyers and aircraft were difficult and dangerous targets, and the isolated successes of Japanese submarines, as with the *Liscome Bay*, came at great cost.

A clear view of the arrangements of a typical breeches buoy. Notice the second line that pulls the pulley to the destination. (Hull Lifesaving Museum)

The fleet lay off the Gilberts protecting the recently conquered islands from Japanese counterattack until 1 December 1943. On that day the *Massachusetts* finally turned south with the *Indiana* and *North Carolina* and Desdiv 92 in Task Unit 50.2.5 to operate 300 miles south of Makin. That morning the *Massachusetts* lost a man overboard. The *Boyd* swung through the battleship's wake and within ten minutes had recovered the man and returned to station. Early that afternoon she came up on the starboard quarter and returned the man by breeches buoy, a process whereby a person transferred by rope between two ships via what today would be called a zip line. The routine back-and-forth cruising continued for several days, the tedium punctuated by false submarine alarms, the occasional sighting of a friendly aircraft, and by refueling on the 5th.

On 6 December Task Unit 50.2.5 was joined by Admiral Lee and Task Group 50.4. The two forces then formed a new Task Group, 50.8, consisting of BatDiv 6 (the *Washington* and *North*

Carolina), BatDiv 8 (the *Indiana* and *Massachusetts*), BatDiv 9 (the *South Dakota* and *Alabama*), the carriers *Bunker Hill* (CV-17) and *Monterey*, and a dozen destroyers of Destroyer Squadron 46 (Desron) and Desdiv 15. The purpose of this powerful aggregate of fast battleships was to dash 300 miles west and bombard the phosphate-producing island of Nauru.

Fast battleships in line preparing to bombard Nauru. Taken from a Bunker Hill aircraft. (U.S. Navy)

Smoke, haze, and a few burning fires on Nauru resulting from the battleship bombardment. Taken by a *Massachusetts* Kingfisher. (U.S. Navy)

The plan called for the carriers to launch strikes against the island and then provide cover against air and submarine threats while the fast battleships formed a line with the *Washington* in the lead and the *Massachusetts* fourth. At the appointed hour, 54 16-inch rifles simultaneously opened fire, sending 74 tons of explosives crashing onto the small island in one sudden and massive blast. As Captain Ruddock noted, "It is realized that the firing of this salvo without preliminary ranging shots probably will result in decreased accuracy. Its primary purpose, however, is to inflict the maximum casualties upon and generally to demoralize enemy personnel." After the first salvo, the *Massachusetts* followed with 29 more three- or six-gun salvos over 30 minutes. After a few minutes, her report noted, "impossible to see Island because of smoke. Fire on shore." She did have a Kingfisher overhead, however, and it reported her gunnery was "right on." The *Massachusetts* targeted the barracks area, the power house, gun emplacements, and supply dumps with her main battery and the airstrip with her secondary battery, expending 135 16-inch and 400 5-inch projectiles. Just at the time of cease-fire one of the carrier fighters looking for targets radioed, "Bombardment looks very effective. I can't see a God damn thing for the fire."

The only damage to American forces occurred when *Boyd* went to rescue an aviator downed two miles off the island. After sighting first an overturned life raft and then an object in the water that lookouts described as a man, she came to a dead stop 4,800 yards offshore, only to discover the object was a smoke float, not a man at all. Suddenly, Lieutenant Commander Sharp saw a flash on the beach and ordered both engines ahead flank, full right rudder. It was too late. At 1142 a shell slammed into the destroyer and exploded in No. 1 engine room, leaving a neat 6-inch hole and killing all personnel in the space except one man who escaped with serious burns. A second shell detonated inside the forward stack, and two shells barely missed. The Japanese battery unleashed a second four-gun salvo that registered two hits on the port side, peppering a large area with splinters, damaging two 5-inch mounts, and seriously wounding two men. The shells contained yellow dye, "which was sprayed over a considerable portion of the ship." As the *Boyd* accelerated and

began chasing salvos, she tried to return fire but was embarrassed by a power failure caused by the first hit. It took a minute before the guns finally opened under manual control. Shifting to a standby supply power, however, remedied the problem, and the *Boyd* finished the action spitting shells in full automatic under director control. The Japanese straddled the destroyer five times before she drew out of range.

The American destroyer fired 306 rounds between ranges of 4,800 to 16,000 yards. The hole in her engine room caused significant flooding, and she was not able to plug it until 1808 after she came alongside the *Alabama*. As Lieutenant Commander Sharp dryly noted: "It is again apparent, as has been reported after other shore bombardments, that shore batteries are seldom permanently silenced by Naval gunfire. Considering the accuracy of the shore batteries fire, I believe that the ship was fortunate to come out with no more damage." Ten men died and nine were wounded in this action. The downed aviator was never found.

Even if the bombardment may not have been as effective as it seemed, the crew of the *Massachusetts* welcomed the opportunity to unleash on the Japanese some of the frustration created by their often dull but dangerous routine. Captain Ruddock wrote: "Although the use of these heavy ships for such a mission might be questioned, it is desired to point out that the action herein reported did more to raise the spirits of the crew of this ship than all the efforts put forth in other ways. . . . [T]he fact that firing was done at a Jap was enough to renew the men's feeling that they were actually in the war."

After the attack on Nauru the task group headed south, arriving at Havannah Harbor, Efate, New Hebrides, on 12 December. She remained at anchor for the balance of the year.

A 16-inch shell pattern taken by a Kingfisher. This off-target salvo was fired during the bombardment of Tarawa. (U.S. Navy Cruise Book)

A Bloody Proving Ground

The U.S. Fifth Fleet opened a significant new front in the Pacific War with the invasion of the Japanese-occupied Gilbert Islands in eastern Micronesia on 20 November 1943. Vice Admiral Raymond Spruance, commanding the fleet from the heavy cruiser USS *Indianapolis* (CA-35), launched Operation Galvanic with simultaneous amphibious assaults against Makin and Tarawa, two coral atolls lying 93 miles apart, slightly north of the equator. Tarawa, gateway to the fortified bomber strip on Betio Island, was the strategic prize. With Betio in U.S. hands, the airfield would bring the Marshall Islands, 550 miles to the west, within range of heavy bombers and reconnaissance aircraft of the Seventh Air Force.

The capture of Betio and Tarawa Atoll was the mission of the Southern Attack Force, commanded by Rear Admiral Harry Hill, and its landing force, the 25,000-man 2d Marine Division, commanded by Major General Julian Smith. Both men knew they faced a well-led, well-armed force of several thousand rikusentai, Japanese Special Naval Landing Forces. They also knew they would have to breech Betio's coral reef at low tide.

The proximity of the Japanese Combined Fleet in the eastern Carolines was a primary concern. Admiral Chester Nimitz, commander-in-chief of the Pacific Fleet, ordered Spruance to "get the hell in and get the hell out" to avoid getting trapped in shallow waters by an enemy counterattack. Timing also was critical. Nimitz grimly reminded Spruance that Tarawa represented a tough but brief stepping-stone for the pending campaign against the more strategically valuable Marshall Islands, slated to begin eight weeks later. The operational tempo was so taut that Spruance could not postpone D-day in the Gilberts even a week in order to gain a more favorable tidal range.

The hurried Betio landing would thus become a storming operation—a frontal assault against a heavily defended island in broad daylight during a dangerously low tide. Success would depend on surprise, simplicity, fire-support coordination, and speed of execution—difficult objectives to attain by even the most experienced amphibious forces. Very few ship captains or troop leaders in the Southern Attack Force had any previous experience in conducting an assault from the sea against a strongly defended beach. Tarawa would provide a bloody proving ground.

Artful surprise and sheer grit enabled the initial U.S. assault waves to gain a foothold on Betio's northwest shore on D-day morning, but the advantage proved temporary. Intense Japanese fire and a freakishly persistent low tide prevented the buildup of firepower and reinforcements ashore. Casualties mounted, communications failed, and chaos ruled the beachheads. The few fragmentary radio reports to reach Hill's flagship described stark conditions ashore. "Have landed," one message reported. "Unusually heavy opposition. Casualties 70 percent. Can't hold." Another message came from the epicenter of the fighting on Red Beach Two: "We need help; situation bad." Hill and Smith sent an urgent message to their common superior, Rear Admiral Richmond Kelly Turner, the Fifth Amphibious Force commander at sea near Makin, requesting commitment of the force reserve, the 6th Marines, to Betio, adding, "Issue in doubt."

The chilling words resonated throughout the chain of command. Desperate U.S. defenders of Wake Island, facing the Japanese landing on 23 December 1941, had signaled "Issue in doubt" in their final radio message. Alarmed, Turner authorized the return of the 6th Marines to the control of the 2d Marine Division.

There was more at stake for the Pacific Fleet in Operation Galvanic than possession of the Betio bomber strip. Defeat at Tarawa would derail indefinitely the promising new U.S. drive through the Central Pacific. Failure of the landing force to seize Betio Island also would discredit the unproven operational doctrine of forcible assault against strongly defended islands.

Tarawa after the landing. This photograph shows what a tremendous impact the sea and air bombardment could have on a target. (U.S. Naval Institute Photo Archive)

TARAWA IN THE PACIFIC WAR

The battle for Tarawa represented a crucial crossroads in the Pacific War. Twenty-three months had elapsed since Pearl Harbor; 17 since Midway. Although the Allies had seized the offensive from the Japanese in January 1943 with difficult victories at Guadalcanal in the Solomons and Buna, New Guinea, they experienced frustrating delays in generating their own offensive momentum. The Allies recaptured the Aleutians in 1943, but their subsequent amphibious campaigns bogged down in the thick jungles of New Georgia and Bougainville. The Japanese regional strongpoint at Rabaul, New Britain, continued to be an unassailable thorn in their side.

Marines on board a Navy transport study a relief map of Betio en route to the invasion. After months of relaxation and training in New Zealand, the Leathernecks were about to engage in one of the toughest island assaults of the Pacific war. (National Historical Center)

The senior officers responsible for waging war against Japan in 1943 faced serious limitations. The Allies had agreed from the beginning that the defeat of Adolf Hitler's Nazi Germany would constitute their primary strategic objective. Although the Combined (U.S. and British) Chiefs of Staff had postponed the long-anticipated cross-Channel assault against Fortress Europe until June 1944, preparations for Operation Overlord still demanded top priority for troops, planes, ships, and landing craft. The Pacific remained a backwater theater, whose few offensive campaigns had been limited in scope and scale.

Admiral Ernest King, representing the U.S. Navy on the Joint Chiefs of Staff (JCS), argued for greater offensive pressure against the Japanese by means of a second front through the Central Pacific. An outspoken advocate of sea power, King believed that the Central Pacific represented the royal road to Tokyo and the U.S. Navy should take the lead in such a maritime strategy. Yet King also insisted that the new front could be undertaken without drawing down European Theater assets by using the troops and shipping already available in the Pacific. At the Trident Conference in Washington in May, the Combined Chiefs accepted the U.S. "Strategic Plan for the Defeat of Japan," which included King's proposed Central Pacific drive.

The new strategy elicited different reactions from the two U.S. theater commanders in the Pacific. Admiral Nimitz, whose realm included enormous oceanic areas dotted with widely scattered small islands, welcomed the concept of his Pacific Fleet attacking west in parallel to General Douglas MacArthur's route through New Guinea and the Philippines. General MacArthur, whose South-West Pacific Area featured narrow seas and large islands, strongly opposed what he perceived to be a wasteful duplication of effort. He argued for a single, concentrated drive to the Philippines under his sole command, fully supported by nearby land-based air and, as needed, by Nimitz's Pacific Fleet. King, however, backed Nimitz, prompting MacArthur's strident warning that the Central Pacific's lack of advance fleet bases and airfields would result in catastrophic defeat—a "reverse Midway."

Proponents of the Central Pacific drive used the verb "whipsaw" to describe the effect of alternating offensives

against the Japanese in the Southwest Pacific and the Central Pacific. In time, with MacArthur steadily advancing up the long coast of New Guinea toward the Philippines and Nimitz attacking through the Marshalls, Marianas, and Palaus, the whipsaw effect would prove its value. The alternating sequence of the U.S. landings at Bougainville, Tarawa, Cape Gloucester, and Kwajalein—within a period of exactly three months—proved the wisdom of this strategy.

Nimitz and Spruance believed that the Marshall Islands were too far away and too unknown to be the first objective of the Central Pacific campaign. Commanders of the 1942–43 landings at Guadalcanal, North Africa, and the Aleutians each had reported the critical need for advance aerial photography of the beaches and inland objectives. Taking advance aerial photos of remote objectives seemed a common-sense preliminary measure, but here, too, the vast Pacific posed vexing problems.

In 1943, existing aerial cameras were still too bulky to fit in carrier-based fighters. In fact, only a bomber the size of the four-engine B-24 Liberator had the capacity and range to collect aerial photographs in the Central Pacific. Seventh Air Force Liberators based in the Ellice Islands could reach the Gilberts, but not the Marshalls. Betio's bomber strip thus became the imperative objective. On 20 July the Joint Chiefs agreed to Nimitz's recommendation that the Gilberts supplant the Marshalls for the opening campaign.

The Joint Chiefs had other pressing concerns about the Central Pacific. Only a few islands in the vast region seemed suitable for airfields or fleet anchorages, and the Japanese, anticipating that any Allied advance would target such objectives, were busily fortifying them. In addition, the coral reefs surrounding most of these strategic islands further complicated amphibious campaign planning. There would be no "cake-walk" landings like those at Kiska or the Russells that had occurred earlier in the year.

Learning from early intelligence reports that the Japanese were fortifying Tarawa Atoll, the Joint Planning Staff advised the Joint Chiefs to undertake the Gilberts campaign with "battle-tested shock troops with amphibious training." Three U.S. divisions in the Pacific met these qualifications in late 1943: the 7th Army Division, veterans of the Aleutians and already earmarked for the Marshalls; and the 1st and 2d Marine Divisions, veterans of Guadalcanal, both currently under General MacArthur's command. With MacArthur preparing for a major amphibious assault of his own against New Britain barely a month after D-day at Tarawa, the JCS compromised, leaving the 1st Marine Division with MacArthur and transferring the 2d Marine Division to Nimitz for the Gilberts assault.

In preparation for the Gilberts, Nimitz chose Spruance to command the newly constituted Fifth Fleet and two countervailing firebrands, Admiral Kelly "Terrible" Turner and Marine Major General Holland "Howlin' Mad" Smith, to command the Fifth Amphibious Force and the expeditionary troops of the V Amphibious Corps, respectively.

LEAN AND FAT YEARS IN THE PACIFIC

The United States fought two wars in the Pacific, a consequence of the strategic priority accorded to the defeat of Germany combined with America's material unpreparedness to wage a two-ocean war in 1941. The first half of the Pacific War featured bare-bones resources, limited offensives, and hit-and-run raids, all conducted under the threat of the Japanese Combined Fleet. The second phase, beginning in late November 1943, finally reflected America's attainment of full wartime production, a tardy but awesome industrial transformation. One herald of this infusion of resources occurred with the arrival of the first Essex-class fleet carriers at Pearl Harbor.

Aircraft carriers were invaluable in the Pacific War. While vulnerable to land-based air attacks from nearby enemy airfields in the constricted waters of the Mediterranean and the North Sea, the carriers proved ideal for the vast expanses of the Pacific. Nimitz fought the first two years with no more than four carriers—sometimes as few as two—but in the war's second phase, the Pacific Fleet would include more than 100 flattops, many of them the highly capable *Essex*-class carriers.

Rear Admiral Charles Pownall would deploy six of these ships as the cutting edge of his Task Force 50 at Tarawa. Escorted by new high-speed battleships and logistic support ships, Pownall's carrier task forces could challenge the Japanese Combined Fleet for command of the seas. More than any other naval factor, the newly created Task Force 50 (soon to become Vice Admiral Marc Mitscher's Task Force 58) would make possible Spruance's stirring victories in the Gilberts, Marshalls, and Marianas.

ADAPTED FROM *NAVAL HISTORY*, DECEMBER 2008

RAIDS AND INVASIONS:
January–May 1944

THE *MASSACHUSETTS* SPENT THREE WEEKS IN EFATE BEFORE weighing anchor on 18 January bound for Kwajalein Atoll in the Marshall Islands, via Funafuti in the Ellice Island Group. She sailed in company with five fast battleships and Desdiv 92 led by Rear Admiral Lee in the *Washington*.

The *Massachusetts* at anchor in solitary splendor at Efete. Two landing craft are visible to the left. (U.S. Navy Cruise Book)

On the 19th the battleships joined the carriers *Bunker Hill* and *Monterey* and four destroyers. The force anchored at Funafuti on the 20th and became Task Group 58.5. This represented the mightiest aggregation of battleship power gathered in the war to date with:

- **Batdiv 6 (*Washington, North Carolina*)**
- **Batdiv 8 (*Indiana, Massachusetts*)**
- **Batdiv 9 (*South Dakota, Alabama*)**
- **Batdiv 7 (*Iowa* [BB-61], *New Jersey* [BB-62])**

The *Bunker Hill* and *Monterey* formed a unit under Rear Admiral Fredrick C. Sherman; the three heavy cruisers *Chester* (CA-27), *Pensacola* (CA-24), and *Salt Lake City* (CA-25), made up another unit under Rear Admiral Ernest G. Small. Sixteen destroyers in four divisions completed the task group.

At Funafuti the *Massachusetts* took on fuel and 2,778 5-inch projectiles. On 23 January TG 58.5 steamed north and two days later met the rest of Task Force 58 three degrees south of the equator. This juncture occasioned another reorganization into four carrier task units. TG 58.1, built around the *Enterprise*, *Yorktown*, and *Belleau Wood* received the *Washington*, *Indiana*, and *Massachusetts* as its heavy support. These six capital ships were screened by just the light cruiser *Oakland* (CL-95), and nine destroyers. The officer in tactical command was Rear Admiral J. W. Reeves Jr. TG 58.1 continued north toward Kwajalein. Several submarine scares along the way proved to be false alarms.

By 29 January the task group was 40 miles southwest of Maloelap Atoll, the site of a Japanese air and sea plane base and a garrison of 3,000 men. TG 58.1's carriers raided the base at dawn, and during the day the battleships screened as the carriers launched and recovered aircraft. That night the force steamed east, and at dawn the next day the carriers struck Kwajalein Island. While this strike was under way the *Massachusetts* formed a line of battle with the *Indiana* and *Washington* while Desdiv 100 screened the capital ships. Their mission was to follow up the carrier strike with a bombardment of the island. Each battleship launched a spotter at 0910 as the line closed their target.

The *Massachusetts* opened fire on Kwajalein Island at 1015 from 11,000 yards. At 1019 a 5-inch battery on the island's western tip answered the battleship. The

The process of recovering an SOC. The ship has made a hard turn to port, creating an area of relatively calm water. The aircraft is coming on fast to hook up with the crane. There is a man signaling at the end of the catapult. Even though this is a routine evolution, it is interesting enough to draw a large crowd of spectators. (U.S. Navy Cruise Book)

This chart shows the movements of the *Massachusetts* from 18 January 1944, when she departed Efate for operations against the Marshall Islands, to 4 May 1944, when she returned to Majuro after operations off Hollandia, New Guinea. The range and speed of U.S. fleet operations are suggested by the vast distances the *Massachusetts* covered literally overnight.

first shells splashed 150 yards short. Between 1020 and 1024 the battery straddled the battleship's wake five times and the ship itself once. Five-inch mounts on all three battleships zeroed in on the imprudent battery and silenced it by 1039. The American attack also caught two Japanese cargo vessels and two small patrol boats in the lagoon. A rain of 5-inch shells from the destroyers and battleships quickly smothered and sank them.

At 1115, after 57 salvos, the battle line turned away to recover seaplanes. According to a fire control officer "firing during Phase I looked erratic—several splashes were seen falling short, while some also were seen to fall over." The battleships launched another spotter while carrier aircraft worked over the island during the break.

Phase II commenced at 1200. Over the course of a half hour, the *Massachusetts* flung 24 salvos at Ebeye Island. The observer remarked, "the 16-inch bombardment of Ebeye looked very good. The island was hit consistently during this part of Phase II." Another 60 salvos on Kwajalein followed up through 1344. The observer continued: "The Phase II bombardment of Kwajalein appeared much better than any of the previous 16-inch firing. All salvos seemed to be landing on the island." One caused what the spotter pilot described as the largest explosion of the bombardment. The battleship's rangefinder operator "snapped a range to the top of the 'umbrella' of smoke and measured it as 3,100 feet. *Massachusetts*'s secondary battery continued in action until 1455. The ship expended 362 16-inch and 1,902 5-inch projectiles throughout the day. Once again, smoke from explosions and fires complicated aim and made spotting a matter of guesswork.

The blast damage the *Massachusetts* suffered as a result of the bombardment alarmed Captain Ruddock. The ship had used reduced charges but it appeared the muzzle pressure from these was greater than the pressure developed by full charges with AP projectiles. More than twenty doors were sprung, broken, or completely blown off, causing "considerable damage to light bulkheads, staterooms, and fixtures within the superstructure." The repeated blast had torn off nearly two dozen vent ducts. Deck bolts worked loose, windows were broken, even the admiral's and captain's chairs sprang free of their bolts and were flung against a bulkhead. One of the SG radar sets went out for 15 minutes, but overall, radar proved more durable than at Casablanca.

The next day the air strikes continued while the *Mississippi* and *Pennsylvania*, with heavy cruisers and destroyers, pulverized the island. The landings went at dawn that day as elements of the 4th Marine Division attacked the northern islets of Namur and Roi, and the 7th Infantry Division assaulted Kwajalein itself.

After the landings a naval gunfire officer wrote: "The effect of naval gunfire on the island of Kwajalein was devastating. The entire island looked as if it had been picked up to 20,000 feet and then dropped. The

A massive explosion sparked by a 16-inch shell send an umbrella of smoke towering 3,100 feet into the sky over Kwajalein Atoll (U.S. Naval Institute Photo Archive)

The fast battleships firing on Kwajalein, taken from the *Massachusetts*. (U.S. Navy Cruise Book)

ground was so torn up that it made even movement by foot difficult . . . Prisoners of war testified that the terrific blasting effect of the heavy and continuous bombardment terrorized the defending forces."

TG 58.1 remained near Kwajalein with the battleships refueling on the night of 1 February. Even routine evolutions were dangerous. One of the ship's ensigns responsible for station keeping remembered: "You had a card which would tell you what the zigzag pattern was. It was very scary because you realized you got 25 or 30 ships out there and you're in the middle of them with aircraft carriers, battleships, cruisers, and a big ring of destroyers all around you and you had to be mighty careful because if you were a few seconds late or a few seconds too soon in giving the order you could get the whole formation into a really bad situation. And that happened." At 0419, with the task force zigzagging at 19 knots, the *Indiana* pulled out of formation to refuel three destroyers. In the process one ship zigged instead of zagging and the *Indiana* accidentally crossed the *Washington*'s bow; lookouts on the flagship did not spot the *Indiana* until the two behemoths were just 1,000 yards apart. Although the *Washington* went full astern and almost had stopped, she still rammed the *Indiana* on the starboard side abreast No. 3 Turret. The impact crumpled the *Washington*'s bow. The *Indiana* suffered major structural damage, and massive flooding

Eating in Action

During her bombardment of Kwajalein, the supply department issued the *Massachusetts*'s crew U.S. Army type "K" ration. According to the after action report, this proved "Highly satisfactory." The ration consisted of eight crackers with butter, a can of pork luncheon meat or processed cheese, a package of "Choclettos," four Chesterfield cigarettes (with matches), salt, a powdered beverage packet, and chewing gum. That sailors dining on this fare probably did not find it "highly satisfactory" is suggested by an account of soldiers

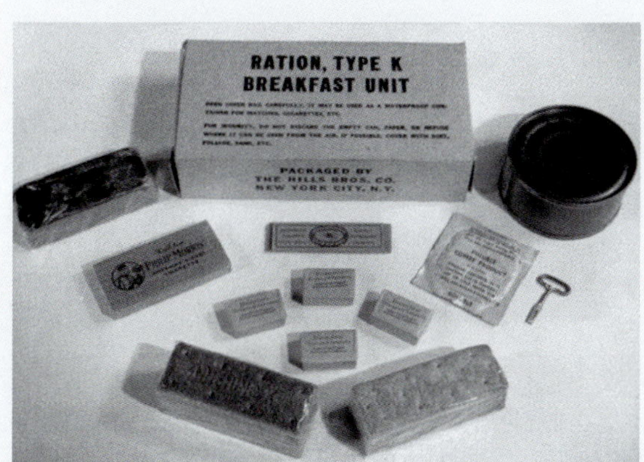

Breakfast version of K rations (U.S. Army Signal Corps)

living off the same rations: "They broke open their K-ration cartons, spread unseasoned potted meat on tasteless crackers and ate . . . in silence, not as one quietly savors a really delicious dinner, but because it was almost impossible to utter an intelligible sound with mouth filled with a substance which tasted like nothing so much as a cotton tablecloth." Indeed, one crewman remembered, "We had a tin can with emergency rations, but we never did get at those; that's for long term use against starvation because they were K rations, sealed up in thick waxy boxes and only broken out as an emergency and we never reached that type of emergency."

occurred on both ships. Escorted by four destroyers, they withdrew at six knots to Majuro for emergency repairs and then to Pearl Harbor. The *Washington* continued on to Puget Sound with a temporary bow. Both returned to service that spring.

On the 2nd the *North Carolina* and two destroyers joined the *Massachusetts* as TG 58.1 remained off Kwajalein. That day the 4th Marine Division overcame the enemy on Roi-Namur, but the Army's 7th Infantry Division required four days to defeat heavier resistance on Kwajalein. TG 58.1 then withdrew south toward Majuro. It was no longer needed off Kwajalein and frequent submarine alarms suggested danger there as there had been in the Gilberts.

TG 58.1 arrived at Majuro on the 4th and anchored in the lagoon. The *Massachusetts* took on 4,000 tons of fuel and 1,211 5-inch rounds and 31 16-inch projectiles. The Pacific command had accelerated the pace of operations to take advantage of perceived opportunities, so the fleet got under way once again on the 12th. The next objective was Eniwetok, 300 miles to the west of Kwajalein. This time the force consisted of Task Group 58.3:

- **Unit 5: Rear Admiral Sherman with the *Bunker Hill*, and the light carriers *Cowpens* (CVL-25), and *Monterey*.**
- **Unit 1: Rear Admiral Lee with the *Iowa* (flagship Batdiv 7): *New Jersey*, *Massachusetts* (flagship Batdiv 8), *North Carolina*, *South Dakota* (flagship Batdiv 9), and *Alabama*.**
- **Unit 2: Rear Admiral Robert C. Giffen with the *Minneapolis* (CA-36) and *New Orleans* (CA-32). Giffen had commanded Task Force 34.1 on the *Massachusetts* a year before off Casablanca. He had been disgraced off the Russell Islands in March 1943 when he lost the *Chicago* (CA-29) to a Japanese air attack, but now, after a stint ashore, he was back at sea in command of a cruiser division.**

Eleven destroyers of Desron 46 and Desdiv 15 screened the force. The ratio of one screening vessel for every capital ship showed how short the supply of destroyers was. Vice Admiral Raymond A. Spruance, in overall command, sailed on board the *New Jersey*. The plan was for the three fast carrier task groups to neutralize the Japanese base at Truk, which was within striking distance of Eniwetok.

On the 14th the Truk Striking Group had reached a point just 43 miles southwest of Eniwetok, and from there it turned toward Truk, steaming more than 500 miles to reach a point 75 miles northwest of the lagoon on the 16th. The carriers began launching strikes while Spruance formed a task unit consisting of the two *Iowa*-class ships, two heavy cruisers, and four destroyers to circle the atoll to hunt ships fleeing the air strikes.

The *Massachusetts*'s major contribution to the operation came at 1902 when she catapulted her two SOCs to rescue a downed *Cowpens* fighter pilot. Lieutenant C. C. Ainsworth landed in the lagoon, picked up the pilot, and took off again, being hoisted aboard just an hour after takeoff. Years later, his radioman, Dale Maudy recalled the rescue. "The first one we picked up he was shot down by an antiaircraft round that hit his propeller and he was going nowhere without a propeller so he landed in Truk lagoon and we landed and picked him up. I was with Ainsworth then. Ainsworth was the senior aviator. He was a great pilot and we were taking off in tremendous swells; I'd say 20-, 30-foot swells. We'd be sitting in the bottom of the swell and we'd look up at a 30-degree angle to the top of the swell coming toward us and, that's a frightening thing but then we'd ride up and bounce, take off for a few feet and then go down and land and then climb up again and we'd gradually frog hop and gradually get up to flying speed and then, we could fly then. Ainsworth was a great pilot."

The battleship avoided some air attacks delivered before dawn on the 19th and fueled that afternoon. Then, with Task Group 58.3 she started steaming north-

northeast for Operation Gateway, carrier strikes against Saipan in the Marianas. Japanese raids followed on the 21st after an enemy reconnaissance aircraft spotted the approaching American armada. The *Massachusetts* took credit for one aircraft shot down at the expense of 74 5-inch projectiles expended. Most of the Japanese effort, however, was directed against American carriers to the north.

On 22 February the task force sent three waves of bombers against Saipan. Following this lightning strike, TG 58.3 turned south. On the 27th the *Massachusetts* anchored at Majuro Atoll, the fleet's new advanced base. There she made further preparations for sea remaining at six hours' notice. Her diary noted that the captain granted "such recreation to the crew as is possible with facilities available."

The fleet spent three weeks resting and replenishing until 22 March when the *Massachusetts* got under way, once again as part of TF 58. The operation this time was Desecrate, a descent on Palau, Yap, and Wileai. The *Massachusetts* led the *North Carolina* in Batdiv 8, commanded by Rear Admiral Davis. Batdiv 9 included the *South Dakota* and *Alabama*. There also were three heavy cruisers and 14 destroyers.

Japanese aircraft spotted Task Force 58 en route and alerted Palau, giving fleet units based there time to withdraw. That day the *Massachusetts* was assigned to TF 58.3, which included the carriers *Yorktown*,

Shore Leave

One crew member speaking of shore leave said, "They'd give us cases of beer and food. The beer was very, very weak. We used to play baseball or tripball or whatever and sit around and just talk and drink beer and have hot dogs and whatever, but that would only last three hours. Then back to the ship and duty. It'd be very hot. Terribly hot." Another man remembered, "There were two beers per man but some ended up with no beers and others with eight beers. On one occasion the liberty boat returned to the *Massachusetts* and there were so many men who couldn't make it up the ladder that they had to lower a cargo net and hoist the eight-beer-men onto deck."

Rest and recreation on the beach at Majuro Atoll. The temperature was consistent yearly with lows in the low 70s and highs in the mid-80s. It rained, on the average, two days out of three. (U.S. Navy)

Lexington, *Langley* (CVL-27), and *Princeton* (CVL-23). The battleships included Batdiv 8 and 9; five cruisers and 16 destroyers rounded out the force. The two other carrier groups included TG 58.1 with the *Enterprise*, *Belleau Wood*, and *Cowpens*, and TG 58.2 with the *Bunker Hill*, *Hornet* (CV-12), *Monterey*, and *Cabot* (CVL-28).

The Japanese attacked the American fleet after dark on 29 March. The *Massachusetts* observed seven separate raids, but none presented "favorable targets for this vessel." Captain Ruddock noted that the only determined attack was made by three aircraft. Two were shot down in flames, and thereafter no aircraft closed nearer than 2,000 yards. The fleet suffered no harm that night. It was the crew's general impression that most of the enemy aircraft were not interested in attacking the battleship, and given her powerful array of antiaircraft weapons, this may have been true.

The smoke and flame emanating from a 16-inch salvo was a spectacular sight. The concussion was also dangerous both to the firing ship herself and her crew. Throughout the war the damage the *Massachusetts* suffered from the blast of her own guns was far greater than the damage inflicted by enemy action. (U.S. Navy Cruise Book)

On 30 March the three carrier task groups attacked Palau. Each launched six strikes starting at 0635. That night the Japanese retaliated with another series of raids. The *Massachusetts* expended 119 5-inch rounds against two groups of boogies, each time from 7,000 yards. She had to cease fire when other ships of the screen fouled her aim at roughly 3,000 yards. Again the fleet escaped unharmed. On the 31st TGs 58.2 and 58.3 hit Palau again while 58.1 attacked Yap. On 1 April all three groups struck Woleai. From there the combined task force headed south-southeast at 22 knots for a refueling rendezvous on the 2nd, 800 miles southeast of Palau. The task force then turned for Majuro Atoll. The weather was heavy on the 4th and 5th with frequent line squalls making air and antisubmarine patrols impossible. The *Massachusetts* entered the lagoon on 6 April, having covered nearly 2,300 miles since the strikes on the 31st. Not surprisingly, she replenished her depleted bunkers with 5,360 tons of fuel.

On 8 April the *Massachusetts* had a change of command as Captain William Walter Warlick, a past commander of Destroyer Squadron 7, relieved Captain Ruddock. Ruddock was promoted to rear admiral and assigned to command Batdiv4, flagship the *Colorado* (BB-45). Warlick did not have to wait long to see action. On 13 April the *Massachusetts* got under way as part of TG 58.3, with the same force composition as during the Palau operation. This time the mission was to support 7th Fleet operations against New Guinea, and a landing on Hollandia.

After a long but largely uneventful passage, keeping well away from Truk, TF 58 made a turn south for New Guinea on the night of the 20th. On 21 April TG 58.3 delivered air strikes against the Wakde Island air base off the coast of New Guinea west of Hollandia, having come 1,850 miles from Majuro. This was followed by attacks on the 22nd, 23rd, and 24th in support of the landings at Humboldt Bay. Army air force units already had pounded these targets, and there was little opposition; TF 58 was just churning mud. On the 25th, being advised that supporting air strikes were no longer required, TG 58.3 and TG 58.1 headed for a rendezvous with six tankers. On the 26th the fleet repeatedly scoped Japanese aircraft at a distance. On every occasion, fighters were vectored out to intercept them. Each time a Japanese plane was shot down, the fleet dispatched destroyers to rescue the survivors. They picked up five enemy aviators during the course of the day. On the 27th the formation headed east a degree or two north of the equator. It then took a sharp turn north for another crack at Truk. The *Massachusetts*, however, made a detour on the 28th in company with the destroyers *Converse* (DD-509) and

Thatcher (DD-514), stopping in Seeadler Harbor in the Admiralties. There Rear Admiral Davis transferred to the *Indiana*, which had returned to the fleet repaired after her collision with the *Washington*. Escorted by four destroyers, the two battleships then headed to rejoin the fast carrier group, something they accomplished on the morning of the 29th. The fast carriers raided Truk on the 30th.

On 1 May the *Massachusetts* with the *Iowa*, *New Jersey*, *North Carolina*, *Indiana*, *South Dakota*, *Alabama*, and 11 destroyers shelled Ponape for 70 minutes. During the first phase, lasting from 1530 to 1551, Big Mamie shot 45 projectiles in 20 salvos. Accuracy was marginal. Salvos 1, 5–9, 14, and 18 all hit in the water. In the next phase, from 1611 to 1629, she expended just 28 rounds in 15 salvos. Finally, the battleship engaged what aircraft had identified as 8-inch coastal guns. This phase commenced at 1637 and lasted until 1647. She discharged six main battery salvos using 14 shells and added 29 5-inch rounds. Any shore batteries present were wise enough to hold fire. There was a report of a submarine contact during the bombardment, however, and destroyers dropped depth charges in the battleship's vicinity.

After the action Captain Warlick remarked, "There were no occurrences of special interest during the bombardment. No enemy gunfire was observed . . . Such casualties as were experienced were minor and were promptly corrected except the failure of the forward Mark VIII radar, which took several hours to repair." TG 58.3 then shaped course for Majuro, where it arrived on 4 May. It had been an active period for the *Massachusetts* and the fast carriers she sailed with. Big Mamie, in fact, had been in active service for two years, and it was past time for refit. On 5 May she transferred 495 rounds of 5-inch ammunition to the *Iowa* and swapped planes with her, and the next day she set sail for Pearl Harbor in company with the carriers *Yorktown*, *Monterey*, and *Princeton* and the seven destroyers of Desron 6.

The force had a quiet five-day passage to Hawaii, arriving on the 11th. This was only a way station on her journey, and the hard-used battleship left the next day bound for Puget Sound Navy Yard at Bremerton, Washington.

Operation Hailstone

After the Gilberts fell, Nimitz prepared to move against the Marshall Islands. Convinced of the continued weakness of Japanese air power in the Central Pacific, the Pacific Fleet commander-in-chief brushed aside the fears of his principal commanders who favored a more cautious approach and aimed for the center of the enemy position—Kwajalein Atoll. Nimitz was proved correct when Kwajalein fell with remarkable ease.

To maintain momentum, it was decided to accelerate the planned invasion of Eniwetok Atoll, which was wanted as a staging base for advances into the Caroline and Mariana islands. With Truk situated 700 miles from Eniwetok, the vaunted Japanese base needed to be suppressed to prevent intervention.

Truk consisted of an enormous coral reef surrounding six principal islands and many islets, "a drowned mountain range inside a coral ring" as described by historian Samuel Eliot Morison. The reef was pierced by four openings covered by coastal defense guns. Hidden from world view, Truk had developed a reputation of nearly insurmountable strength. One air group commander would say, doubtless rhetorically, that his first impulse on learning the target was to jump overboard.

Fear of the unknown had magnified the threat, as Truk's reputation was greatly overblown. Only 10,000 to 12,000 Japanese soldiers and sailors garrisoned the atoll; also, Truk had just 40 antiaircraft guns, all of which lacked radar. But there was no shortage of aircraft. At the time of the raid, about 160 planes were ready for immediate deployment with another 180 ready for delivery to Rabaul and elsewhere.

The Truk raid, Operation Hailstone, would be conducted by the fast carriers of the U.S. 5th Fleet commanded by Vice Admiral Raymond A. Spruance, the victor at Midway. In January 1944, only weeks before the operation, Rear Admiral Marc A. Mitscher assumed command of the carriers,

replacing Rear Admiral Charles A. Pownall, whose conduct of operations in the Marshalls was considered insufficiently aggressive by Nimitz's headquarters. Having grown up with naval aviation from its earliest days with service on board the Navy's first carrier, the *Langley* (CV-1), Mitscher enjoyed unequaled respect from the carrier commanders. They particularly appreciated his style of command, which was succinctly described by Mitscher: "I tell them what I want done. Not how!"

One of the few not pleased with the change was Spruance, who thought well of Pownall and resented his removal at the instigation of Vice Admiral John H. Towers, Nimitz's commander of naval air forces. Towers and Spruance clashed about how the carriers should be employed, with Towers' more aggressive outlook finally prevailing. Spruance would come to fully appreciate the talents of his new commander, judged by Morison to be *facile princeps* (easily first) of America's carrier leaders.

To develop information about Truk, two Marine PB4Y-1 Liberators flew 850 miles from Bougainville to photograph the base. Although clouds obscured the view, many warships and cargo vessels were observed in the lagoon. Admiral Mineichi Koga, successor to Admiral Isoroku Yamamoto, already had recognized Truk's vulnerability and had begun to withdraw the Combined Fleet. After the Marine planes were observed, this movement was accelerated and soon completed, with Koga himself departing with part of the fleet to Japan.

Rescue in Truk Lagoon. An SOC with three downed aviators perched on its wings. (U.S. Naval Institute Photo Archive)

Spruance's 5th Fleet included 12 carriers organized in four carrier groups. Expecting no important naval opposition at Eniwetok, just one carrier group was sent there. The other three groups, organized as TF 58, centered on five heavy carriers and four light carriers, headed for Truk. Hoping to engage Japanese vessels fleeing the lagoon, Spruance transferred his flag to the battleship *New Jersey* (BB-62) in preparation for a surface action. Since that hardly seemed necessary, Spruance's chief of staff wondered if his commander was essentially on a sightseeing trip, curious to see the base that had long dominated naval planning. Spruance's biographer, Thomas B. Buell, speculated that the admiral might have wanted to flaunt American naval dominance by sailing a victory lap outside the Japanese equivalent of Pearl Harbor.

The first success was scored the day before the raid when the American submarine *Skate* (SS-305) spotted and sank the light cruiser *Agano* as she left the lagoon. A Japanese destroyer saved most of the *Agano*'s crew, but nearly all of them would perish during the raid when their rescuer was sunk.

Sailing undetected to a point 90 miles east-northeast of Truk, TF 58 launched 72 F6F Hellcat fighters that arrived over Truk at 0800 on 17 February. Mitscher's strategy called for the Hellcats to fully engage the enemy fighters and soften up the ground defenses, clearing the way for the bombers. That idea worked perfectly, as 30 of the 80 A6M Zeros that rose were downed against the loss of just four Hellcats. After brushing the air opposition aside, the F6Fs headed for three principal airfields, where they destroyed about 40 planes. On the heels of the Hellcats, 18 TBF Avengers dropped incendiaries on the airfields.

One witness to the destruction was legendary Marine aviator Major Gregory "Pappy" Boyington, en route from Rabaul to captivity in Japan. Landing on Truk at the start of the attack, Boyington was hustled into a concrete slit trench as a Hellcat destroyed the aircraft in which he had arrived.

With Truk softened up, the attack on shipping began. Although the Combined Fleet was gone, the lagoon was crowded with ripe targets. Present were about 50 cargo ships and auxiliaries, delayed there because of weather, plus many naval escorts including three light cruisers and eight destroyers. Mitscher's fighters, dive bombers, and torpedo bombers carried out 30 strikes, each more powerful than those at Pearl Harbor. Air opposition was minor and sporadic, the only substantial resistance coming from antiaircraft fire.

When he received news that enemy ships were fleeing the lagoon, Spruance formed a task group centered on the *New Jersey* and *Iowa* (BB-61). With the admiral in tactical command, the ships circled Truk in search of prey, but with results that were hardly commensurate with the risks. A crippled cruiser and destroyer were dispatched, and two smaller naval vessels were engaged and sunk. In the process, a Japanese bomb nearly hit the *Iowa*, and torpedoes fired by the crippled destroyer straddled the *New Jersey*. Although an essentially cautious commander, Spruance was anything but that in needlessly exposing his capital ships at Truk.

That evening, the Japanese sent six radar-equipped B5N Kate torpedo planes against Mitscher's carriers. After being held off for about two hours, one Kate eluded the night fighter defense to deliver a torpedo that struck the *Intrepid* (CV-11). Eleven crewmen were killed and 17 wounded by the hit, which flooded several compartments and jammed the carrier's rudder. Withdrawing to Eniwetok under her own power, the *Intrepid* would be sidelined for several months.

Meanwhile, above the lagoon, 12 radar-equipped TBF-1C Avengers conducted the first nighttime bombing of shipping by U.S. carrier aircraft. Able to locate enemy ships in the darkness, the Avengers made 25 runs at masthead level, scoring 13 direct hits.

The onslaught continued after daylight. With light antiaircraft fire now the only opposition, attacks were directed primarily against airstrips, hangars, storage tanks, and ammunition dumps. Then, with Mitscher and Spruance concerned that the Japanese might repeat their success against the *Intrepid* if the warships remained after dark, TF 58 departed at noon on 18 February.

Spruance's raid cost 12 fighters, seven torpedo bombers, and six dive bombers, most lost to antiaircraft fire, plus the *Intrepid*'s damage and casualties. Twenty-two downed airmen were rescued thanks to efficient lifesaving efforts by submarines, destroyers, and aircraft. The price was minuscule in relation to the results.

Sixteen Japanese naval vessels were sunk, including three light cruisers, four destroyers, and nine auxiliary vessels; in addition, 19 cargo *marus* and 5 tankers were destroyed. In all, Japan lost nearly 200,000 tons of badly needed shipping. Still, Morison believed that with air opposition essentially absent, the score should have been higher. He traced the problem to overemphasis during pilot training on aircraft interception and amphibious support with too little attention to vessel attacks.

Of greatest consequence was the toll on Japanese aircraft. More than 250 planes were destroyed or damaged, leaving fewer than 100 intact. With his air defenses shattered, Koga recognized that he lacked the strength to defend the Central Pacific while the attrition of aircraft continued at Rabaul. Two days after Hailstorm, the Combined Fleet commander ordered his aircraft in the South Pacific to leave for Truk.

OPERATION HAILSTORM: FROM *NAVAL HISTORY*, FEBRUARY 2014

After the attacks on Truk, the fleet is steaming at speed to refuel and rearm. (U.S. Navy Cruise Book)

REFIT
May–August 1944

ACCOMPANIED BY TWO DESTROYERS, THE *MASSACHUSETTS* TRANSITED THE EASTERN PACIFIC FROM 12 TO 19 MAY.

The *Massachusetts* at anchor, view from the foredeck looking aft. (U.S. Navy Cruise Book)

Fresh from the yard, the *Massachusetts* is under way at 15 knots off Point Wilson, Washington, on 10 July 1944. (U.S. Navy)

She raised the coast of Washington State at 0342 on the 19th, passed the Tatoosh Light 90 minutes later, and anchored in Sinclair Inlet at the Bremerton Navy Yard at 1705. There the *Massachusetts* unloaded ammunition, completing the task by 0515 on the 20th. Afterward, she entered dry dock.

The process of getting the battleship ready for another deployment involved much more than scraping her keel and slapping on a new coat of paint. The crew enjoyed a welcome break from their routine. Most men received 20 days' leave; some were assigned temporarily to training schools, and only enough officers and crew to carry on yard work remained on board.

The refit process also included correcting defects, repairing accumulated damage, and making improvements and alterations as authorized by the commander of the Service Force, Pacific. There also were occasional setbacks. On 10 June a worker who was cutting through a bulkhead with a torch ignited a fire that smoldered for several hours, burning through the electrical insulation in the area.

On 25 June the ship emerged from dry dock and was moored to continue yard work and to complete her overhaul. The process continued through 4 July, when she undertook dock trials for main engines and auxiliary machinery.

The crew gathers at the rails for the first view of U.S. coast in a year, 19 May 1944. (U.S. Navy Cruise Book)

With the successful completion of trials, the crew started loading stores, which took five days. The U.S. Navy undertook the whole refitting process with a sense of extreme urgency, with shifts running 24 hours a day. On 0806 on 10 July, the *Massachusetts* was finally under way under her own power. She sailed into Puget Sound and commenced full-power trials, also firing 5-inch mount No. 9 to test its structural integrity. Next came high-speed tests of the steering control and rudders. At 1734 she anchored in Sinclair Inlet, and the crew started loading ammunition and more stores.

On 14 July the process was completed. The *Massachusetts* departed for the battle zone at 1108 with 76 yard workers still on board completing last-minute tasks. The crew spent the day calibrating the ship's degaussing equipment, determining the standard compass compensation, calibrating her radio direction finder, and receiving a draft of men for the 5th Amphibious Force for transport to the western Pacific. On the 15th, the workmen departed and Big Mamie was under way once again for Pearl Harbor, escorted by two destroyers.

The underway period was filled with drills and exercises and checking all the equipment, such as radar and fire control directors, to be sure they were working as required. All the guns were fired, and the escorting destroyers simulated torpedo attacks and helped the battleship conduct night combat exercises.

On 21 July the *Massachusetts* entered Pearl Harbor. There she embarked on a "limited availability period" to finish work not completed in Puget Sound. This phase lasted until 1 August when, in company of four destroyers, the *Massachusetts* set out for Eniwetok. A week of gunnery and tactical drills at sea followed as the ship steadily coursed west, reaching Eniwetok Atoll at noon on 8 August. There, in the words of her war diary entries for 10 August to 16 August 1944, she "anchored in Berth 423. Port War Watch is set, normal port routine being followed. Making all preparations for sea and maintaining a schedule of repair, maintenance and upkeep of equipment as permitted by Condition of Readiness for getting under way. Conducting routine training, drill, and recreation schedule." This schedule lasted until 31 August, when the *Massachusetts* entered the war once again, steaming out in company with Task Force 34.

Clockwise (all photos on this page, U.S. Navy Cruise Book): The *Massachusetts* in dry dock, her first destination after unloading ammunition and stores at Bremerton—she remained docked for a month and five days; slinging aboard stores and supplies for the next deployment, a process that seemed to attract a large audience of all ranks; Port of Seattle during the war. The city had a population of approximately 400,000 at the time, and the nearby port of Bremerton was, next to San Francisco, the most important naval yard on the West Coast.

WE SHALL RETURN:
September–December 1944

THE *MASSACHUSETTS*'S NEXT THRUST INTO JAPANESE-HELD WATERS kicked off on 31 August 1944, when she sailed as a part of TG 34.10: five fast battleships, Crudivs 14 and 13, and Desrons 52 and 50. They headed west along the equator practicing battle line maneuvers. As Captain Warlick told his men, "It is Admiral Halsey's hope that he can smoke out the Japanese fleet on one of these operations." As the carriers attacked Palau, the *New Jersey*, with Halsey on board, joined the battle line. They continued to practice tactical exercises through 9 September, keeping roughly 200 miles southeast of Palau while the carriers proceeded to hit Mindanao.

Puffs of smoke from exploding shells mark an antiaircraft barrage overhead as Japanese aircraft attack the fleet. (U.S. Navy Cruise Book)

On 11 September Halsey dissolved the battle line, and the *Massachusetts* was assigned to TG 38.3: the carriers *Essex*, *Lexington*, *Langley*, and *Princeton*, and the battleships *North Carolina*, *Washington*, *Indiana*, and *Alabama*. Crudiv 13 and Desrons 50 and 55 rounded out the force. On the 12th and 13th the carrier air groups raided targets in the central Philippines. The *Massachusetts* helped down a Japanese fighter that penetrated the screen and unsuccessfully bombed the *Princeton*. The strikes continued on the 14th. On that day one of the battleship's Kingfishers rescued a downed *Wasp* pilot. After recovering aircraft that evening, the task force headed southeast by south to keep a fueling rendezvous.

On 21 September TF 38 began launching fighter sweeps and air strikes on Japanese airfields, shipping, and shore installations around Manila Bay. Thereafter the weather deteriorated, and the *Massachusetts* refueled on the 23rd. On the 24th, with the target still the central Philippines, the battleship's Kingfisher rescued a *Princeton* pilot. Then, along with the *Alabama* and *Washington*, the *Massachusetts* joined TG 38.2 and headed for Saipan, where she anchored on the 28th. After one day in the Marianas the *Massachusetts*, *Alabama*, and *Washington*, along with the *Iowa* and *New Jersey*, weighed anchor for Ulithi.

The fleet reached Ulithi on the morning of 1 October. The next day Rear Admiral G. B. Davis, ComBatdiv 8, hoisted his flag on the *Massachusetts*. On the 3rd Big Mamie had to depart Ulithi on an emergency basis as a strong tropical storm blew up. The battleship successfully conned her way through the narrow channel using Mark 8 radars. She returned to Ulithi the next day after the weather moderated.

On the 6th the *Massachusetts* was under way as part of TG 38.3 with the *Essex*, *Lexington*, *Langley*, *Princeton*, *Washington*, *South Dakota*, *Alabama*, three cruisers, and Desrons 50 and 55; course 335 degree (true), speed 18 knots. The group's task was to support landings in Leyte Gulf by first striking airfields on Okinawa and Formosa, from which the Japanese could stage reinforcements, before turning against the Philippines. On the 10th, all four task groups of TF 38 united for the first time since June to launch massive raids on Okinawa's complex of airfields. As Captain Warlick informed his crew, "This new operation, as usual, will lead to a landing. When and where I cannot tell you until later. It is enough for us to know that Task Force 38 leads off, as usual, with a damaging blow to some important enemy position. The purpose of this blow is to weaken the enemy's ability to counter the landings when they come."

The arrival off Okinawa achieved tactical surprise; there were no enemy attacks the first day. The fleet then pivoted six degrees south the next day, as the ships fueled. The *Massachusetts* took on 458,041 gallons and dispensed 153,560 gallons to the destroyers *Healy* (DD-672) and *Laws* (DD-558). Then, with replenished bunkers, TF 38.3 ran in at 24 knots toward Formosa. The carriers launched planes on the 12th, but this time the Japanese were ready. Hundreds of fighters met the Americans in the skies over Formosa, and waves of bombers descended on TF 38. Little of this affected the *Massachusetts*. That evening, her antiaircraft batteries went into action just twice, as the Japanese did not

"A Display of Expert Seamanship." There appear to be three cruisers between the *Massachusetts* and the aircraft carrier in the background. (U.S. Navy Cruise Book)

press any attacks against TG 38.3. The 13th was a repetition. The *Massachusetts* went into action briefly at 1834, but the only American ship to suffer harm was the heavy cruiser USS *Canberra* (CA-70), part of TG 38.1. A Japanese aircraft from a specially trained night attack unit torpedoed her, and she had to be towed from the area. This necessitated a third day of fighter sweeps to help the crippled ship escape.

On 14 October Japanese aircraft torpedoed the light cruiser *Houston* (CL-81), part of the *Canberra*'s escort. On that day the fast carriers—except TG 38.1, which stayed to cover the cripples—turned southeast and withdrew at 24 knots. After dark a Jill, presumably from the Japanese TAF special attack force, penetrated the screen and dropped a torpedo at the *Langley*. The *Massachusetts* shot her down in flames a short distance off the starboard bow. A second Jill met the same fate. A third, however, crashed into the fantail of the cruiser *Reno* (CL-96), causing a few casualties and minor damage. After refueling on the 15th, TF 38 sent searchers north, believing the Japanese fleet was at sea.

At 1600 on the 16th, scouts reported a carrier and battleships far to the north, but a night search found nothing. That day Captain Warlick told the crew, "Admiral Halsey has made a change in plans for our Task Force. This change has been brought about by the enemy's reaction to our sustained strikes on Formosa, or rather it has been brought about by the enemy's opinion of the effectiveness of his counterattacks upon us. . . . The enemy apparently believes that he has sunk 53 of our ships, including 17 carriers. As we all know, that is all the carriers we brought along. . . . Two cruisers have been torpedoed, and are being towed out of the battle area. They are escorted by cruisers, destroyers and a carrier. It will be surprising if these cruisers and their escorts do not suffer additional damage during their retirement. They have fought off all attacks for two days. In the meantime our striking power is undiminished. . . . Admiral Halsey has moved Task Force 38 to a position where he can make a flank attack upon any enemy surface force leaving Japan to attack that group."

Rear Admiral G. B. Davis hoisted his flag on the *Massachusetts* on 1 October 1944. Here he is inspecting a division. Note the dark trousers and caps of the crewmen. (U.S. Navy Cruise Book)

Air Battle off Formosa - A Japanese Perspective

"The Battle off Formosa," by Vice Admiral Shigeru Fukudome, from U.S. Naval Institute *Proceedings*, December 1952 (78/21/598)

Immediately prior to the Battle off Formosa, we had an air raid by American carrier forces on Okinawa on October 10. On the previous day, October 9, one of our long-range patrol planes had disappeared far to the east of Okinawa. Except for that incident, we did not have a single indication of the enemy's approach. The attack on Okinawa was, therefore, a complete surprise. To make matters worse, we had stationed no planes on Okinawa at the time. We had not been fully prepared for launching counterattacks from Kyushu either. Consequently, we could not help sitting by as spectators to what was going on in the Ryukyu Islands.

Judging from the circumstances of the Okinawa air raid, we believed that the enemy would soon attack Formosa. On the 11th, for the first time, our scouting planes were successful in discovering the enemy carrier groups. Convinced that a major enemy air raid would be launched upon Formosa early on the morning of the 12th, I ordered my forces to complete all the following measures during the 11th, thus to be made ready for the impending battle.

October 12th dawned quietly, but at 0810 hours a radar station on the east coast of Formosa detected a great formation of enemy planes. This was the first wave of the enemy attack. All of our fighters took off from their bases at once; one group circled above Takao and the other above Taihoku to wait for and counterattack the enemy.

Although I was thoroughly aware of the manifest inferiority of our airmen's military skill as compared with that of the enemy flyers, I was confident that, as far as the defensive fighting in the air over Formosa was concerned, the odds would be in our favor at a six-to-four ratio. My confidence was based on two facts: First, we were able to use simultaneously as many as 230 fighters, a number which would, in all probability, exceed the number of planes the enemy carrier task force could dispatch at one time; and secondly, we were able to take advantage of our defensive position for counterattacking the invaders on our home ground. I expected that the foregoing two points would surely work in our favor, and that, therefore, no matter how superior the enemy flyers might be to our own men in military skill, there was no fear of our losing the fight.

What actually happened, however, was utterly contrary to what I had expected. As I watched from my command post, a terrific aerial combat began directly above my head. Our interceptors swooped down in great force at the invading enemy planes. Our planes appeared to do so well that I thought I could desire no better performance. In a matter of moments, one after the other, planes were seen falling down, enveloped in flames. "Well done! Well done! A tremendous success!" I clapped my hands. Alas! to my sudden disappointment, a closer watch revealed that all those shot down were our fighters, and all those proudly circling above our heads were enemy planes! Our fighters were nothing but so many eggs thrown at the stone wall of the indomitable enemy formation. In a brief one-sided encounter, the combat terminated in our total defeat. Looking up at the enemy planes which continued their perfect formation intact throughout the combat, I could not help heaving a deep sigh. It was a total surprise to me to see that, while our planes caught fire the instant they were hit, enemy planes, though momentarily smoking, did not catch fire, presumably because of their perfected fire-preventing devices.

Since our interceptors could not put up any real resistance, the enemy went on ravaging to his heart's content and inflicted terrific damage to our ground installations through strafing and bombing.

Though the number of fighters we lost in the first waves of the enemy attack was only about one-third of our strength, the real effect was much severer than the mere number suggests, since among those lost were many of the leader-planes. Consequently, when the second wave of the enemy assault came, as few as between 60 to 70 of our fighters in the aggregate throughout Formosa took to the air to meet the enemy. Worse still, none of them could offer resistance of any value. Finally, when the third wave came, none of our fighters could take to the air. In the meantime, our forces based in Kyushu unleashed a daring offensive against the enemy at sea. The offensive was launched on the 12th by 101 planes of the Second Air Fleet, utilizing Okinawa as a relay base. The sortie was made in a large formation in broad daylight and claimed, though dubiously, that two enemy carriers had been hit by bombing, with some damage. With reinforcement from the Third Fleet carrier squadrons, we repeated daylight formation sorties with about 400 planes on the 14th and with about 170 planes on the 15th. But the last two-day sortie claimed no perceivable result, with most of the planes having failed to sight the target.

It was the TAF (specially trained poor-weather attack force) alone which was credited with giving an appreciable blow to enemy surface forces. Beginning with the night attack on the 13th, the typhoon-trained air unit conducted sneak attacks on three successive nights until the night of the 15th. Each night about 30 planes were used. Immediately after the Battle off Formosa, Japanese Imperial General Headquarters announced that 12 enemy ships—cruisers and above—had been sunk and another 23 enemy ships had been otherwise destroyed. Most of this result was credited to the TAF.

THE EVALUATION OF THE BATTLE RESULT

As we have seen, the announced result of the Battle off Formosa was originated from the report by the TAF, which, under the command of Captain Kuno, was then based in Kyushu, away from my personal direction, though, as the Second Air Fleet commander, I was officially responsible for it.

After the war ended in 1945, I was told that of the ships in the U.S. Fleet only two cruisers had sustained serious damage. Why on earth had such an exorbitant exaggeration been made in our report? Having been informed of the real damage, I was startled indeed at the great discrepancy, nor can we shrink from the responsibility for having made such a report.

The losses on our part were really great. Against the surface units of the enemy carrier task forces, we made 761 sorties in all, and lost 179 planes in these sorties. In addition, we lost about 150 planes in the air and on the ground in Formosa. The damage to the military installations was also very severe. My original confidence in our ability to fight out the battle with six-to-four odds in our favor was shattered. The battle was fought with nine-to-one odds in favor of the enemy.

The results achieved by air forces were always exaggerated by airmen. As I have explained elsewhere, the TAF was the cream of my fleet strength and had been trained for night attack. I was convinced that such a trained unit could achieve one-third of what they claimed.

As a matter of fact, however, the real result they had obtained was less than one-tenth of what they claimed. The exaggerated report caused the Imperial General Headquarters to commit, though temporarily, a mistake in its estimate of the war situation. It made the nation indulge in a false celebration and created the illusion that the Empire could turn the tide of the war.

For my part I ascertained through the reconnaissance planes' report on the 16th that the damage done to the enemy was slight, and I was convinced that a major invasion of the Philippines would soon be launched. As soon as the Battle off Formosa was over, I made all haste in preparations for our move to the Philippine theater.

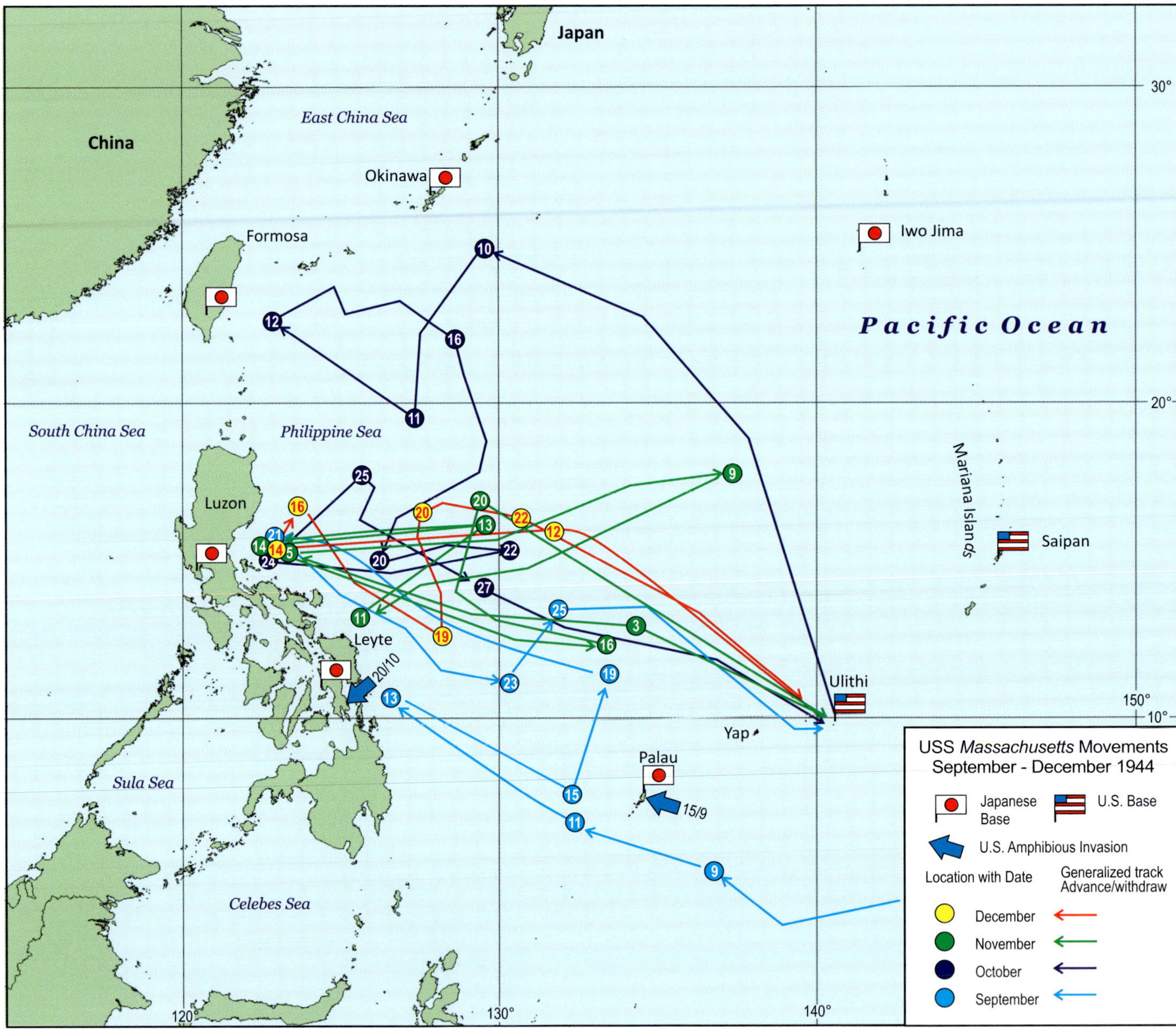

This chart shows the movements of the *Massachusetts* from September through December 1944. The major action during this period was the Battle of Leyte Gulf. The weblike density of the battleship's movements over a relatively short period stands as a testimony to the ability of the U.S. Navy to extract the most from its assets.

Although portions of TG 38 struck North Luzon and the Manila area over the next three days, the *Massachusetts* and TG 38.3 remained approximately 400 miles east of Manila, steaming in "strategic support of the Philippine Operations" and awaiting news that the Japanese fleet was at sea.

Four American divisions landed on Leyte on 20 October. TG 38.3 conducted air operations against the northern Visayas on the 21st, but generally it was careful to keep its bunkers topped and await developments. Early on 24 October reports arrived that as many as seven enemy battleships were approaching. TG 38.3's combat air patrol intercepted a Japanese air strike at 0755 that day, but at 0837 a second group penetrated the patrol and roughly 30 bogeys closed the task group. The light carrier *Princeton* was recovering aircraft. According to her report:

"The gasoline detail commenced fueling the planes which had just landed aboard. At 0912 the *Essex* had just reported a possible "bogey," together with a friendly plane . . . but there were no further reports by any ships of unidentified aircraft within a radius of about 25 miles of the formation." However, "At 0938 a single Japanese VB aircraft type 'Judy' was sighted by the *Princeton* lookouts diving on this vessel from out of the low cloud cover ahead of the ship. . . the enemy plane dropped a single bomb which scored a direct hit about 15 feet off the centerline to port."

At first the damage did not seem critical as the carrier returned to station and maintained speed, but in fact the bomb exploded between the main and second deck. The detonation ignited the fuel in six torpedo bombers in the hangar deck ("fitted with torpedoes and full auxiliary wing tanks in addition to

Smoke rises from an explosion in the *Princeton*'s hangar deck at 1000.5 hrs. on 24 October 1944, shortly after she was hit by a Japanese bomb while operating off the Philippines. (U.S. Navy)

The Battles of Leyte Gulf

[The Japanese plan] Sho-1 aspired to repulse the invasion of the Philippines by bringing the Imperial Navy's still-formidable surface action forces into contact with Kinkaid's amphibious units in Leyte Gulf. To execute this agenda, the Japanese reverted to the complicated tactics Spruance had anticipated at Philippine Sea. During the ensuing battle, U.S. forces referred to Japanese formations according to their relative positions. Northern Force, commanded by Vice Admiral Jisaburo Ozawa, consisted of the heavy carrier *Zuikaku*, three light carriers, two hybrid battleship-carriers, three cruisers, and eight destroyer types. Powerful as this force would appear from the air, it embarked only 116 planes. Its mission, expected to entail its annihilation, was to draw Halsey northward away from Leyte Gulf while two gunfire groups converged on Kinkaid. Center Force, the strongest Japanese formation, was commanded by Admiral Kurita. Composed of the superdreadnoughts *Musashi* and *Yamato*, three lesser battleships, 12 cruisers, and 15 destroyers, it would thrust through San Bernardino Strait to enter Leyte Gulf from the north. Southern Force was to transit Surigao Strait to enter the gulf from the south. It advanced in two echelons. The first, under Vice Admiral Shoji Nishimura, included two battleships, a cruiser, and four destroyers; the second, under Vice Admiral Kiyohide Shima, three cruisers and seven destroyers. Land-based naval aircraft in the Philippines were to support the operation

Early on 23 October submarines sighted and reported Center Force on its way toward the Philippines. The next morning U.S. air searches located Center Force and Southern Force, but, ironically, not Northern Force. While Kinkaid began concentrating his fighting ships at Surigao Strait, for which Southern Force was clearly bound, Halsey launched five strikes against Center Force as it pushed across the Sibuyan Sea. Although no Japanese ships were sunk in these attacks, the mighty *Musashi* sustained so many hits that she went down hours later, and at 1400 Halsey's pilots reported that Center Force had reversed course. In case it should double back, at 1512 Halsey issued a preparatory command detailing the composition of a battle line, Task Force 34, that, upon the order to execute, would be formed under Admiral Lee. Unfortunately, Admiral Kinkaid, whose communicators intercepted the signal, assumed that TF-34 had actually been called into being.

Throughout the day Halsey and the Third Fleet staff had puzzled over the apparent absence of carriers from the enemy order of battle. The mystery was solved around 1700, when they learned that aerial reconnaissance had discovered Northern Force off Cape Engano, the northeastern tip of Luzon, approximately 400 miles from Leyte Gulf. In contrast to the orders given Spruance before the invasion of the Marianas, which directed him only to "capture, occupy, and defend" specified islands, the operations plan issued to Halsey for Leyte included the stipulation that "In case opportunity for destruction of major portion of the enemy fleet offer [sic] or can be created, such destruction becomes primary task." At the moment, that opportunity seemed to beckon. For three hours Halsey and his staff considered their options. At 2000, convinced by aviators' reports that Center Force had been hurt too badly to inconvenience anyone, Halsey decided to take his entire force to attack the enemy carriers. The wording of the message announcing that decision left Kinkaid under the impression that TF-34 was guarding San Bernardino Strait.

Almost exactly three hours before Halsey began to move north, Kurita swung his Center Force back toward the east. Several U.S. air searches reported the Japanese advance between 1935 and 2320. This intelligence inspired some of Halsey's subordinates to conclude that Northern Force was indeed a decoy (a possibility his staff had weighed and rejected) and that part of TF-38 should remain behind to prevent Center Force from debouching through San Bernardino Strait.

An hour earlier, Nishimura had led Southern Force into Surigao Strait. Inside the strait, Kinkaid had extended a gauntlet of 39 patrol torpedo (PT) boats and 28 destroyers. Across its eastern exit, in position to cross the T of an enemy approaching from the west, he placed Seventh Fleet's six old, shore-

bombardment battleships—all but one veterans of Pearl Harbor—in a line flanked by eight cruisers. The issue was never in doubt. Both Nishimura's battleships and three of his destroyers were blown out of the water. Shima's echelon, following 40 miles astern, prudently retired. By 0430 on 25 October, the southern arm of the Japanese pincers had been eliminated by the mighty U.S. force.

The elation felt in Seventh Fleet over this victory was extinguished a little more than two hours later, when the pagoda masts of Center Force's battleships appeared on the horizon north of Rear Admiral Clifton F. Sprague's Taffy 3, one of three groups of escort carriers operating off Samar. One of the epic actions in naval history was about to unfold. While Sprague's six little 18-knot carriers made away at flank speed, chasing rain squalls and the towering, color-coded splashes of Japanese shells, aircraft arose from all three Taffies to harass the oncoming enemy, and the three destroyers and four destroyer escorts constituting Sprague's screen advanced with utmost gallantry to engage Kurita's battleships and cruisers. The small boys' attack threw the Japanese formation into confusion and disabled at least one cruiser. The Taffies' aircraft also scored, forcing three cruisers to drop out of the battle. Ultimately, however, it was inevitable that Center Force's superior speed and bigger guns would tell. By 0910 the *Gambler Bay* (CVE-73) had become the second carrier in the war to succumb to gunfire, the destroyer *Hoel* (DD-533) had also been sunk, and the destroyer *Johnston* (DD-557) and destroyer escort *Samuel B. Roberts* (DE-413) were sinking.

Throughout these desperate hours, Kinkaid bombarded Halsey with calls for help. Informing him of events in Surigao Strait in a message sent at 0412, Kinkaid had sought confirmation that TF-34 was covering San Bernardino Strait. Halsey, who had given the order to form TF-34 during his run north, did not receive this communication until 0648. Perplexed by Kinkaid's query, Halsey replied that TF-34 was with his carriers, "now engaging enemy carriers," against which Mitscher had begun launching an hour earlier. By the time his answer reached Kinkaid, Center Force was engaging Taffy 3. Halsey learned of the action under way off Samar from a signal received from Kinkaid at 0822 and followed eight minutes later by an urgent request for the fast battleships. To a vexed Halsey it seemed that Kinkaid's 18 escort carriers and six old battleships should be able to cope with Center Force. Furthermore, whatever damage Center Force could do would have been done long before the fast battleships could reach the scene. Nevertheless, at 0848 he ordered TG-38.1, which had been trying to overtake the battle from an opening position 600 miles east of the Philippines, to make "best possible speed" to strike Center Force. Kinkaid was not assuaged, and at about 1000 his appeals climaxed in an anguished, plain-language WHERE IS LEE X SEND LEE.

Within minutes, Halsey received an even more electrifying signal. Sent by Admiral Nimitz, with information copies to Kinkaid and King, it read: WHERE IS RPT WHERE IS TASK FORCE THIRTY-FOUR RR THE WORLD WONDERS.

Halsey ordered all six fast battleships and TG-38.2 to turn south. At that moment, only 42 miles separated Northern Force from TF-34's big guns. Mitscher was left to press the action with two carrier groups and a surface action group of four cruisers and ten destroyers.

The terrible irony was that, although it would not be evident for hours, by then the crisis off Samar had passed. At 0911 Kurita broke off the pursuit of Taffy 3, convinced that it was one of Halsey's task groups. Apparently, he intended merely to reform his force, disordered by the Taffies' counterattacks, but at 0945 a false report from naval headquarters in Manila inspired him to go looking for another U.S. carrier group supposedly located not far to the north. The phantom force eluded him, and, after a series of fruitless countermarches during which three heavily damaged cruisers went down, Kurita decided to withdraw. At 2140, Center Force reentered San Bernardino Strait. The van of TF-34 reached there at 0100, in time to sink a laggard destroyer.

ADAPTED FROM "... 50 YEARS AGO: LEYTE GULF," U.S. NAVAL INSTITUTE *PROCEEDINGS*, OCTOBER 1994

their normal gasoline load.") Failures in water pressure and the automatic sprinkler system allowed the fire to rage uninterrupted. Heavy black smoke entered the forward engine room, filling the space "to the point of suffocation and darkness."

The *Princeton* was the first carrier to be hit while under Big Mamie's protection. As she burned, enemy air attacks continued. At 1017 bombs from a Judy near missed the *Langley*. Other strikes at 1300 and 1510 inflicted no additional damage. The *Princeton*, however, was a lost cause. Secondary explosions also damaged the *Birmingham* (CL-62) and *Morrison* (DD-560), which had come alongside to remove personnel.

To the north, the Battle of the Visayna Sea was under way, which resulted in the loss to the Japanese of the large battleship *Musashi*. As the *Massachusetts*'s war diary noted, the commanders of TF 38, particularly Halsey, placed too much reliance on the overly optimistic reports of their airmen: "Preliminary reports indicated that our planes had done extensive damage to units of the Jap force in waters east of Mindoro Island."

Thus, when scouts finally spotted Japanese carriers acting as a decoy force to the north, and believing that the surface threat had been dealt with, Halsey collected his full available strength, which included the *Iowa*, *New Jersey*, *Washington*, *Massachusetts*, *South Dakota*, and *Alabama*, along with six cruisers led by Rear Admiral Whiting in the *Vincennes* (CL-64) and Desrons 50 and 52, and on 25 October TG 34.1 steamed north together to chase down this perceived threat.

The plain prose of the battleship's war diary captures best what happened next.

"While reports from our planes indicated that severe damage had been inflicted upon the portion of the Japanese Fleet to the north of us, other reports from Commander Seventh Fleet revealed that a considerable force of enemy ships had passed through San Bernardino Straits during the night and was attacking Seventh Fleet Forces in waters east of Samar Island." This unexpected

Coming into Ulithi Anchorage on 24 November 1944, during a break in operations off the Philippines. Photographed from the USS *Wasp*; Fleet Admiral Chester W. Nimitz has autographed the original print (U.S. Navy)

Liberty on the beach at Ulithi. On this day, at least, swimming and sunbathing seem to be the only activities under way. (U.S. Navy Cruise Book)

attack finally caused Halsey to order TG 38.2 and the battleships to turn south. It was too late even though he pushed ahead with his two 33-knot battleships and left the *Massachusetts* and her four 27-knot sisters to follow.

The only surface action that the mighty surface forces of the Third Fleet saw came when Whiting's Crudiv 14 caught the Japanese destroyer *Nowaki*, which was straggling after rescuing survivors from the Battle off Samar. The *Vincennes*, followed by the *Biloxi* (CL-80) and *Miami* (CL-89), annihilated her in five minutes. Whiting erroneously reported that the enemy vessel was a heavy cruiser of the *Aoba* or *Atago* class.

On 27 October the fast battleships rendezvoused with nine tankers and their attendant escort carriers. After that, the *Massachusetts*, in company with TG 38.3, headed for Ulithi. The first phase of the Philippine campaign was over. It was not particularly successful for Big Mamie as she had missed the long anticipated surface action, and in her only serious air action, one of the carriers in her care had been sunk.

The *Massachusetts* anchored in Ulithi on 1 November, but she did not stay long, being called to support TG 38.1 as it hit targets on northern Luzon from the 4th through the 6th. This group consisted of the *Wasp* (CV-18), *Hornet*, *Cowpens*, *Monterey*, *Massachusetts*, *Alabama*, three cruisers, and Desrons 61 and 46. There was a submarine scare on the 5th. Also on that day a kamikaze crashed the *Lexington* of TG 38.3; she was still able to maintain her place in formation.

An approaching typhoon caused the task force to break off operations on the 8th and head north. On the 11th, however, TG 38.1 was back on the line, hitting Ormoc Bay through which the Japanese were reinforcing Leyte. The *Massachusetts* and her group kept a fueling rendezvous on the 12th, followed by two more days of air strikes in the central Philippines.

In the early morning of 19 November an Emily got near enough for the *Massachusetts* to engage the aircraft with her 5-inch battery. The plane veered away, and a night fighter finally splashed it. This was the last day in the task group's offensive against the central Philippines. On the way back to Ulithi, the *Massachusetts* and *Alabama* exercised their main batteries by taking turns firing on each other's wakes. The *Massachusetts* spent the rest of November at anchor.

On 1 December the *Massachusetts* got under way as part of Task Group 38.1: the *Yorktown* (flagship of Rear Admiral A. E. Montgomery), *Wasp*, *Langley*, *Cowpens*, *Massachusetts* (flagship of Rear Admiral G. B. Davis), *Alabama*, Crudiv 6 with four cruisers, and Desron 53, but she immediately lost a propeller shaft due to a hot spring bearing. Her men fixed this

Halsey's Typhoon

The sea was anything but pacific when I stepped on the *Nehenta Bay*'s (CVE-74) bridge to take over the watch again at 0800. Never before had I seen a day like that one. Mountains of angry water rushed against one another, surging and writhing together. Masses of water, unbelievable in size, hurled themselves at the ship, tossing it about like an autumn leaf in the wind. The water boiled, and from the top of every wave, the full gale, which was howling so that one had to shout to be heard, blew sheets of spray to mingle with the rain and thick mist that hung low on the water. Visibility had dropped to a few hundred yards.

Soon after this watch began it was apparent that we'd been overtaken by a typhoon—the most dreaded force in the Pacific. Already, all plans for completing the refueling had been abandoned, as had any thought of launching any aircraft, though we were close to some of Japan's most powerful airbases. Controlling the ships themselves had become the principal consideration on the bridges of all vessels in the area, of which there must have a hundred.

The barometer, 29.40 at 0900, was steadily dropping; every quarter-hour check showed it lower. The wind was now a steady 60 knots, with gusts up to 75. The waves, where they could be distinguished through the shroud of mist, were rising to 40 and 50 feet. As they took the ship from behind, running up under her, they lifted the screws clear of the water and flung the carrier head down into the churning trough.

Soon . . . we were alone. We could see nothing but the pall of the mist and the savage anger of the sea. The latter was now lashed into such a fury of foam that the blown spume across the ragged shapes of the waves looked like the streaked drifting of blizzard-driven snow. The barometer was down to 29.20 and still tumbling. (It would reach 29.12 before I left the bridge that day.) The wind was causing the arrow on the gauge to hit the top—80 knots—and quiver there, and its sound had become a penetrating shriek that rose by piercing octaves. A man could not stand against that wind. The crew on the flight deck, striving desperately to lash down those of our aircraft that we had not been able to take below, lay on the deck and clung to lines like men in the tide of a wave, and where the driven spray struck the face or other uncovered skin, it stung like needles.

The feeling on the bridge was tense as we stood peering ahead and seeing less than our own ship's length through the thick mist that swirled and eddied around us. Every man was walled off from the others about him by the roar of the tempest; each was thinking his own thoughts and seeing his fears reflected in the taut faces of the others.

One could see that the ship could not hold together if we continued much longer as we were going. She was shaking all over with each rush into the trough of the sea. Already, seams were opening. One in the side plating on the hangar deck had given way, fortunately well above the waterline. Another opened in the deck on the fantail, over which green sea water was pouring. The men in the steering engine room, just below the latter, were calling for a bucket brigade to help them bail.

The ship had to be brought into the wind and held there with only enough speed to maintain steering control. Word was passed to all hands by means of the public announcing system that we were to come about. No one had to be told what to expect when the ship came broadside to a sea like that.

The ship's skipper had taken the con, and he now gave the order to the helmsman. Slowly, the ship began to swing into the wind. Every man clung to his support until his knuckles were white. For several long minutes, the tension lasted while nothing particularly remarkable happened. Then, suddenly, as though the sea had only just observed that we had put ourselves in its grasp, an enormous wave coming up on the quarter picked up the ship as a puppy picks up an old shoe. Lifting us aloft so that the screws, free of the water, caused the ship to vibrate to its keel, the wave threw us crashing into the teeth of

a crosswave toward our starboard bow. Down went the bow, engulfed in green seawater, as the ship shuddered and we held our breaths, clinging to our supports until our arms ached.

For agonizing seconds, the ship lay on her side. Twenty feet above the flight deck, those of us on the bridge, feeling the full effect of the roll, waited with something tight about our hearts, seriously wondering whether the ship would right itself. Finally, hesitantly at first and then more surely, the uproll began. Then came the list in the other direction, seldom so bad as that to starboard because of the weight of the carrier's island. Then down again to starboard, as another wall of water struck the bow and a shiver went through the ship, but she did not go down so far this time. Over again to port and back to starboard, shuddering and quaking so that her groans and the grinding of steel on steel could be heard even over the howl of the gale.

Slowly, however, the *Nehenta Bay* was coming about. The ship, nevertheless, was in irons, locked in the teeth of the typhoon. We had full control of engines and rudder, yet from that moment until the storm began to abate, she was out of our control.

Then, to turn terror into near-panic, reports began to come up from radar plot of ships about us. Suddenly there were vessels on all sides coming toward us. One went by to starboard only a half-mile away. That's too close for comfort with heavy ships in low visibility. Almost immediately another went by to port, even closer this time. Then there were ships ahead coming directly toward us. We lay there in irons, unable to maneuver, as radar plot reported minute by minute.

"Ship, dead ahead, 800 yards, closing."

It was now apparent that, in coming about into the wind, we had turned directly into the path of Task Force 38 steaming downwind before the storm. We were surrounded by ships in all directions.

"Ship, dead ahead, 600 yards, closing."

There, slightly off the port bow, a battleship loomed through the mist only a few hundred yards ahead.

ADAPTED FROM "BATTLING THE PACIFIC'S MOST DEADLY FORCE," *NAVAL HISTORY*, OCTOBER 2008

The bow of the *Massachusetts* pushing through green seas during a Pacific typhoon (U.S. Navy Cruise Book)

problem at sea, but the battleship returned to Ulithi on 2 December nonetheless. She did not return to action until 10 December. After several days of exercises, TG 38.1 approached Luzon on the 14th and launched a series of attacks that continued through the 17th. The Japanese did not retaliate to these strikes. On 18 December another typhoon struck the fleet, making it impossible to refuel. The *Massachusetts* diary gives only a dry taste of what it must have been like: "By 0800 visibility was limited to a few hundred yards and the storm had increased to such proportions that some of the ships began to report personnel lost over the side and the sustaining of material damage. At 0912 the *Monterey* reported all the planes on her hangar deck to be on fire and the loss of a gun director. Shortly thereafter she reported loss of steering control and that she was dead in the water." The *Cowpens* also suffered a fire on her hangar deck. She dropped out of formation. "At 1030 an unidentified ship was detected by radar drifting through the formation. Avoiding action was taken, and at 1035 a CVE, apparently dead in the water was sighted about 500 yards off the starboard bow. An unsuccessful effort was made to communicate with the ship, later identified as *Rudyard Bay* (CVE-81)."

Conditions improved that afternoon and on the 19th fueling commenced. However, the storm had overwhelmed the *Hull* (DD-350), *Spence* (DD-512), and *Monaghan* (DD-354). Four light carriers, one light cruiser, and ten destroyers suffered significant damage. As the cripples headed out for Ulithi the fleet turned toward Luzon for more strike operations, steaming back through the same storm-churned waters looking for survivors. However, as the *Massachusetts*'s diary commented, "apparently the course followed toward tomorrow's strike position is taking the Task Force closer to the typhoon and into heavy swells resulting from it." Shortly after midnight on the 21st Halsey canceled the strike, and the fleet sought safer waters to the south. That morning one of the *Massachusetts*'s destroyers picked up 13 survivors from the *Hull*, "all in good condition with the exception of one man who had been bitten by a shark." TG 38.1 met the tankers on the 22nd and conducted exercises on the 23rd and 24th as it continued south toward Ulithi. The *Massachusetts* docked on Christmas Eve and remained in port provisioning and repairing the dings and bangs incurred by continuous operations and violent weather.

She was under way again on the 31st, however, and almost immediately suffered a casualty when a leak in the main condenser caused the boilers to begin salting. The *Massachusetts* dropped out of formation to correct the defect, accompanied by the *Maddox* (DD-731) and *Taussig* (DD-746). She locked No. 3 shaft at 1844 and started repairs. Thus passed New Year's Eve on the battleship.

Murderers' Row: Third Fleet aircraft carriers at anchor in Ulithi Atoll, 8 December 1944, during a break from operations in the Philippines area. The carriers are (from front to back): the *Wasp*, *Yorktown*, *Hornet*, *Hancock* (CV-19), and *Ticonderoga* (CV-14). The *Wasp*, *Yorktown*, and *Ticonderoga* are all painted in camouflage Measure 33, Design 10a. (U.S. Navy)

ASIA AND THE HOME ISLANDS:

January–August 1945

NEW YEAR'S DAY 1945 FOUND THE *MASSACHUSETTS* STEAMING FROM ULITHI toward Formosa with Task Group 38.1: the carriers *Yorktown* (flagship of Rear Admiral A. W. Radford), *Wasp*, *Cabot*, and *Cowpens*; Batdiv 8 with the *Massachusetts* (flagship of Rear Admiral J. F. Shafroth Jr.) and *South Dakota*; Crudivs 6 and 10; and two destroyer squadrons. After taking on 204,758 gallons of fuel on 2 January, the *Massachusetts* screened the carriers as they began launching fighters on the 3rd. Squally weather and a low ceiling, however, forced cancellation of bomber operations that day and the next. TF 38 then turned south to hammer airfields in Northern Luzon. These raids continued throughout the 6th and 7th as Formosa remained socked in. On the 8th the *Massachusetts* refueled. Standing by the carriers was thirsty work, although she was dispensing oil to destroyers nearly every day herself.

Japanese ships aflame near Kamranh Bay, French Indochina, 21 January 1945, after being attacked by planes of the USS *Wasp* (U.S. Navy)

The carriers finally were able to hit Formosa on 9 January. On the 11th TF 38 began a high-speed run south toward Kamranh Bay (Cam Ranh Bay) in French Indochina. Captain Warlick told the crew: "As you all know, we have now entered the South China Sea. This is a step of tremendous importance in advancing the war. It is of greater importance, for example, than the first raid on Truk and Saipan." He went on to explain how sea power was the control of maritime lines of communication and how by the fleet's advance, Japan's routes to the resource-rich areas of the south would be cut. "In a sense we may consider that the Navy's objective in crossing the Pacific Ocean has been to arrive at this goal. . . . Tomorrow morning we will be in a position to strike at the dense shipping which skirts the coast of Indochina, carrying the riches of the Indies to Japan. In the next few days we shall destroy the seaborne trade of Japan from Saigon to Hongkong."

The Americans hoped to confront the Japanese carrier-battleships *Ise* and *Hyuga*. The fast battleships gathered to take them on, but the Japanese had no interest in fighting the American battle line with a couple of hybrids, and a surface battle did not materialize. TF 38's bombers, however, caught three convoys at sea and sank nine escorts, seven tankers, and four cargo ships. They dispatched another nine vessels

A dramatic image of the *Massachusetts* pushing through heavy seas, taken from one of her escorting destroyers. A light carrier is visible beyond her. (U.S. Navy Cruise Book)

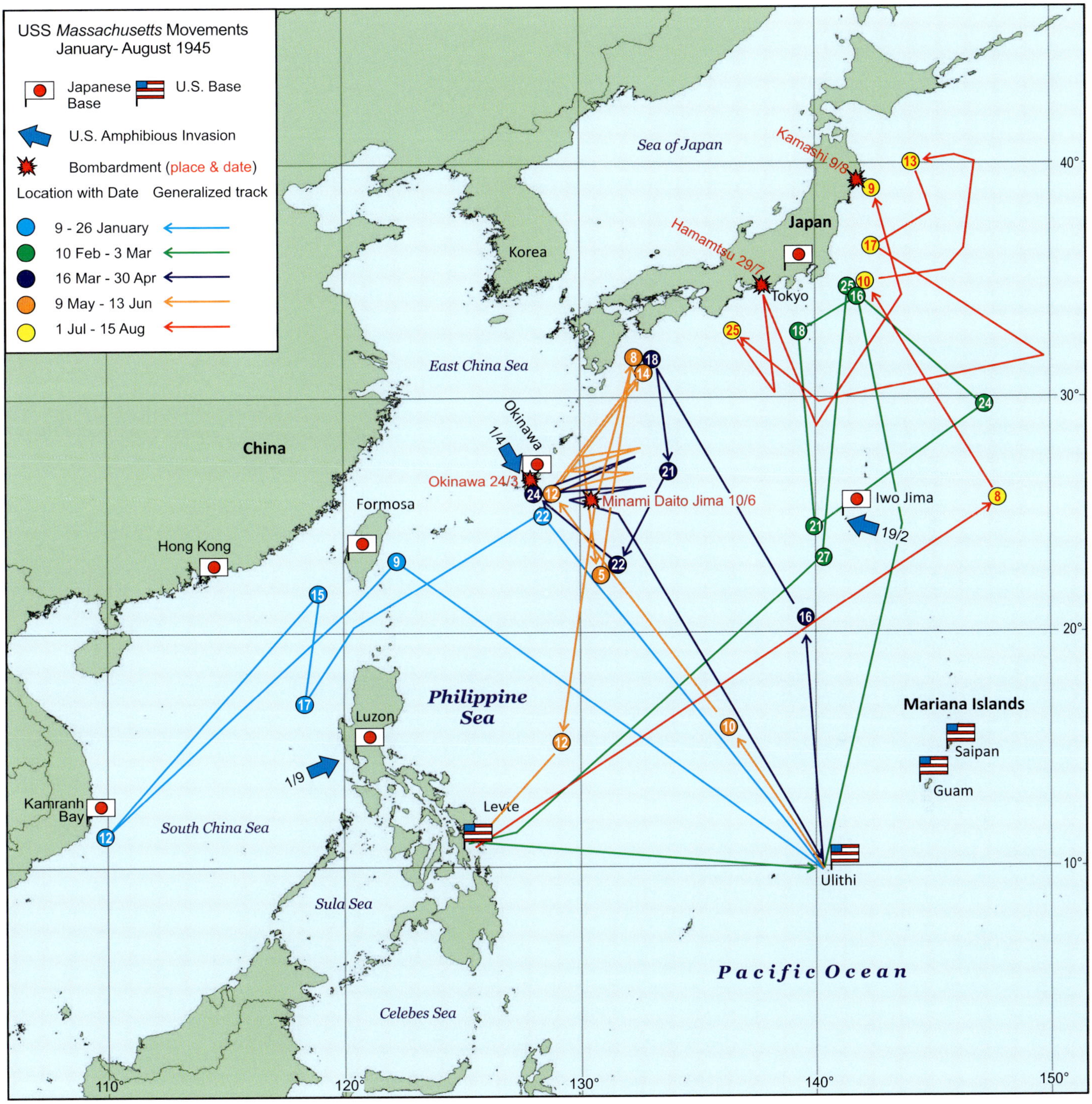

This chart shows the movements of the *Massachusetts* from 9 January 1945 when she departed Ulithi to support aerial strikes against Formosa to the end of the war. During these months she rampaged over a massive area extending 40° of longitude from west to east and 30° north to south supporting the strikes of the fast carries, conducting four bombardments and supporting three landings.

in port. The French light cruiser *Lamotte-Picquet* was swept up in the carnage and sent to the bottom as well. TF 38 then retired unscratched. As it withdrew north it struck Hong Kong, Amoy, and the Swatow area of southern China along the way on 15 and 16 January.

On 17 January the fleet experienced heavy swells off Luzon. Fueling operations had to be suspended, and the weather damaged several destroyers. After conditions improved the 3rd Fleet debouched into the Philippine Sea on the 20th. That day the Japanese made several air attacks, and for the first time in 1945 the *Massachusetts* fired her 5-inch, 40-mm, and 20-mm weapons on a single aircraft that had the temerity to approach her starboard bow. As the fleet launched strikes against Formosa on the 21st, the *Massachusetts* observed Japanese aircraft attacking other units, but no targets approached within range of her guns.

On 26 January the *Massachusetts* entered Ulithi and anchored. She took on supplies, repaired her main injection valve grid, and granted such liberty as the atoll's slender attractions could offer.

On 10 February the *Massachusetts* was under way as part of TG 58.1, heading north to support the landings on Iwo Jima. Once again Captain Warlick addressed his men. He explained that the Philippine campaign was over for the *Massachusetts* and that they were returning to the Central Pacific Campaign. "We are now en route to our usual task of paving the way. Where the landing will be will become clear in a few days."

On 16 February TG 58 began launching fighters for a predawn sweep over airfields in the Tokyo-Yokohama area. This was the first U.S. carrier air strike on Japan's capital since the Doolittle Raid in April 1942. Dive and torpedo bombers followed. At 0710 the *Massachusetts* detected an enemy picket boat 15,000 yards away. This proved to be *Patrol Craft 36*, which the destroyer *Haynesworth* (DD-700) dispatched expending 292 rounds in the process. The *Haynesworth* then took care of the picket boat *Wafu Maru* and rescued 11 survivors. No enemy aircraft approached within 25,000 yards of the battleship. The Americans repeated their strikes the next day and then set course for Iwo Jima to help soften up that island. Those strikes occurred over 20 and 21 February. Japanese aircraft attacked elements of TF 58 but kept clear of the *Massachusetts*.

On 23 February the *Massachusetts* bunkered 279,755 gallons of fuel oil and then, following exercises, she turned north for another go at Tokyo. The carriers launched strikes on the 25th, but heavy snow in the target area minimized their effectiveness. The task group headed toward Kobe, but the weather was bad there as well. The ships retired south having accomplished little in their second attack against the Japanese Home Islands.

The first of March saw TG 58.1, now consisting of the *Hornet*, *Wasp*, *Bennington* (CV-20), and *Belleau Wood* with Batdiv 8, the *Massachusetts* and *Indiana*; the cruisers *Vincennes*, *Miami*, and *San Juan*; and Desrons

Few images capture the might and power of the late-war U.S. Navy better than this one of the fleet at anchor in Ulithi (U.S. Naval Institute Photo Archive)

Boxing match held while under way. Boxing was probably the most popular spectator sport in the fleet. (U.S. Navy Cruise Book)

A carrier pilot successfully plucked from the sea by a *Massachusetts* SOC. (U.S. Navy Cruise Book)

The USS *Haynesworth* (DD-700), a *Sumner*–class destroyer, joined the 3rd/5th Fleet at Ulithi in December 1944 and was one of the *Massachusetts*'s regular escorts for the next three months. (U.S. Navy)

The *Massachusetts* under way with Task Force 58.1 on 12 February 1945, en route to raid Tokyo. Ships of Task Group 58.3 are in the background. (U.S. Navy)

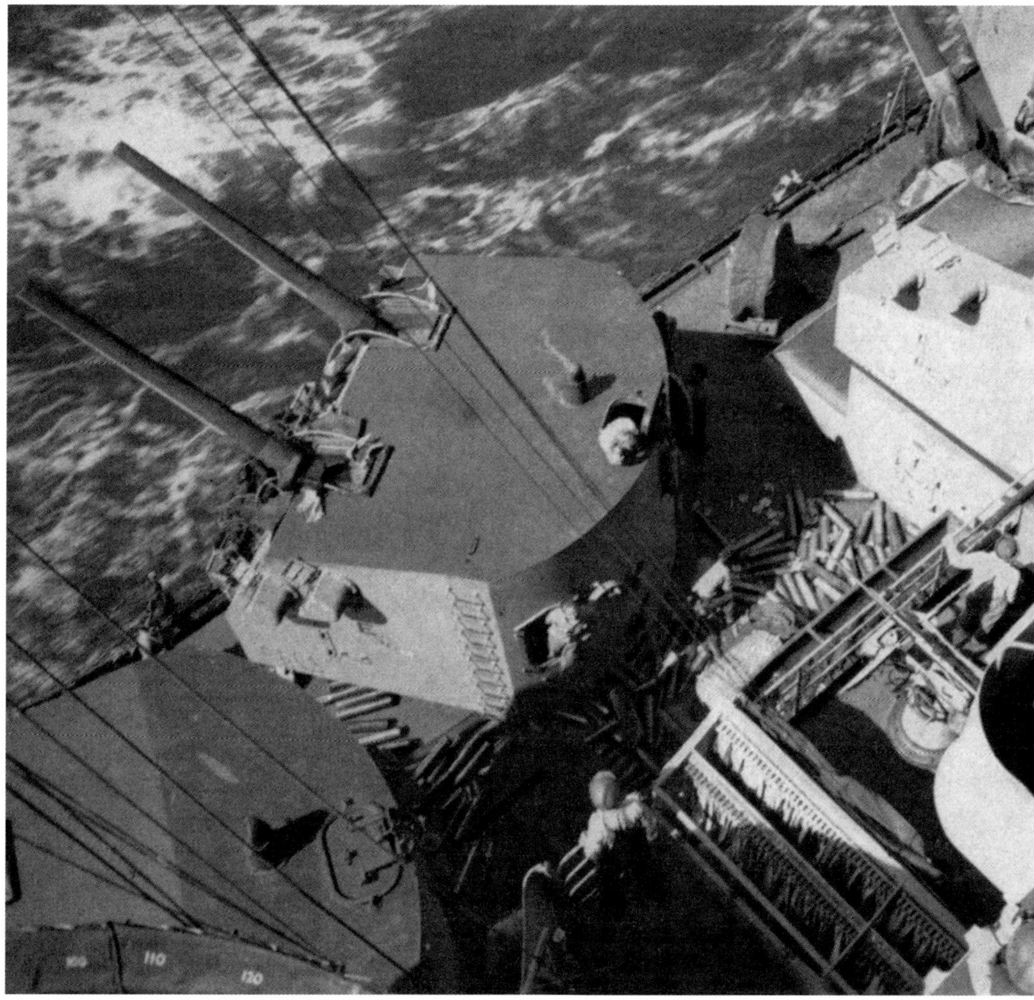

A 5-inch mount with ejected shell casings littering the deck around it. Firing in full automatic a 2-gun mount could generate 40 such casings in just a minute. (U.S. Navy Cruise Book)

61 and 25 launching air strikes on Okinawa—the relentless American offensive's next target. On the 1st a *Massachusetts* Kingfisher rescued a *Bennington* pilot who had splashed southwest of Okinawa.

On the 3rd, during the return to Ulithi, the battle line formed to practice surface warfare evolutions. The mighty force included eight fast battleships, eight cruisers, and nine destroyer divisions. The big ships improved their gunnery skills as the destroyers simulated torpedo attacks. On 16 March, after a quick turnaround in Ulithi, the *Massachusetts* was again a member of TG 58.1, with much the same organization as during the strikes off Tokyo. Just before dawn on 18 March, when TG 58.1 was 240 miles east of Kyushu, Japanese aircraft attacked. This was the largest air raid the *Massachusetts* had experienced in months. One plane buzzed the battleship, and Big Mamie damaged another that crossed her stern heading for the *Wasp*. This Nell crashed just 50 yards short of the big carrier. At 0725 the *Massachusetts* shot down another dive bomber that was after the *Hornet*. During that day the carriers struck Japanese facilities on Kyushu. At 1311 the *Massachusetts* shot down another aircraft attacking the *Hornet*. Her Kingfishers also plunked a downed USS *Franklin* (CV-13) pilot from the drink. In her final action, the *Massachusetts* fired on a group of bogies at 2226 and saw one aircraft burst into flames and crash 8,000 yards off her port quarter.

The next day, 19 March, was just as frantic. The battleship engaged enemy night bombers at 0418. At 0708 "an enemy plane dove out of the clouds and dropped a bomb which hit the *Wasp*. . . . This ship took the enemy plane, a Judy, under fire but was not able to destroy it." The bomb penetrated the flight deck amidships and the hangar deck and exploded after passing through the second deck, blowing a 16-by-24-foot hole in the second deck and a 19-by-22-foot hole in the third deck. Two aircraft were destroyed and 30 damaged, and 102 men died, but the carrier was back in action within an hour. However, on this strike TF 58

Taken from the USS *Wasp*, a Japanese aircraft literally dropping from the sky. The flash of antiaircraft fire can be seen from the battleship on the lower right-hand corner of the photograph. (U.S. Navy Fold 3); (inset) The USS *Wasp* at the moment she was hit by a Japanese bomber. (U.S. Navy Fold 3)

Okinawa

The World War II battle for Okinawa is unique in the annals of warfare. For it was there in the spring of 1945 that one nation attempted to annihilate the sea and air forces of her enemies by the almost exclusive use of suicide attacks. For 82 days the battle raged. For 82 days the finest young men of Japan flew off to certain death in the skies and waters about Okinawa. And for 82 days the officers and men of the U. S. Navy fought savagely and brilliantly to fend them off. It is a fact that the kamikazes left their mark; it is also a fact that they could not dislodge the "fleet that came to stay."

Okinawa is the largest, most populous island in the Nansei Shoto (Ryukyu) chain. Situated only 350 miles from industrial Kyushu, 845 miles from Tokyo, and 1,210 miles from U.S. B-29 bases on Saipan, it offered numerous sites for airfields from which almost any type of plane could operate. It also provided several excellent naval anchorages, and its possession by the Allies would lead to the severance of Japanese communications with Formosa, Korea, and the Chinese mainland. But Okinawa's greatest importance stemmed from the fact, well understood by the Japanese, that it would provide the necessary staging area for the planned invasion of Japan.

The desperate situation which would threaten the Japanese if the U.S. assault on Okinawa were successful stimulated them to their greatest and most fanatical effort. One hundred twenty thousand men stood ready to defend the island, with every possible plane, and the remnants of the Imperial Fleet. Allied forces, under the command of Admiral Raymond A. Spruance, USN, consisted of 548,000 men of the Army, Navy, and Marine Corps, 339 combatant ships (including 21 units of the British Pacific Fleet), and 1,139 auxiliary vessels. Of the Okinawa operation Fleet Admiral E. J. King wrote, "from any standpoint [it] was the most difficult ever undertaken by our forces in the Pacific." The Japanese were convinced that suicide attacks were the only means at their command which might prove effective against U.S. ships. But in order to understand the reasons behind this belief, it is necessary to go back six months to October 1944, and the Battle for Leyte Gulf. At that time the odds were tremendously against Japan. Her early supremacy, based on control of the sea, had long since waned. In June 1944, in the Battle of the Philippine Sea, the Japanese fleet had suffered an overwhelming defeat. Japan's only offensive resources were her land-based air fleets, whose pilots were pitifully inexperienced, and the fire power of her surface ships, which lacked the support of carrier planes. Everyone was aware that it would take a miracle to save the empire from disaster. It was becoming apparent that neither surface, carrier, bomber, nor submarine forces could perform that miracle.

An entry dated 18 October 1944, in the personal diary of Admiral Kimpei Teraoka (at that time Commander, First Air Fleet) summed up the Japanese feeling.

"We can no longer (resist) by adhering to conventional methods of warfare. . . . Instead, we must steel ourselves against weakness. . . . If fighter pilots set an example by volunteering for special attack missions, other units will follow suit. These examples will, in turn, inspire surface and army forces. . . . We conclude that the enemy can be stopped and our country saved only by crash-dive attacks on their ships."

On 25 October the Japanese were able to compare the relative effectiveness of conventional and suicide attacks; for on that day 93 fighters and 57 bombers inflicted no damage, while six kamikazes scored hits on three escort carriers. During the first three months of their operation, the kamikazes scored 121 hits and 53 damaging near-misses. The superiority of special attacks was manifest, and the Japanese belief was proven true. These early reports of kamikaze success caught the fancy of military leaders and the public—and the craze was on.

The USS *Bunker Hill* on fire after being crashed by a kamikaze aircraft off Okinawa on 11 May 1945. The USS *The Sullivans* (DD-537) is in the foreground. She closed the carrier and rescued 166 men forced over the side by the fire. (U.S. Naval Institute Photo Archive)

The first major action of the Okinawa campaign occurred between 18–21 March 1945, when the 82 ships of Task Force 58 carried out air strikes against Kyushu airfields and fleet units at Kure and Kobe. Five hundred twenty-eight enemy planes were destroyed; 16 enemy surface craft were damaged; and scores of hangars, factories, and warehouses were destroyed or damaged at a total cost of 116 American planes. This attack resulted in the Japanese being unable to mount any strong air attack against our forces for almost a week after the initial landings on Okinawa.

On 1April the assault troops landed over the Hagushi beaches and drove toward Yontan and Kadena airfields. On 6 and 7 April the divine wind struck with all the fury of an empire on the brink of disaster. In this first of nine general kamikaze attacks, 355 special attack planes, accompanied by almost as many conventional fighters and reconnaissance planes, bore down on Okinawa. In the two days of vicious battle, 22 kamikazes succeeded in crashing ships. Total Japanese losses are unknown, but it is estimated that nearly 300 were stopped at the picket line; and of this number it is estimated that 275 fell victim to Navy carrier pilots. But U.S. forces were not unscathed. Two destroyers, one high-speed minesweeper, and one LST went to the bottom; while 11 destroyers, one high-speed minesweeper, three escort vessels, three minesweepers, and the aircraft carrier *Hancock* were damaged.

During the next two months the U. S. Navy absorbed a pounding unlike any it had ever experienced. The divine wind struck no fewer than eight more times in general attacks; but after each onslaught the Navy buried its dead, cared for its wounded, replaced its sunken and battered ships, and rose to fight again.

By 10 June the battle was all but over, and the fast carriers set their course for Leyte Gulf. On June 21, 1945, 82 days after the initial landings, organized resistance came to an end, and the Island was declared secured.

EXTRACTED FROM "DIVINE WIND OVER OKINAWA," U.S. NAVAL INSTITUTE *PROCEEDINGS*, JUNE 1957

A formation of Curtiss SB2C Helldivers flying in formation. By 1944 they had replaced the SBD Dauntless in front-line units. (U.S. Navy Cruise Book)

suffered more damage than in any other attack during the war to date, inasmuch as the *Enterprise* and *Yorktown* also were hit by bombs and a kamikaze crashed the *Intrepid*. The *Franklin*, however, was roughed up worst of all. Two bombs struck her, and explosions ignited huge fires. Only heroic damage control saved the ship. The *Santa Fe* (CL-60) and *Hickox* (DD-673) suffered damage when they were alongside helping to fight the fires. The *Pittsburgh* (CA-72) towed her south at 6 knots, and the fleet stayed in company despite the danger to all. But the Japanese were only able to mount one more small attack several hours after dark. A large group of Bettys tried to attack on the 21st; American fighters intercepted and claimed the destruction of 26 bombers and 11 fighters. No enemy aircraft got within 10,000 yards of an American ship. The *Massachusetts*, however, did suffer a freak accident. At 2010, while making a sharp turn, a large wave broke over the stern and knocked the Kingfisher on the port catapult onto the deck, damaging it beyond repair.

While the crippled and damaged ships withdrew to Ulithi, TF 58 reorganized into three groups. FG 58.1 lost the *Wasp* but gained the *San Jacinto* (CVL-30), and on 23 March the fleet was back in action attacking Okinawa. The next day eight fast battleships bombarded shore installations. The *Massachusetts* opened fire at 0943 but left the line after three hours to recover her spotter aircraft. When the plane touched water a float collapsed and the aircraft nosed over. A destroyer rescued the pilot and radioman.

Following the bombardment, the crew was anxious to see the object of the ship's anger. One crewman recalled, "Nothing was firing back at us. We were experiencing no difficulties. We were practically dead in the water. We had been pounding them for some time with our 16-inch guns and we secured from general quarters. Well, everybody wanted to go and see the island. See what we'd been doing. So everybody rushed topside and were on the starboard side looking out over the island and the ship started to roll a bit and all of a sudden the 16-inch guns which had been heading out toward the island were heading closer and closer to the water. And they had to call general quarters again to right the ship. Two thousand men on one side, plus the guns, of course, were out that way too. That struck me as pretty funny."

Operations off Okinawa continued until the 28th when TF 58 took another swing north to hit Kyushu on the 29th. This time the fast carriers did not linger, beginning their retirement south at noon that day. Air strikes against Okinawa resumed on the 31st.

The landings on Okinawa occurred on 1 April. The *Massachusetts* was still part of TG 58.1, which consisted of the *Hornet*, *Bennington*, *Belleau Wood*, *San Jacinto*, Batdiv 8, Crudivs 10 and 14, and Desrons 61 and 25. Air operations continued through the 6th, with the *Massachusetts* firing one time on the 2nd at an enemy aircraft that buzzed the fleet before dawn. On the 6th a kamikaze missed the *Bennington*. The *Massachusetts* shot down a Zeke trying to attack the *Vincennes* and

later another attacking the *San Jacinto*. No ships in TG 58.1 were damaged that day. On the 7th TG 58 spent its full strength attacking the *Yamato*, which had sortied from the north. The giant battleship absorbed terrific punishment but finally succumbed to at least 6 bombs and 11 torpedoes delivered by 380 carrier-borne aircraft.

On 8 April, in a demonstration of the ever-improving efficiency and scope of the U.S. Navy's underway replenishment capabilities, the *Massachusetts* took on 14 16-inch projectiles, 440 5-inch projectiles, and 464,795 gallons of fuel oil while under way. The next day she returned to the operational area, defending the carriers.

On 12 April TG 58.1 shot down two Zekes that tried to crash the *Indiana*. On the 13th a *Massachusetts* Kingfisher rescued another pilot. Despite a warning to expect heavy air attacks, none developed. On the 14th, however, Japanese aircraft broke through the fighter cover and one Zeke was shot down near the *Indiana* and another astern of the *Bennington*. No ships were damaged. There was another heavy air attack on the 16th. Lookouts on the battleship could observe fighters engaging Japanese aircraft 12 to 15 miles from the formation. Then several broke through. At 1201 an aircraft dove on the *San Jacinto* but broke off after the *Massachusetts*'s guns filled the skies around it with steel. Another Zeke drove on the *Massachusetts* at 1400 but was destroyed by fighters. It fell into the water 6,000 yards away.

On the 17th the *Massachusetts* took on 3,232 40-mm rounds, 58 16-inch rounds, and 532 5-inch rounds, along with 926,252 gallons of fuel oil. She continued to support operations ashore as part of TG 58.1, refueling destroyers every day and taking on more fuel and ammunition herself on the 22nd. There was a submarine scare on the 25th, an event that had become rare. She received more fuel and ammunition on the 27th. Finally, on 28 April, after nearly six weeks of sustained operations, the *Massachusetts* turned south for Ulthi, anchoring there on 30 April.

On 2 May there was another change of command ceremony as Captain John R. Redman relieved Captain Warlick. Redman had served as the communications officer on the staff of Admiral Chester Nimitz. The stopover in Ulthi was relatively brief. On 9 May the

On 2 May 1945, the last wartime captain of the *Massachusetts*, John R. Redman, replaces Captain Warlick. Redman had been the communications officer on the staff of Admiral Chester Nimitz. Rear Admiral J. F. Shafroth is on the left. (U.S. Navy Cruise Book)

Massachusetts was under way as flagship of Rear Admiral Shafroth and Task Unit 58.1.5, with the *Indiana*, *Alabama*, six cruisers, and three destroyer divisions. On 12 May Captain Redman addressed his crew. He told them the war was progressing well, but new challenges awaited as TF 58 headed north to seek strategic targets on Japanese soil. He also warned of new threats, such as the Baka bomb, a manned bomb dropped from a Betty and guided to its target by a suicide pilot.

On the next day, TF 58.1, which the *Massachusetts* had rejoined, was launching attacks on airfields in Kyushu. These had proved to be dangerous waters. On the 14th the battleship's antiaircraft batteries helped down three attackers that had penetrated the screen, including one that had targeted the battleship. On the 16th the *Massachusetts*'s Kingfisher rescued a downed carrier pilot. By the 17th TG 58.1 was off Okinawa again, supporting operations there. By this time the battleship's Kingfishers were accompanying fighter strikes so as to be at hand should rescues be required. This activity continued through 26 May with periodic refueling breaks. During this time Japanese air strikes failed to damage any ships in TG 58.1; in fact, attacks were fairly rare, with the *Massachusetts* only using her guns on the 25th.

On 28 May Vice Admiral Spruance hauled down his flag and Admiral Halsey took command, TF 58 becoming TF 38. The *Massachusetts* continued with TG 38.1, essentially the same formation as on 1 April. TG 38.1 continued to operate off Okinawa through the first days of June. The routine was interrupted on 4 June when, in the midst of refueling, orders came to retire southeast by south to avoid a typhoon reported to be southwest of the force. As the battleship's diary

A Japanese Betty twin-engine bomber rigged to carry a Baka manned rocket-propelled bomb. This weapon was first used off Okinawa but as fearsome as the weapon seemed, it accounted for relatively few U.S. ships. In its first operational use on 21 March 1945, the 16 carrier Bettys were all shot down before they could release their Bakas within the required 25 miles of a target. (U.S. Naval Institute Photo Archive)

tersely noted, "By 0100, 5 June 1945, the barometer had dropped to 29.42, the wind was force 7, causing a heavy swell. . . . At about 0630 the wind increased to an estimated 100 knots. A number of ships reported having serious difficulty, *Pittsburgh,* losing her bow and *Duluth* (CL-87) having her bow buckled." The *Massachusetts* passed through the eye of the storm at 0700. Although the wind dropped and the visibility rose, "seas in the typhoon's eye were mountainous, being much greater even than those encountered when the wind was estimated at 100 knots." However, despite the damage to the fleet, which included the loss of several destroyers, the *Massachusetts*'s principal casualty was only the loss of one Kingfisher.

Despite a general battering, the fleet continued to operate, and on 8 June TF 38's fighters swept over Kyushu. On the 10th Batdiv 8—the *Massachusetts, Indiana,* and *Alabama*—and Desdiv 121 bombarded Minami Daito Jima. The main battery fired 15 salvos, expending 81 16-inch shells, from 0620 to 0724. This damaged or destroyed several buildings. The secondary battery fired from 0728 to 0800, expending 100 rounds in 20 salvos, targeting a radio tower, an ammunition dump, and the town. Afterward the *Massachusetts* started south, and on 13 June she anchored in San Pedro Bay, Leyte Gulf. Here on the 19th Rear Admiral Shafroth transferred his flag to the *South Dakota.*

On 1 July the *Massachusetts* raised anchor and headed north in company with the *South Dakota* and *Indiana,* five cruisers, and ten destroyers. She joined with TF 38 the next day and on 3 July once again became part of TG 38.1 with the *Bennington, Lexington, Hancock, Belleau Wood,* and *San Jacinto.* In addition to the three battleships there were seven cruisers and Desrons 61 and 25. On 9 July Captain Redmon addressed his crew. He said that the Okinawa operation was concluded and no longer required TF 38's support. However, "continuous pressure must be exerted against the enemy. . . . Task Force 38 is stronger than ever this time. We have three groups each containing five carriers. We have a total of eight fast battleships, many new cruisers, and a much more comfortable number of destroyers than last time. Tomorrow morning at dawn from waters east of Tokyo we will send many air strikes against that area. . . . There may be a violent reaction to our visit. It is our job to take care of any that get by the aircraft patrols." He then informed the crew that they would be heading north after that to bombard Hokkaido and, finally, although "there has been nothing official, I feel certain . . . we will be the next fast battleship to go back [to the States for maintenance]."

The air strikes against targets in the Tokyo area commenced on 10 July. Despite expectations, the *Massachusetts* did not face any retaliatory raids. On 14 July the *South Dakota, Indiana,* and *Massachusetts,* two heavy cruisers, and four destroyers separated to bombard iron works at Kamaishi on the island of Honshu, north of Tokyo. Land was in view by 0842. The *Massachusetts*

Shelling Japan

There were no planes, no ships and only a timid spattering of fire from shore batteries to oppose them. The big battlewagons, their 16-inch guns pumping ton after ton of high explosive shells into targets that flamed erupted and collapsed, paraded brazenly only a few hundred yards off shore, completely ignoring the fact that the shore was the enemy's Japan.

For two ear-splitting hours, beginning at noon on 14 July, the 35,000-ton battleships *Massachusetts, Indiana,* and *South Dakota,* the cruisers *Chicago* and *Quincy,* and the destroyers *Black, Erben, Heermunn,* and *Southerland* pounded away at Kamaishi, vital steel port on the island of Honshu 275 miles north of Tokyo

Targets, for the 16-, 8- and 5-inch rifles of the fleet were the huge Kamaishi steel mill and dockyards sprawling along the water's edge. When the ships finally put back to sea, after steaming in sight of the coast for more than five hours, the steel mill was completely demolished and adjacent coke ovens were blazing furiously.

The assault was the first surface attack on Japan since 1863, when three American warships destroyed a shore battery that had been firing on neutral shipping.

Just as had carrier-borne aircraft in previous attacks, the fleet caught the enemy completely by surprise. Following a heavy carrier raid on Tokyo four days before, Tokyo radio confidently gushed that the 3rd Fleet was heading south, only to have it turn up in the north with more bombs dropped in coordination with the fleet shelling.

ADAPTED FROM *ALL HANDS*, AUGUST 1945

A Kingfisher being hoisted aboard the *Massachusetts*. (U.S. Navy Cruise Book)

A salvo of six 16-inch shells fired against the iron-works at Kamaishi, Japan. (U.S. Navy Cruise Book)

opened fire at 1213, and through 1409 she expended 300 HC 16-inch rounds. On the 15th the air targets were located in northern Honshu and Hokkaido. Once again, the battleships cruised unmolested off the Japanese coast. On the 17th, after refueling, the fast carriers launched waves of bombers and fighters that blanketed Japanese air installations in the Tokyo area. The strikes continued on the 18th. The worse threat the *Massachusetts* faced this entire time was a drifting mine that passed close aboard to starboard. One sailor remembered, "There was a Marine stationed on the bow. He had earphones. He'd spot the mines and he shot 'em with his rifle, but you had to hit 'em right on the little peddle. So, we're heading right for this mine, the battleship, and he was shooting but couldn't hit it so we did an emergency turn, the right side full speed ahead and the left side reverse and we just turned on a dime and the ship lay over and as it lay over the [wash] hit the mine and the shrapnel just sprayed on the deck. We had a few injuries on that one. That was pretty spooky."

After retiring several hundred miles to refuel "re-ammunition," and perform some maintenance (the *Massachusetts* fixed a condenser leak), the fleet steamed toward southern Honshu to hit the Japanese fleet units in the inland sea. These strikes commenced on 25 July and were repeated on the 28th. On the 29th the fleet once again targeted Tokyo. The only ammunition the *Massachusetts* expended was in drills and practice shoots.

The big guns went into action on 29 July when, in company of the *South Dakota* and *Indiana* and with four heavy cruisers and destroyers, the *Massachusetts* headed for Hamamatsu, south of Tokyo, her target being the Japanese Musical Instrument Company. She opened fire with her main battery at 2319 on the 29th and continued firing until 0028 on the 30th, expending 270 rounds. The ship experienced no casualties to materiel or personnel; however, Big Mamie narrowly avoided a collision with the *Lexington* that evening. She refueled the next day and on 3 August, TF 38, which had been cruising south of Honshu, met with a logistic group. There was little action for the fleet in the early part of August, as fog and rain twice caused operations to be canceled. The crew anticipated orders to head east toward the United States at any time. There was a back-and-forth as ships transferred personnel to her for

The battleships contributed Marines and sailors for the first landing forces sent to the Japanese mainland following the Japanese surrender. (U.S. Navy Cruise Book)

The crew of the *Massachusetts* inspecting the Japanese battleship *Nagato* in Tokyo Bay. (U.S. Navy Cruise Book)

transportation home and took equipment and supplies as the ship was cannibalized. But Big Mamie's war was not over yet.

On 9 August she participated in another bombardment of Kamashi, opening fire at 1254 and expending 265 HC 16-inch rounds through 1445. There were no casualties. At 1603 her antiaircraft battery went into action against a Judy, the first aircraft the ship had engaged in months.

There were air strikes against targets in northern Honshu and on Hokkaido on the 10th. Despite rumors of an imminent Japanese surrender, more raids on the Tokyo area followed on the 13th. The carriers launched strikes on the 15th, when word arrived from Third Fleet command that offensive operations against the Japanese had ceased and all strikes were recalled.

On the 16th "the three Task Groups of Task Force 38 and the British Task Group closed distance and were maneuvered simultaneously by signal direct from ComTask Force 38 in order that pictures might be taken from aircraft from 1100 to 1200." TF 38 remained off the coast of Japan; the carriers continued to fly combat air patrols and the battleships performed gunnery exercises. On the 19th the *Massachusetts* sent her Marine detachment of 95 men for temporary duty with the American forces making the initial landings on Japan. One officer recalled, "every ship provided a small contingent to go ashore and secure the Japanese home islands. It was a little strange, to put it mildly. All we had were some old Springfield rifles. We did have a Marine contingent, and they went ashore. They must have looked pretty good, but our bluejackets, they didn't know anything about marching, they didn't know anything about handling a rifle, and the Japanese must have thought why did they quit when they did when they saw this motley crew coming ashore."

On the 23rd Captain Redman disappointed his crew, telling them their return to the States for overhaul had been postponed. "We can only do the job we have and see what happens." Over the next week the *Massachusetts* supported the carriers operating off North Honshu. Finally, on 28 August word arrived that the *Massachusetts* would be going home. It had been a long war. She had been there when the very first U.S. troops engaged in combat on foreign soil in the Old World, and some of her crew were the very first to land in Japan at the very end.

The diary entry for 3 September 1945 reads: "At 0800 set course of 045°(T), speed 16 knots and departed from area enroute Puget Sound via great circle." Ten days later, she dropped anchor in Washington.

WRAP-UP

THE *MASSACHUSETTS* SAILED FOR PUGET SOUND ON 3 September 1945, where she received her second overhaul and refit. The sense of urgency that had marked her first refit, 15 months earlier, was gone, and not until 28 January 1946 did she sail for California and then for Hampton Roads, arriving there on 22 April 1946.

Once in Virginia the ship began the protective mothballing process, which involved dehumidifying the machinery spaces and placing metal cocoons over the gun emplacements. The *Massachusetts* decommissioned on 27 March 1947, after slightly less than five years of service, and became a member of the Atlantic Reserve Fleet at Norfolk. During this period the Navy considered various plans to refurbish the battleship, including one to raise her speed to 33 knots by removing the after turret and expanding her machinery spaces. All such

The *Massachusetts* under way at six knots in Puget Sound, Washington, after her final overhaul, 22 January 1946. (U.S. Navy)

The *Massachusetts* laid up at the Norfolk Naval Shipyard, Virginia, on 3 January 1963. At that time she had been stricken from the Naval Vessel Register, but was awaiting preservation as a memorial. The USS *Uvalde* (APA-88) is at right. (U.S. Navy)

ideas, however, proved prohibitively expensive, and nothing came of them.

On 1 June 1962, the Navy announced plans to scrap the *Massachusetts*. This news galvanized a group led by an association of former crew members to try to save the ship. Their original intention was to dock her alongside the frigate USS *Constitution* in Boston, but no site there would accept her; in fact, it seemed that no one wanted the ship at all. Finally, the crew's association approached the mayor of Fall River, Massachusetts, and sold him on the idea of hosting what hopefully would turn out to be a major tourist attraction in the city, which had in the past decades seen its tax base eroded by a loss of industry. Once the site had finally been determined, there remained the problem of moving the ship there. Over a two-year period, the *Massachusetts* Memorial Committee raised $100,000 to pay for the cost of insuring and towing the battleship from Virginia to Fall River, with over half the contributions coming from Massachusetts schoolchildren. On 14 August 1965, the *Massachusetts* was towed to Fall River, where she became a memorial for the state's World War II dead. The crew's association began the long task of refurbishing the ship, which had suffered from a lack of maintenance, and restoring her, at least in appearance, to her World War II condition.

Since 1965 the *Massachusetts* has been the center of Battleship Cove: America's Fleet Museum and Maritime Museum, one of the most successful warship and maritime museums in the world. Battleship Cove's collection of ships has grown and today includes the destroyer USS *Joseph P. Kennedy Jr.* (DD-850), the submarine USS *Lionfish* (SS-298), the Soviet missile corvette *Hiddensee*, and PT boats *617* and *796*. More than 80,000 people visit the *Massachusetts* each year to view her unique and immersive compartments and exhibits. She actively preserves the memory of her service in the words of many of the men who served on board her and the memory of a period in American history where the deeds and accomplishments of the nation were truly epic. Even nearly 80 years after her keel was laid, she remains a marvel of engineering and technology.

FROM BATTLESHIP COVE

Following Operation Torch, *Massachusetts* transferred to the Pacific and spent the remainder of the war there, save for a brief overhaul at Bremerton in the middle of 1944. She decommissioned in March 1947 and rested for 18 years in the Portsmouth VA reserve fleet. Thanks to the intervention of former crew members, legislators, private citizens, and schoolchildren, she escaped several appointments with the scrapyard in the early 1960s and began her new life in Fall River, MA, on August 15, 1965, as our state's official World War II memorial.

Fast-forwarding to the present, *Massachusetts* is queen of the fleet at what is now known as Battleship Cove. Over the more than half century since her arrival, she's been joined by submarine *Lionfish*, destroyer *Joseph P. Kennedy, Jr.*, Russian-built corvette *Hiddensee*, PT Boats *617* and *796*, *LCM 56*, and two helicopters.

The challenges inherent in maintaining the latter are many in what is essentially a 24/7 operation. Beyond managing expected physical plant issues, staff and volunteers work continuously to create and maintain safe and sensible wayfinding and engaging interpretation for our visitors, preserve our huge collection of artifacts and documents, and most importantly, *keep the rust at bay*.

As for all of our peers in the museum-ship business, creative programming is key to sustainability. Our ships offer remarkable educational opportunities related to science, technology, history, and the humanities, and we strive to integrate these into our interpretations and public interactions. Related activities include behind-the-scenes tours, living history (re-enactor) weekends, and public and private school collaborations. Most significantly, our overnight camping program that debuted in 1972 remains relevant today as grandchildren and great-grandchildren seek knowledge about their forebears.

Ultimately, our vessels are memorials to those who served on and in them. As we move further away in time from those generations, we are focused more than ever on our primary mission to safeguard their memories. We consider it a privilege.

Christopher J Nardi
Chief Operating Officer
USS *Massachusetts* Memorial Committee Inc.

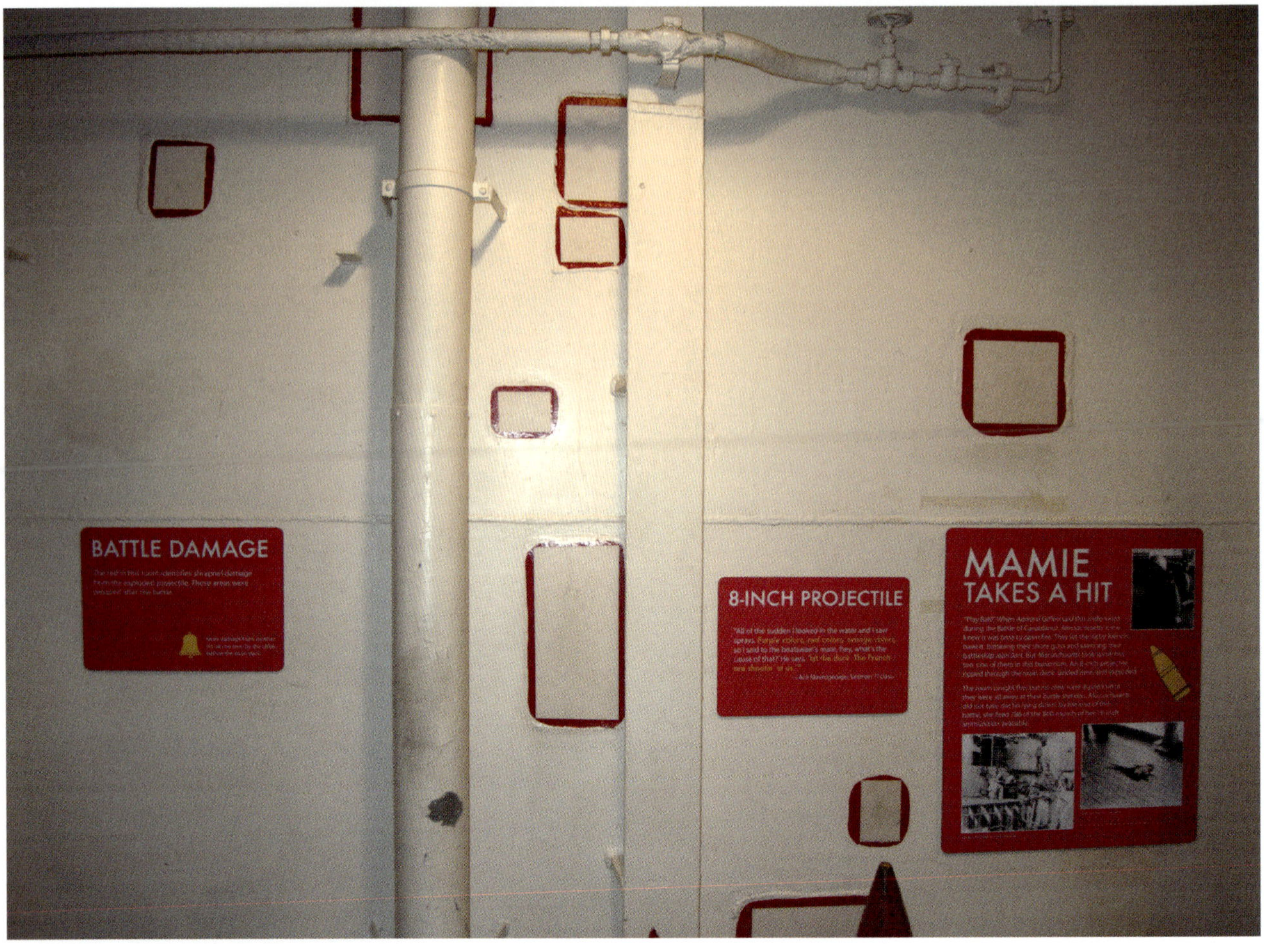

Damage from 8-inch projectile to inboard bulkhead of living space A-208L. (Christopher J. Nardi / USS *Massachusetts* Memorial Committee Inc.)

Looking up at patch in main deck where 8-inch shell penetrated from within an outboard bunkroom on the port side of A-208L. (Christopher J. Nardi / USS *Massachusetts* Memorial Committee Inc.)

Damage to bunk stanchion in outboard bunkroom on port side of A-208L. (Christopher J. Nardi / USS *Massachusetts* Memorial Committee Inc.)

Exhibited section of main deck where 8-inch shell penetrated and exploded within an outboard bunkroom on the port side of A-208L. (Christopher J. Nardi / USS *Massachusetts* Memorial Committee Inc.)

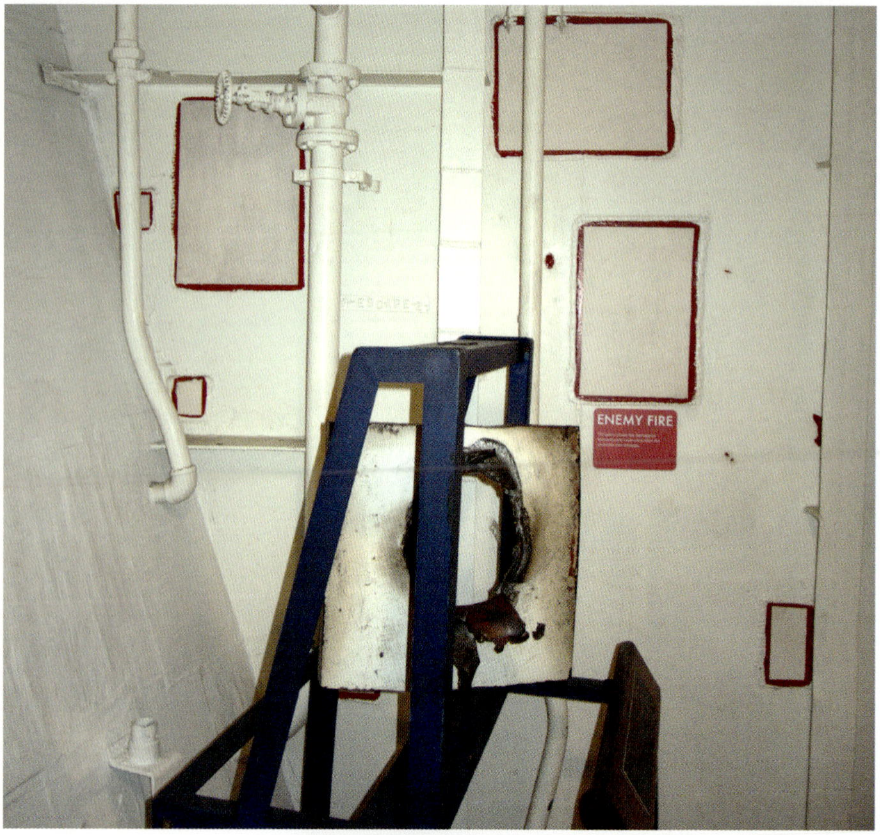

Damage to forward athwartships bulkhead in outboard bunkroom on port side of A-208L. (Christopher J. Nardi / USS *Massachusetts* Memorial Committee Inc.)

16-inch projectile fragment recovered from Casablanca battle area. (Christopher J. Nardi / USS *Massachusetts* Memorial Committee Inc.)

Damage to bulkheads of 5-inch Mount 9 and boat crane machinery room. This area is adjacent to the after quarterdeck. (Christopher J. Nardi / USS *Massachusetts* Memorial Committee Inc.)

(Photos by Edward Hayes)

World of Warships is a free-to-play, naval warfare–themed, massively multiplayer online game produced and published by Wargaming. Like their other games, *World of Tanks* (WoT) and *World of Warplanes* (WoWP), players take control of historic vehicles to battle others in player-versus-player or play ccooperatively against bots or in an advanced player-versus-environment (PvE) battle mode. *World of Warships* (WoWs) was originally released for PC in 2015; the PlayStation 4 and Xbox One console versions, titled *World of Warships: Legends*, followed in 2019, and it was released on the PlayStation 5 and Xbox Series X/S in April 2021.

Developed by Lesta Studios in St. Petersburg, Russia, *World of Warships* (PC) currently has more than 44 million registered players—playing on five main servers across the globe. More than 500 dedicated staff members work on a four-week update cycle to bring new features, ships, and mechanics to the game—keeping gameplay fresh and inviting to new players. The game features more than 400 ships, spread across 12 different in-game nations. Ships are designed based on historical documents and actual blueprints from the first half of the 20th century, and it takes from two to six man-months on average to create each of these ships. There are more than 20 ports to choose from, and 10 of them are re-created based on historical harbors and port towns.

There are four different ship classes: destroyers, cruisers, battleships, and aircraft carriers, with each class offering a different gameplay experience. Submarines have been in testing cycles since 2018, and based on testing results and player feedback, they have undergone significant changes that should allow them to launch as the fifth class in the near future. Ships are arranged in tiers between I and X, and players must progress through ship classes and tiers to reach tier X. Ships of tier X represent the pinnacle of naval engineering from World War II and the early Cold War era. Each warship needs a naval commander to lead it into the battle. There are many commanders to choose from in *World of Warships*, including more than 10 iconic historical figures. In *World of*

Warships players can battle on more than 40 maps. There are seven different permanent or seasonal Battle Types to choose from: Co-op Battles, Random Battles, Ranked Battles, Clan Battles, Brawls, Scenarios, and Training. Additionally, within Battle Types there are four different Battle Modes available: Standard, Domination, Epicenter, and Arms Race.

Massachusetts made her *World of Warships* PC debut in June 2018 as an American tier VIII; since then she has become a fan favorite. Her decent armor, speed, and guns make her a formidable opponent. In-game, her guns are less accurate than her sister, *Alabama*, but it is her dual-purpose 5-inch battery that really shines. *Massachusetts* has some of the best secondary battery performance in the game—enemy ships really need to think twice before approaching her. *Massachusetts* was removed from sale on PC in early 2021, but she is still available in *World of Warships: Legends*—on console. See *Massachusetts* in person, then take her into battle today in *World of Warships*.

Developed by the team behind *World of Warships* for PC, *World of Warships: Legends* is a completely new entry in Wargaming's flagship nautical franchise that takes full advantage of the power and capabilities of home consoles. *World of Warships: Legends* brings the online naval action loved by millions to home consoles for the very first time, alongside a host of content and features exclusive to the console experience. *World of Warships: Legends* is now available for download from the PlayStation® Store and Microsoft Store. Players can now wage wars across a variety of maps, in numerous warships, and enjoy stunning oceanic vistas with glorious HDR support on PlayStation®4 and Xbox One X. Full 4K support is available on PlayStation®4 Pro, PlayStation®5, and Xbox One X too! *Legends* also supports standard high-def on PlayStation®4 and Xbox One, with more intriguing graphics on the horizon.

Wargaming proudly supports various charitable causes that members of the gaming and history community care deeply about. Supporting veterans and servicemembers: Operation Lifeboat (2020) raised $150,000 USD for Stack Up's mental health awareness helpline; Remembrance charity drive

(2020) raised $45,000 USD for Help for Heroes, which supports UK veterans and servicemembers; and Project Valor (2017) saw WoWS, WoT, and WoWP collectively raise $75,000 USD for a veteran housing program. Preserving historical ship museums: *World of Warships*, in partnership with museums across the world to support the preservation of naval history and the education of the global community, raised $50,000 USD for the restoration of USS *Batfish* (2019) and $400,000 USD for the restoration of USS *Texas* (2017). Finally, supporting the local community: a 24-hour charity livestream (2019) raised $43,000 USD for the Save the Children organization, and also raised $78,000 USD for Team Rubicon and the victims of Hurricane Harvey in 2017.

The United States Naval Institute (USNI) has been a proud partner of *World of Warships* and Wargaming since December 2019. Wargaming has a made a commitment to naval history through various programs and events over the past years. It produces excellent video content with its *Naval Legends* series on YouTube, and hosts events on board museum ships where members of the gaming and naval history communities can get together and experience living history in person. *World of Warships* and Wargaming are also great sponsors of the Historic Naval Ships Association (HNSA). USNI thanks Wargaming and *World of Warships* for their continued support of the naval history community and their participation in this Naval History Special Edition. Please see the back cover for a special offer for *World of Warships* PC and *World of Warships: Legends*.

In 1940, during the war, the United States began looking for a replacement for the obsolete and weak Browning AA machine guns. The 20-mm automatic Oerlikon, significantly improved by that time, proved to be very useful. In 1941, production began in the United States, and soon the Oerlikons were mounted on almost every warship, from boats to battleships. USS *Massachusetts* carried 35 of these weapons during World War II.

The Mark 12 5-inch/38-cal gun would prove invaluable to the U.S. Navy in World War II. The MK 29 and 32 dual-purpose mounts were a highly efficient artillery system. A heavy-duty power drive and reliable mechanism ensured a fast horizontal and vertical aiming speed—perfect for use in the antiaircraft role. The mount had a nominal rate of fire of 15 shots per minute, but that could be increased for a short period of time, shooting up to 22 shells per minute. Each 5/38 shell weighed more than 50 lbs. USS *Massachusetts* was built with 10 MK 32 mounts, 5 per side.

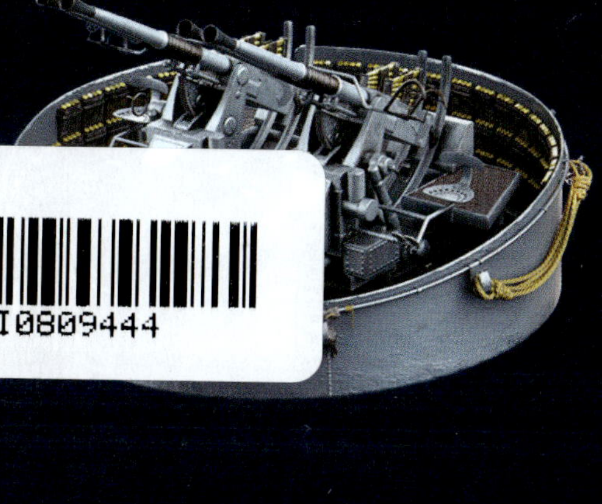

The 40-mm Bofors was produced in a variety of versions: with air and water cooling; in twin, quadruple, and single mounts; with manual aiming; and with power drive. More than ten thousand mounts were manufactured for the Navy and Coast Guard and more than twenty thousand for the Army, and around nine thousand were supplied to allied countries. USS *Massachusetts* was equipped with seven quad-mounted 40-mm Bofors during World War II.

Marines. And hand-to-hand combat erupted again, as on Betio, only this time in the morning light. At the conclusion of the skirmish on 27 November, none of the last 175 Japanese rikusentai at Tarawa had survived. Murray lost 32 killed and 59 wounded from 2/6.

Smith could now send the division's scouts to other nearby islands and atolls to ensure no Japanese were left behind in the Gilberts to surveil or harass the occupation garrisons, construction battalions, or aircrews. Although a few Japanese were located, they escaped to an unknown fate at sea before they could be killed or captured. With this last action, the Gilberts were finally secure from any land-based threat on 1 December 1943, just short of the two-year anniversary of the first appearance of Japanese units after the attack on Pearl Harbor.

TBFs from USS *Monterey* in flight during the Nauru Island Strike, 8 December 1943. (U.S. Naval Institute Photo Archive)

Nauru

Some of the ships that had been part of Turner's carrier forces remained nearby and formed Task Force 50.8 to pound Nauru on 8 December. The attacking ships included the new fast battleships *Alabama* (BB-60), *Indiana* (BB-58), *Massachusetts* (BB-59), *North Carolina* (BB-55), *South Dakota* (BB-57), and *Washington* (BB-56), and the aircraft carriers *Bunker Hill* (CV-17) and *Monterey* (CVL-26). Nauru may not have been invaded as part of Galvanic, but it was made to suffer now and for the rest of the war, because it was isolated and abandoned by Japanese leaders who had far more pressing concerns elsewhere.

New Air Bases

The next stage for Tarawa, Makin, and Abemama was the beginning of a rapid transformation from wrecked battlefields to air bases for the coming reconnaissance and bombing missions to the Marshall Islands, already set for invasion at the end of January 1944. The Seabees of the 3rd Battalion, 18th Marines, had been performing combat, construction, and repair work almost since the battle for Betio had begun on 20 November. As more of their bulldozers and other equipment began to arrive toward the end of the battle, they could begin to repair the airfield and assist Marine infantry units by sealing Japanese fortifications that were thought to be temporarily clear, yet might be infiltrated at night or even harbor unseen stragglers who could attack the Marines from behind.

The construction units built two airfields at Tarawa Atoll: the repaired Japanese field on Betio, now called Hawkins Field for Lieutenant William Deane Hawkins, and another new one on the island of Buota, to be known as Mullinnix Field for the admiral killed on the *Liscome Bay*. Abemama's new airfield would be O'Hare Field, for Lieutenant Commander Butch O'Hare of the USS *Enterprise*. Makin's new Starmann Field featured a 7,000-foot runway that had to be covered partially with steel matting due to the poor soil; it was named for U.S. Army Air Forces Second Lieutenant John W. Starmann, a fighter pilot who died attacking Mili Atoll in December 1943.

Collectively, these airfields cut in half the distance between the main existing U.S. Army Air Force base at Funafuti and the Japanese stronghold at Kwajalein Atoll in the Marshalls. Bomb weight could be added in place of the fuel that had been required for the lengthy flights from Funafuti, and smaller land-based aircraft could be added to the mix. A variety of fighters, medium bombers, and heavy bombers were stationed at the new air bases. The Seventh Bomber Command completed the move of its headquarters to Tarawa by 7 January 1944. Land-based fighter protection for the bombers could be provided for the first time in this region. Constant missions over the Marshalls beginning in December 1943 enabled far more sophisticated and precise aerial photoreconnaissance of those atolls than had been possible for the Gilberts.

AFTERMATH

PRESS AND MEDIA RESPONSES TO TARAWA

No matter the outcome of the Battle of Tarawa, it was almost guaranteed to get an outsized share of U.S public attention at the time, since it occurred during a lull in urgent news from other fronts. Media accounts around 20 November 1943 told of an immense (but inscrutable) struggle under way in the Soviet Union, which would result in the liberation of Gomel in Belarus. In Italy, British and U.S. forces under General Dwight Eisenhower, who had not yet relocated to the United Kingdom in order to lead the invasion of France, were making little progress against stiff German resistance and the Italian terrain. Allied air raids over Germany were taking a daily toll on its largest cities, including Berlin and Ludwigshafen, on the eve of Tarawa.

And then Operation Galvanic erupted onto the front pages. The *Alabama Journal*, for instance, dedicated a banner headline to the invasion on 22 November: "Yanks Gain Foothold in Gilberts." This was set in all caps, and whatever was reported next also would have the full attention of the American public.

Beachhead Scene, Marines at Tarawa **by Kerr Eby. (Naval History and Heritage Command)**

The Marine Corps had decided to chronicle the assault on Tarawa to an unprecedented extent and to facilitate the presence of civilian media representatives as well. As a result, it is one of the most richly documented combat experiences of the entire U.S. war effort, especially for such a brief (if also furious) engagement.

Reporters, photographers, and artists landed during the first few hours of D-Day at Tarawa. Five civilian correspondents came ashore with the first waves of LVTs and LCVPs on 20 November: Robert Sherrod (*Time/Life*), Frank Filan (Associated Press photographer), William Hipple (Associated Press), Don Senick (Fox Movietone News cameraman), and Richard Johnston (United Press). All had close brushes with death, but none were wounded or killed. Their job at first was complicated by the same factors hindering the Marines: they were pinned to a very small portion of Betio, usually behind the seawall. Only as the battle wound down were they able to make their way to ships in the transport area to begin typing stories or shipping their film back to Hawaii. So while the news of the battle reached U.S. newspapers quickly, eyewitness accounts by civilian and Marine correspondents alike took many days to begin appearing in U.S. newspapers.

The Marine Corps dedicated a unit to memorializing the assault on film, both in still and motion pictures. Its commanding officer had been a Hollywood star before the war, Captain Louis Hayward (most famously of the film *The Man in the Iron Mask*, 1939). Viewed suspiciously by some of the assault commanders as "Hollywood Marines" who would get in the way, Hayward's unit earned respect by coming ashore early and being prepared, had it been necessary, to pick up rifles and fight. Cinematographer Staff Sergeant Norman Hatch, for instance, arrived on Red 3 with Major Crowe's 2/8, and captured footage of the dramatic final assault on "Bonnyman's Bunker" on D+2.

Combat artists, too, were accommodated. They included Gilbert Bundy of King Features, whose LVT, to which he had transferred from an LCVP, was hit by Japanese artillery, killing 21 of 23 in the craft with him and pinning him under a pile of Marine bodies. He and the other survivor freed themselves and struggled to the front cab, where they remained until they were rescued hours later by a passing U.S. boat, shortly after nearly being mistaken for Japanese snipers. Kerr Eby, an artist who had already experienced combat in World War I, came ashore and produced some of the grimmest images

Tarawa No. II by Kerr Eby. (Naval History and Heritage Command)

***Ebb Tide, Tarawa* by Kerr Eby. (Naval History and Heritage Command)**

of Marines struggling to gain a foothold on Betio and proceed inland despite all odds.

These images, even today, are shocking. But was the American public shocked by them at the time? The evidence is mixed. The Navy and Marine Corps leadership may well have expected a strong negative public reaction and tried to get control of the narrative by quickly portraying Tarawa as the first of many tough tests to come in the Pacific. On 4 December 1943, soon-to-be Commandant of the Marine Corps Lieutenant General Alexander Vandegrift began to lay the groundwork for a fuller reporting of the experience and a reckoning with high casualty numbers. "There will be more Guadalcanals," he stated, "more Bougainvilles, and—let us be honest—probably more Tarawas."

By 13 December, Robert Sherrod's employer, *Life* magazine, was taking the same line: It listed a reasonably accurate figure for Marine and Navy deaths (1,026), noting that they had occurred in 76 hours, whereas 954 had been lost at Guadalcanal in six months. "The price of progress" in the Central Pacific, *Life* warned, would be high. It documented that cost by publishing photos of dead Japanese troops alongside dead Marines, and one of a salvage boat from the transport USS *Sheridan* (APA-51) next to Marines using a pole to recover from the lagoon the bloated body of a fellow Marine.

Colonel Merritt Edson was returned to Washington to help manage the story. About to be promoted to brigadier general and named the new assistant division commander of the 2d Marine Division, Edson rebutted stories that were circulating about Marine difficulties at Tarawa's reef. He stated that the tide had been a known problem beforehand, and that 80 percent of casualties had occurred ashore rather than in the lagoon. Edson got to the crux of the matter when he summarized "the psychology of the people we are fighting—to make the campaign as costly as possible because they don't believe we can take it."

Being shocked at Tarawa's high casualties was, to follow Edson's logic, doing Japan's work for it. Newspapers across America seemed to accept this perspective. That winter they were filled with pride at the stories of local boys who served, were wounded, or died in the Gilberts, but none argued that their lives were wasted by poor planning or leadership. For instance, on 14 January 1944, the Ada, Oklahoma, *Evening News* reported on the community's fallen native son, Marine Sergeant James Maples Jr., age 20, on its front page. Maples, who had been buried at sea, left behind a wife and a child he had never met. Yet there was no statement or implication by the newspaper that something untoward had been present in Navy and Marine Corps tactics or strategy in the Central Pacific. The story revealed an unspoken pride in Maples' sacrifice during what the newspaper called an "epic battle," "the hardest in U.S. Marine history." In a similar vein, on 23 December 1943, the *Oakland Tribune* editorialized against "lurid stories" that "Marines were deliberately thrown into a death trap." It blamed the open access given to the correspondents for graphic descriptions of the Marines' difficulties and a naïve expectation that the United States could win the war with light casualties. To these newspapers, Tarawa was less a mistake than a harbinger of battles sure to come.

Although photos such as the ones in *Life* were already appearing just three weeks after the battle began, it was the release of motion pictures, some with color footage, that would make the reaction to Tarawa unique among U.S. battle coverage thus far. By 4 December 1943, Elmer Davis, director of the Office of War Information, was already promising "knockout" footage of the Gilberts action in coming newsreels. When the United News (U.S. government) newsreel appeared in U.S. theaters in mid-December 1943, it showed about five minutes of film introduced by an assertion that Tarawa was "vital to the Allied offensive" in the Pacific, without going into specifics. It documented the variety and fortitude of Japanese emplacements, even as it seemed to boast of the ability of U.S. firepower to demolish them. Japanese dead were shown and their total estimated losses stated, but no fallen Americans were seen, and no casualty figures mentioned. After five minutes, the newsreels switched to reports on the meetings of President Roosevelt in Cairo and Tehran with Winston Churchill, Chiang Kai-shek, and Joseph Stalin.

There was plenty of film footage of dead Americans to match the still photos already appearing in *Life*. Yet there was also a strong taboo about showing it (only on 23 September 1943 had stills of U.S. killed in action first appeared in a U.S. publication, *Life*). A 20-minute documentary, *With the Marines at Tarawa*, was released to the public in early March 1944. Sherrod later expressed the belief that a talk he and Franklin Roosevelt had in January 1944 might have helped persuade the president to order the gruesome Tarawa films shown. Featuring footage shot by Hatch and other Marines of Hayward's unit, the motion picture avoided commentary on the battle's strategy and did not mention the tide. It made evident the savagery of the three days on Betio through not only combat scenes but also images of dead Marines and Japanese troops. Staff Sergeant Hatch shot one powerful scene that showed, for the first and only time in the war, U.S. and Japanese troops in the same frame of a motion picture as they are engaged in combat. Marine bodies are then seen bobbing in the lagoon, yet the film ends on a triumphal note as surviving Marines salute a U.S. flag raised over Betio and then march off to board boats back to their transports. The vividness and novelty of such footage helped the film win the 1945 Academy Award for Best Documentary (Short Subject).

There would be no Hollywood feature films during the war, or afterward, that focused solely on Tarawa. The battle did, however, play a prominent role in *Sands of Iwo Jima* in 1949. Colonel David Shoup was assigned to serve as a technical advisor and made a cameo appearance as himself, instructing 2/8's Major Henry Crowe, also playing himself, on how to prepare for the first night's fighting. But Iwo Jima, and star John Wayne's portrayal of his character's death on it, were the film's real focus. By the end of the war, Tarawa had been eclipsed on the scale of sacrifice by Iwo Jima and other battles.

The 1955 film *Battle Cry* dramatized the book of the same name by Tarawa veteran Leon Uris (of 2/6) and employed Crowe as a technical advisor. Yet it documented 2/6's journey around the atoll for less than one minute of screen time. No combat there was re-created, and the death of one of the minor characters was narrated rather than shown. The real action of the film was saved for its scenes depicting the Battle of Saipan.

One final feature film, *Tarawa Beachhead* (1958), simply reused footage from *Sands of Iwo Jima* for all but close-up shots during the Tarawa battle scenes. It did not convey an accurate historical sense of the flow of battle. The combat was mainly a vehicle to bring to a resolution the dramatic conflict between the two main characters.

Even a recent major attempt to raise public consciousness of the U.S. Marine Corps' efforts against Japan, the ten-part HBO miniseries *The Pacific* (2010), failed to recount the fighting at Tarawa, while giving lengthy treatment to Guadalcanal, Cape Gloucester, Peleliu, Iwo Jima, and Okinawa. While perhaps not totally forgotten or trivialized in films, Tarawa may certainly have been overlooked.

LESSONS LEARNED

Naval Bombardment and Fire Support

The Marines did not get the type, scope, or duration of preliminary bombardment, from the air or the sea, that they requested and believed they needed. There is

A Cinematographer Comes Ashore on D-Day with 2/8

"WHAT WAR WAS LIKE" BY NORMAN HATCH, *NAVAL HISTORY*, DECEMBER 2008

Off to our left was a Japanese machine-gun turret firing at the amphibian tractors. The shooter was apparently scaring the life out of the amtrac drivers. On our right, a pier ran out about 600 yards, and amtracs were bunching up against it.

All [2/8 battalion commander Henry "Jim"] Crowe could visualize was his landing craft unloading on an unprotected beach. So he told the coxswain to put his boat into the water. But the coxswain ran it up on the reef, and the ramp wouldn't go down. Everybody had to go over the side.

In the LCVPs, the gunwales up at the top and on the sides were almost shoulder level for most of those people who were six feet tall, like my assistant, Bill "Kelly" Kelleher, and I were. At least we were tall enough to see over the damn thing without having to hold on.

Everybody had to go over with 80 pounds of gear and drop in the water. The kids who were short had to start swimming right away, whether they knew how to swim or not. When Kelly and I went over the side, we had the Navy guys put the cameras and film canisters over. We could not get into the water with the film and the cameras. Jokingly, I told Kelly that if he fell into a hole and got those cameras wet, I was going to kill him.

In the end, neither of us fell, and we walked in. Many of the guys who came out of the LCVP did a lot of dog-paddling, because we were being shot at by the Japanese from under the pier as well as by the guy with the machine gun.

When we reached the beach, both Kelly and I were exhausted. After 15 minutes or so, we got our breath back and got oriented to where we were. Jim Crowe was walking up and down, yelling at his troops to "get over that goddamn seawall! They can't hit you, what are you hunkering down here for?"

They eventually moved up and went over the seawall, but a lot of guys had wound up under the pier because they had lost their weapons and didn't know what to do. Eventually, a couple of junior lieutenants got the troops doing what they were supposed to do.

Of course, I started shooting film. Crowe was directing things from the stern of an amtrac that tried to crawl up over the seawall but didn't make it. That became his permanent command post during the 76-hour battle.

Then-Staff Sergeant Hatch mans his trusty 35-mm Bell & Howell Eyemo, the motion picture camera he used to capture combat scenes for the Marine Corps' graphic Oscar-winning film. (Courtesy of Norman Hatch)

no doubt that their success in only 76 hours against a densely fortified and fanatically held island fringed by a coral reef with unpredictable tides would have been impossible without bombardment before and during the Marine attack. The bombs and shells killed the Japanese leadership, isolated their strongpoints, and prevented coordinated counterattacks by destroying their communications.

But the 2d Marine Division's planners had wanted many days of bombardment and their own artillery landed on Bairiki in advance of the main landings. They got neither, nor did the Army Air Forces receive the message that the 2d Marine Division wanted 2,000-pound "daisy cutter" bombs dropped on the beach just before the landings, ordnance that might have killed any Japanese not totally hunkered down.

The Navy learned from its failure to destroy fortifications that it needed to:

- arrive days, not hours, in advance for preliminary bombardments;
- focus its fire on specific fortifications until they were eliminated, rather than blast entire areas and assume destruction would follow; use base-fuzed (slightly delayed detonation) armor-piercing shells of the sort normally fired against enemy ships, rather than the point-detonating (immediate detonation) high-explosive shells previously believed to be suitable for targets on land;
- fire its rounds with less propellant at steeper, plunging angles in order to penetrate the thickest fortifications;
- do much more work on coordinating on-call fire to points requested by Marines or Army troops ashore;
- time its preliminary bombardment far more carefully, so that the enemy would be given no rest prior to the arrival of amphibious troops on the invasion beaches, and employ rocket launchers among the landing craft, of a sort that got a limited, unsuccessful trial at Makin.

What the Marine Corps and Army Learned on the Ground

The lessons learned on the ground at Tarawa, Makin, and Abemama, and then employed in subsequent amphibious assaults in the Central Pacific, were costly. Yet lives lost and casualties endured in the first campaign would save later lives and enable an accelerated timetable for operations moving toward

Japanese steel pillbox. (Hatch Collection, National Museum of the Pacific War)

Japan—far sooner than anyone could have expected in early 1943. Moving faster would prevent Japanese commanders from fortifying their positions, which amounted to saving more U.S. lives and shortening the war. Someplace had to be first, and somewhere the U.S. infantry leadership had to learn in what ways the theories of amphibious warfare that had been developed abstractly during the previous decade did not work so well in actual practice.

To begin with, there were intelligence shortcomings. Aerial photography had provided some stunning overhead and oblique views of the islands to be assaulted. But the photographic missions were limited in number, and they did not reveal information about the tides. Accurate knowledge of the tides could have been even more persuasive about the need to plan for inaccessible beachheads for much of the day during the chosen time frame for the assaults. Underwater demolition teams ("frogmen"), whose primary mission might have been to clear lanes for landing craft through mines and obstacles, could also have been useful in determining tidal features, the slope of the coral, and the best routes for the initial waves. They would be used later, but doing without them in the Gilberts and the chaotic arrival of Marines at Tarawa demonstrated how vital frogmen would have been and could be again in future attacks.

The decision to press for LVTs at both Tarawa and Makin was more than validated by events. Thousands of Marines and soldiers were placed on shore within the opening minutes. On Betio, their immediate presence was one of a few factors that can be cited as absolutely essential to eventual victory. But the vehicles had addressable problems that were apparent even before the Gilberts operation. They were in poor mechanical condition, under-protected, and easily forced out of action. Ninety of the 125 LVTs at Tarawa broke down, wrecked, or were disabled or destroyed by enemy fire. The armor placed at the front was either wholly inadequate (on LVT-2s) or useful only against the smallest caliber Japanese weapons (on LVT-1s). The disembarking procedure was nearly comical: Marines threw themselves over the sides and dropped many feet onto land or into water, whereas on LCVPs a front ramp was lowered and allowed for a quick and orderly exit. The LVTs were entirely thwarted by the coconut log seawall on Betio, which prevented their passage, caused them to become stuck, or exposed their thin bellies to destructive fire. The new LVT-4s, ready by the next summer's Marianas campaign, would feature a rear exit ramp to help with some of these problems. As for the numbers to be made available for successful assaults, Julian Smith reported that he believed 300 LVTs per assault division was the minimum, or more than double the 125 the 2d Marine Division had operated at Tarawa.

Far better preparation for facing hardened Japanese fortifications was needed. The Marine advance on Betio faced an immediate hurdle when men who had made it to the beach were stymied by emplacements just inland. If engineer teams assigned to infantry battalions became casualties, then their flamethrowers and demolitions were lost and the Japanese emplacements were extremely costly to defeat. V Amphibious Corps believed that in future operations, each rifle platoon should have a flamethrower. Bazookas, a staple of later fighting in the Pacific, had not been made available to the 2d Marine Division in time for training and deployment at Tarawa. The 37-mm guns on the Marines' antitank pieces and on the Stuart light tanks were of little use against fortified positions. While the 75-mm pack howitzers were more effective, they were difficult to maneuver to an appropriate firing position. The solution seemed to be far more Sherman medium tanks than the 16 that had arrived at Betio.

Supply and resupply created serious problems. Tarawa revealed major shortcomings in existing practices. The lack of any sort of beachhead to enable secure arrival, offloading, and distribution of supplies on Betio delayed victory and increased casualties. There was confusion just off the reef about which boats with what kind of supplies should be given priority for getting to the pier, and also about how to move supplies onto the island. Should the pier be used, or should an LVT shuttle supplies over the reef? Portable pontoon piers would have helped overcome the problems in using the partially wrecked Japanese main pier. The chaos of battle revealed that the shore party responsible for moving supplies from the beach to fighting units did not have enough manpower. Individual Marines in rifle units had too much of some things (food) and too little of others (water and grenades). Many lost their packs coming ashore, or dropped them immediately as an extravagance for the kind of fighting in which they were engaged.

Communications were disastrous. Both Ralph Smith at Makin and Julian Smith at Tarawa were often out of touch with key subordinates, and they struggled to get accurate information about the flow of battle and the best way they could help. One tactical communication difficulty revealed by Tarawa occurred during combined tank-infantry attacks, since each type of unit used a different kind of radio. Efforts to remedy this included attaching phones to the outside of tanks, thereby allowing infantry to speak with tank commanders. Batteries in handheld radios drained too quickly in actual combat conditions. The Marines' TBX model radios, on which they counted for coordinating their efforts, were often damaged by water coming ashore. Meanwhile, their TBY model radios were a complete failure. Thus, survivable radio equipment would become a prerequisite for and hallmark of later amphibious assaults.

Julian Smith's and Harry Hill's presence on the battleship *Maryland* proved to be an immediate mistake. The first counterbattery fire from the *Maryland* just after 0500 on D-Day disrupted Hill's radio communication with other elements of the task force—in particular the mysteriously absent Navy aircraft that (it was thought) were due at 0542. Future amphibious assaults would be directed from specially designed command ships such as the USS *Rocky Mount* (AGC-3), which would be Turner's flagship in the Marshalls and Marianas.

Lessons in the Air

Close air support for the soldiers on Butaritari and the Marines on Betio was provided by Navy planes from fleet carriers, light carriers, and escort carriers. Additional scouting, reconnaissance, and fire-spotting duties were carried out by floatplanes catapulted from battleships and cruisers. Their work was considerably eased by the lack of any fighter-escorted Japanese air attacks.

Yet in the air, too, problems were legion. Friendly fire incidents were common. U.S. pilots had not been trained to act in close

Supply

The supply situation turned out to be adequate at Tarawa, but only because the battle was so short. Sufficient quantities of the items that the Marines needed most badly could be delivered to allow them to continue to apply and maximize pressure on Japanese soldiers isolated in their fortifications. These supplies were chiefly ammunition and weapons of all sorts—for example, pack howitzers, 75-mm rounds for the howitzers and the medium tanks, flamethrowers, and demolition charges—vital medical supplies, and water, although water was often fouled with traces of kerosene or gasoline, and was delivered only very late to extremely thirsty Marines fighting in the equatorial sun and heat.

The basic principle for supplying amphibious units ashore called for the establishment of a beachhead under the direction of a Navy officer, the beachmaster. A Marine shore party (in this case, battalion 2/18) would then move the supplies to where frontline Marines or medical staff needed them. At Tarawa there was never a beachhead, because no area relatively secure from Japanese fire could be established on the flat island of Betio. Whatever system might have been developed in theory or in rehearsals for delivering supplies had to be abandoned, and use had to be made of what Betio had to offer: an 800-yard-long pier.

Lieutenant Colonel Chester Salazar, battalion commander of 2/18, set up his command post at the pierhead, where supplies arrived on landing craft. Salazar's Marines had to quickly determine if these were priority items, since the unloading from transports and cargo ships had not occurred in an order related to the needs of the landed Marines at any given moment. Instead, the Navy had decided that the transports and cargo ships had to be unloaded as quickly as possible and started sending everything into the lagoon. The enthusiasm was commendable, but Colonel Shoup, for one, was irate that when he requested certain types of items for immediate resupply, he could not get them because the landing craft already had other items on board. After the battle, Salazar noted that some of the earliest boxes that arrived contained mops and the cleaning agent Blanco.

During the first two days, Salazar's Marines had to locate the higher priority items, stack the rest on a pier sometimes under fire, and then find rubber boats to float in the most desperately needed items. Toward the end, vehicles such as Jeeps arrived and were driven off onto the seaplane ramp at the end of the pier and down the pier, still sometimes under fire. Throughout the battle, Japanese infiltrators occasionally reappeared under the pier, and fires started on it that the shore party had to extinguish, occasionally by using their helmets as buckets to throw lagoon water on the flames. It was one of many times during the battle that the Navy and Marines improvised to great effect; but it was also a lesson in how to be much better prepared for future operations so as to ensure that the supplies most needed were delivered when called for by commanders ashore.

support of the units they would be assisting, since in the months preceding Operation Galvanic they had been engaged in other operations in or near the Solomons, or in raids throughout the Pacific. In future amphibious attacks, Holland Smith wanted Marine aviators who were specially trained in close support of fellow Marines to be flown from carriers. This occurred in many later battles in the Pacific.

Timing of the final air attacks prior to H-Hour revealed severe shortcomings at Betio, where H-Hour had been delayed by 40 minutes. Planes that were supposed to strike until the last minute in fact finished their final runs from 10 to 22 minutes before the initial waves of LVTs came ashore. The recommended practices for future assaults would base the timing of the final aerial attacks on the location of the first waves, rather than on the time the first waves were supposed to land. In coming operations, the planes were to cease firing only when the first LVTs were 100 yards from the beach.

Strafing had proved inadequate against beach fortifications, and a gasoline-based bomb was recommended to suppress fire from such locations in the future.

Preliminary bombardment of the Gilberts by the B-24s had not done much to protect the arriving waves of Marines. Yet Warrant Officer Kiyoshi Ota, the highest ranking of the few Japanese prisoners from Betio, recalled the stunning effect of the heavy bombs. Twenty antiaircraft guns and several heavier guns were destroyed; fires were started that destroyed gasoline supplies; and some ammunition stockpiles were obliterated. The morale effect was substantial: Ota reported that 300 of his men were wounded, and the others had "pale faces." Yet when the Marines appeared, the Japanese still fought capably. High-level saturation bombing plainly did not have much impact on the combat effectiveness of surviving enemy troops, nor did such bombing diminish their numbers substantially.

JAPAN'S NEW POSITION AFTER THE GILBERTS

The rationale that had drawn Admirals King and Nimitz to the Gilbert Islands was now obvious to Japanese leadership. That is, once the Gilberts were in U.S. hands, the Marshall Islands were highly vulnerable and clearly the next target. Not just the target itself was evident, but also how it might be attacked. Because the Japanese garrison at Tarawa had been able to radio out a report that the Marines had unexpectedly approached through the lagoon, the Japanese now had to contend with another direction of possible assault in preparing their island defenses.

Knowledge of U.S. tactics would do the Japanese little good if they could not get men, supplies, aircraft, and construction supplies to the Marshalls—even if they could correctly predict which of the many atolls the United States was likely to attack first. The 7th Air Force repeatedly attacked Japanese bases and airfields in the Marshalls in December 1943 and January 1944, and its B-24 bombers could, for the first time, be escorted by land-based U.S. fighters. Moreover, U.S. submarines could pick off cargo and troops destined for the Marshalls.

Thus, Japan could not do enough in time to counter an enemy who had learned much from Tarawa and was eager to put the battle's lessons to good use. Without a carrier force that actually had planes and experienced pilots, Japan was helpless to prevent an American invasion force from appearing at a time and place of its choosing. The best Japan could hope for, in the Marshalls, Marianas, and points west, was to make the cost of setting foot ashore so high that the United States would be reluctant to try again. At the cost of appalling casualties on their own side, they attempted to exact such a price from the invaders at places such as Roi, Namur, Kwajalein, Saipan, Tinian, Guam, Peleliu, Iwo Jima, and Okinawa. In spite of ever-increasing casualties and the savagery required in fighting the Japanese, the United States continued through each of these islands to the doorstep of Japan, guided by knowledge and experience won first at Tarawa, Makin, and Abemama.

CEMETERIES AND REMAINS

The care taken today to enable grieving family members to quickly bury loved ones who have died in service abroad is a testament to the small scale of modern wars by comparison with World Wars I and II, as well as to the transport capacity—airlift especially—that can be dedicated to non-combat tasks such as returning those who have perished in combat theaters.

In 1943, as action in the Gilberts concluded, there was no such capacity and no such expectation that the armed services could send the fallen home immediately. Those who died on ships were buried at sea, because there was no suitable storage available on board. Those who died on land would be buried near the place of their death and, if all went well, somebody (a chaplain perhaps, or an organized graves registration team in more efficient operations) would document the location of each American's grave and then take care with that documentation.

At Tarawa, it quickly became apparent that no great amount of thought had been given in advance to the question of burying the dead. After the battle had commenced, chaplains were ordered to make their main duty such burials and did the best they could by themselves, since every other Marine was engaged in the effort just to hold on. The first cemetery on Betio was established near Shoup's command post behind Red 2, and a bulldozer was spared from combat duties long enough to excavate a trench to bury Marines and sailors side by side. No individual graves could be prepared during the fighting. This first cemetery held 112 Marines.

The next day, the second cemetery to be excavated was filled with the bodies of 66 more Marines. On occasion, they could not be identified or were just body parts. Some Marines who had been evacuated while still alive but subsequently died were buried at sea; at least 90 were honored in this fashion. Others who were killed in the lagoon sank or drifted away, never to be seen again.

Ultimately, U.S. personnel were buried in 43 separate locations around Betio. Usually a marker of some kind

Funerals

Fifty-seven servicemen killed at Tarawa have been identified since 2014 alone. They include Silver Star recipient Lieutenant George Bussa, discovered on Betio and identified from DNA comparisons made with relatives and from effects found with him. Bussa was buried at Arlington National Cemetery in October 2017, just weeks before Corporals Walter G. Critchley and Anthony G. Guerriero, similarly identified from Betio, were interred at Arlington. Dozens of other such funerals preceded these. None, however, garnered more attention than that of Medal of Honor recipient Bonnyman in Knoxville, Tennessee.

Until 2015, Bonnyman was the only Medal of Honor recipient from Tarawa who neither returned alive (Shoup) nor was repatriated. The remains of William Deane Hawkins and William J. Bordelon had been taken to the National Memorial Cemetery of the Pacific, known as Punchbowl, on Oahu; in 1995 Bordelon was disinterred and reinterred at Fort Sam Houston

1st Lt. Alexander Bonnyman Jr., USMCR. (Naval History and Heritage Command)

National Cemetery in his hometown of San Antonio, Texas. Bonnyman's family had desperately and earnestly sought the return of his body for many years after the war, but had run into an indifferent bureaucracy that could not and would not tear Betio apart to search for the missing remains.

As the decades went by, the memories of combatants deteriorated. Marines and sailors present in 1943 who might have helped locate Bonnyman's body had conflicting recollections. History Flight's dogged pursuit of Cemetery 27, thought to contain Bonnyman's remains and those of 39 other Marines, took years. It finally paid off in the courtyard of a Betio business in March 2015. Bonnyman's identification did not require the use of DNA due to the unique and expensive dental work he had had performed prior to his death, along with the personal effects found with his body.

In September 2015, Bonnyman's funeral took place at the plot his father had purchased on a hilltop in Knoxville many decades earlier. A Marine Corps band and honor guard from Marine Barracks Washington, led by Major General Burke W. Whitman, helped Bonnyman's daughters and other family members gain the closure denied to his parents and siblings just after his death. Now Bonnyman rests near the marker his father erected in 1949. Its inscription echoes what the Pentagon told the family after giving up its search: "Buried at Sea."

A bulldozer prepares a trench to be used for Marines' graves. (Hatch Collection, National Museum of the Pacific War)

Many were not to be found at all. By 1949 the Army gave up and declared their efforts at an end. Any families of the missing who had put their hopes in the idea of a funeral at home had to slowly come to the sad realization that there would never be any formal closure for them to the Battle of Tarawa. Those American dead who had been found but not identified were ultimately returned to the National Cemetery of the Pacific War in Honolulu, along with many others who were identified but whose families did not request repatriation. Even as late as March 2017, the Defense POW/MIA Accounting Agency stated that 491 of the 1,049 it listed as killed in action at Tarawa were "not accounted for."

with the name of the fallen was erected, however crude and hurried. Yet anyone who knew the full story of who had died— as well as where, when, and how— no matter how tenderly they might have initially cared for the remains, was gone from Betio within a few days. Construction battalions, garrison troops, and airfield personnel arrived. They had a different mentality about upcoming missions, no connection to the fallen, and no expectation that anyone down the road would be especially concerned about construction over cemeteries or moving the remains around without careful documentation. Morale among these rear area units plummeted as the Central Pacific war reached the Marianas within seven months. No one was looking out for the cemeteries.

It therefore should not be surprising that when the war was over and U.S. Army Graves Registration teams came to locate the Marines and sailors who had died on Betio, they could not come close to finding them all, despite published photos of immaculate cemeteries with neatly lettered crosses. In a 1946 mission to locate buried servicemen on Betio, a team that included two of the chaplains who had served during Galvanic located only about half of the bodies they believed to be buried on Betio. The technology and science of the time allowed just 58 percent of those to be identified. Some markers had been placed over "graves" that were actually empty. On the other hand, some graves had no markers.

Much of the energy behind recent efforts to find Marines' remains at Tarawa came from two American pilots—one a Marine veteran, William Niven; the other a civilian, Mark Noah. They led separate efforts to locate the lost cemeteries on Betio and to persuade the Defense Department—now preoccupied with the dead and missing of wars from Vietnam forward—to pay renewed attention to Tarawa.

By the 21st century, however, the major problem was that Betio had become one of the most densely populated places on Earth. Searching for lost U.S. personnel would create a serious disruption for citizens of the nation of Kiribati, the successor to the British colony of the Gilbert Islands. Their backyards, the soil under their houses, and everywhere else on the island was as good a place to look as any other.

Even locating cemeteries whose location was fairly well documented in 1943 would be challenging. Establishing the likelihood that remains were present before digging was even more difficult. And then there was the probability that any remains located would be Japanese rather than American, due to the disparate killed-in-action ratio from 1943. Thus, on its face, what Niven and Noah set out to do was audacious. But by the end of the first decade of the new millennium, it was paying off. Marines were being found and brought home.

Noah, in particular, was indefatigable. He had previously founded an organization called History Flight

Tarawa grave markers for IMAC tank Marines William I. Sheedy and Edwin H. Vancil. (WFI Research Group)

to offer rides in restored vintage aircraft to World War II veterans. He and his organization turned to finding missing pilots, aircrew, soldiers, sailors, and Marines from World War II. His interest in Tarawa started in 2007, when he first learned that as of that date almost half of the Marines who had died there had not been located and repatriated.

Noah traveled to Tarawa many times and developed contacts with local government officials. He raised funds for ground-penetrating radar surveys and archaeological digs to locate remains in what was now an excessively dense and difficult urban environment. Where the U.S. Defense Department had not made Tarawa's Marines a priority, Noah filled the gap. By 2015, History Flight's historians, archaeologists, and search personnel had located dozens of Marines' remains, most famously those of First Lieutenant Alexander Bonnyman, the only one of the three posthumous Medal of Honor recipients from Tarawa who had, until that date, not been located and repatriated.

Grave marker of 1st Lt. William I. Sheedy, National Memorial Cemetery of the Pacific, Honolulu. (Courtesy of the Author)

World of Warships is a free-to-play, naval warfare–themed, massively multiplayer online game produced and published by Wargaming. Like their other games, *World of Tanks* (WoT) and *World of Warplanes* (WoWP), players take control of historic vehicles to battle others in player-versus-player or play ccooperatively against bots or in an advanced player-versus-environment (PvE) battle mode. *World of Warships* (WoWs) was originally released for PC in 2015; the PlayStation 4 and Xbox One console versions, titled *World of Warships: Legends*, followed in 2019, and it was released on the PlayStation 5 and Xbox Series X/S in April 2021.

Developed by Lesta Studios in St. Petersburg, Russia, *World of Warships* (PC) currently has more than 44 million registered players—playing on five main servers across the globe. More than 500 dedicated staff members work on a four-week update cycle to bring new features, ships, and mechanics to the game—keeping gameplay fresh and inviting to new players. The game features more than 400 ships, spread across 12 different in-game nations. Ships are designed based on historical documents and actual blueprints from the first half of the 20th century, and it takes from two to six man-months on average to create each of these ships. There are more than 20 ports to choose from, and 10 of them are re-created based on historical harbors and port towns.

Developed by the team behind *World of Warships* for PC, *World of Warships: Legends* is a completely new entry in Wargaming's flagship nautical franchise that takes full advantage of the power and capabilities of home consoles. *World of Warships: Legends* brings the online naval action loved by millions to home consoles for the very first time, alongside a host of content and features exclusive to the console experience. *World of Warships: Legends* is now available for download from the PlayStation® Store and Microsoft Store. Players can now wage wars across a variety of maps, in numerous warships, and enjoy stunning oceanic vistas with glorious HDR support on PlayStation®4 and Xbox One X. Full 4K support is available on PlayStation®4 Pro, PlayStation®5, and Xbox One X too! *Legends* also supports standard high-def on PlayStation®4 and Xbox One, with more intriguing graphics on the horizon.

Wargaming preserves naval history by making a series of documentaries on museum ships. Since 2014, Wargaming Saint Petersburg published 50 episodes devoted to the world's most popular museum ships in the United States, Great Britain, Canada, France, Japan, Germany,

Greece, Australia, Sweden, Poland, Russian Federation, and China. Documentary videos cover all main classes of warships engaged in world wars such as aircraft carriers, battleships, cruisers, destroyers, and submarines. If you are interested in learning about the birth and development of U.S. naval aviation, please scan the QR-code below with your cell phone or simply find the respective video on YouTube by typing its name: "Naval Legends: Birth and Development of US Naval Aviation."

The United States Naval Institute (USNI) has been a proud partner of *World of Warships* and Wargaming since December 2019. Wargaming has a made a commitment to naval history through various programs and events over the past years. It produces excellent video content with its *Naval Legends* series on YouTube, and hosts events on board museum ships where members of the gaming and naval history communities can get together and experience living history in person. *World of Warships* and Wargaming are also great sponsors of the Historic Naval Ships Association (HNSA). USNI thanks Wargaming and *World of Warships* for their continued support of the naval history community and their participation in this Naval History Special Edition. Please see the back cover for a special offer for *World of Warships* PC and *World of Warships: Legends*.

Naval History Special Editions

8½ x 10¾ | Paperback | **$19.95**

Building upon the expertise of the authors and historians of the Naval Institute Press, the *Naval History* Special Editions are designed to offer studies of the key vessels, battles, and events of armed conflict. Using an image-heavy, magazine-style format, these Special Editions should appeal to scholars, enthusiasts, and general readers alike.

Battleship *Massachusetts*

BY VINCENT P. O'HARA

978-1-68247-635-2

Aircraft Carrier *Intrepid*

BY ANDREW FALTUM

978-1-68247-740-3

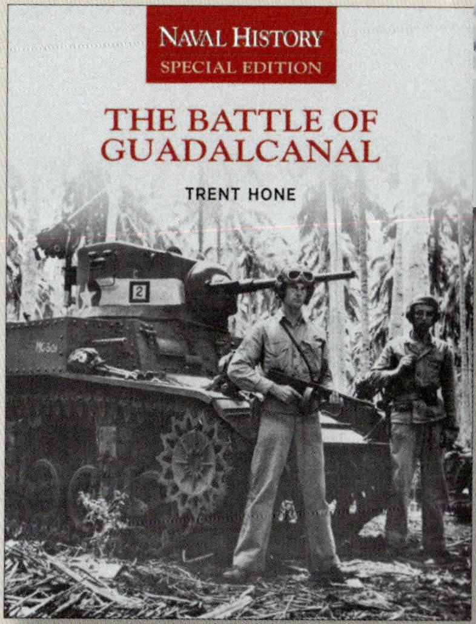

The Battle of Guadalcanal

BY TRENT HONE

978-1-68247-731-1

Heavy Cruiser *Prinz Eugen*

BY VINCENT P. O'HARA

978-1-59114-872-2

Battleship *Tirpitz*

BY VINCENT P. O'HARA

978-1-59114-870-8

Battleship *Iowa*

BY LAWRENCE BURR

978-1-59114-910-1